Waging Peace:
Global Adventures of a
Lifelong Activist

David Hartsough

with Joyce Hollyday

PM

Waging Peace: Global Adventures of a Lifelong Activist
David Hartsough, with Joyce Hollyday
© 2014 PM Press.

Unless otherwise noted, all photos are from David Hartsough's photo collection.

ISBN: 978-1-62963-034-2
Library of Congress Control Number: 2014908061

Cover by John Yates / www.stealworks.com
Interior design by briandesign

10 9 8 7 6 5 4 3 2 1

PM Press
PO Box 23912
Oakland, CA 94623
www.pmpress.org

Printed in the USA by the Employee Owners of Thomson-Shore in Dexter, Michigan.
www.thomsonshore.com

Contents

Foreword by John Dear   v

Introduction by George Lakey   ix

Acknowledgments and Thanks   xii

CHAPTER 1 The Seeds Are Sown: A Childhood Experiment with Nonviolence   1

CHAPTER 2 One Common Humanity: Meeting Dr. King and a Lunch Counter Showdown   13

CHAPTER 3 Crossing Borders: Citizen Diplomacy in Cuba and Yugoslavia   25

CHAPTER 4 Bridging the Divide: Forging Peace at Checkpoint Charlie   34

CHAPTER 5 Meeting the "Enemy": Making Friends with Russians During the Cold War   50

CHAPTER 6 Taking a Stand: Life as a Conscientious Objector   66

CHAPTER 7 Blockade: Standing in the Way of Bombs Headed for Nam   83

CHAPTER 8   Reversing the Blueprint: Saying No to Nukes   99

CHAPTER 9   Accompaniment: Into the Central American
War Zones   112

CHAPTER 10   Assault on the Tracks: Facing Violence with Love
and Courage   128

CHAPTER 11   The World Is Watching: Facing Down Death Squads   148

CHAPTER 12   A Force for Peace: Creating a Nonviolent Army   161

CHAPTER 13   Taking the Long View: Active Nonviolence in
Palestine and Averting War with Iran   177

CHAPTER 14   Transforming Our Society from One Addicted to
Violence and War to One Based on Justice and Peace
with the World   193

Proposal for Ending All War: An Idea Whose Time
Has Come   209

Resources for Further Study and Action:
What You Can Do   213

Ten Lessons Learned From My Life of Activism   219

Hartsough's Sentencing Statement for Nonviolent
Protest Opposing Drones at Beale AFB   222

Suggested DVDs, Books, and Websites for
Further Study and Action   225

The Six Principles and Six Steps of Kingian
Nonviolence   237

Afterword by Ken Butigan   239

About the Authors   242

"Peace will only come when all of us become the change we wish to see in this world. David Hartsough became that change and has spent the best part of sixty years working to bring peace to our troubled world. His book, *Waging Peace: Global Adventures of a Life-Long Activist* is one that every peace-loving person must read and learn from."
—Arun Gandhi, president, Gandhi Worldwide Education
Institute (grandson of Mahatma Gandhi)

"It has been my privilege to work with David Hartsough over the years and to be arrested and go to jail with him doing nonviolent civil disobedience challenging wars and nuclear weapons. His riveting and inspiring stories in *Waging Peace* of his lifelong efforts to speak truth to power and to oppose injustice and work for peace confirm for me what I've long felt about him: that his has been a life lived nobly. I highly commend *Waging Peace* to every American who wishes to live in a world with peace and justice, and wants to feel empowered to help create that world."
—Daniel Ellsberg, *The Pentagon Papers*

"For courage, perseverance, and commitment to a nonviolent world, David Hartsough is my teacher. So I treasure this long-awaited memoir where, in his unassuming, ordinary way, he takes us along with him on extraordinary encounters that challenge our notions of what one person in one lifetime can do. From Guatemala to Kosovo, from Moscow to Palestine, he lets us see the kind of adventures that are possible for us as well, when we share his faith in the power of truth and nonviolence."
—Joanna Macy, author, *Active Hope: How to Face
the Mess We're in Without Going Crazy*

"When great events happen, such as the falling of the Berlin Wall, we must never forget that people like David Hartsough and many others have worked hard to prepare the ground for such 'miracles.' David's belief in the goodness of people, the power of love, truth, and forgiveness, and his utter commitment to making peace and ending war and militarism will inspire all those who read this book."
—Mairead Maguire, Nobel Peace Laureate,
Peace People, Northern Ireland

"*Waging Peace* is a collection of powerful and moving stories about how one remarkable person has acted on his belief that peace is possible. It's a must-read for anyone who wants to help create the world we all hope and pray for. Be prepared to be empowered!"
—Parker J. Palmer, author, *Healing the Heart of Democracy*, *Let Your Life Speak*, and *The Courage to Teach*

"Over thirty years ago, when with great trepidation I went through nonviolence training in order to join the blockade at the Diablo Canyon Nuclear Power Plant, David Hartsough was my trainer, and his personal stories inspired me to put myself on the line for what I believed in. Later, I went on to become a trainer myself, and for some years Hartsough and I were in a training collective together. Now he's compiled his tales of moments of crisis and his life story into this wonderful book. *Waging Peace* will inspire anyone who is concerned with social and environmental justice, and will help you formulate your own approach to the activism so crucial now for the world!"
—Starhawk, author, *The Fifth Sacred Thing*

"In this highly readable memoir, David Hartsough personifies the adage 'Love life enough to struggle.' A man whose passion for justice and love for humanity has taken him to many parts of the world into the heart of some of the most significant struggles of the past sixty years, this book provides a personalized account of some of the greatest moments in popular movements for peace and justice."
—Stephen Zunes, professor of politics, University of San Francisco

"Permit me to congratulate you for your persistent and steadfast acting out truth in the face of power."
—Staughton Lynd, author of *Accompanying: Pathways to Social Change* and *Lucasville: The Untold Story of a Prison Uprising*

"Committing one's life to being a witness for peace takes courage and discipline. A life of activism can also be a source of joy, good humor and blessed community, as David Hartsough's inspiring stories so clearly illustrate. *Waging Peace* offers insight into the ways in which nonviolence can transform tyranny into justice, violence into peace—a timely reminder that one person *can* make a difference."
—Shan Cretin, general secretary, American Friends Service Committee

"Hartsough's heartfelt memoir is a testament to the far-too-often forgotten legacy of courageous dissent. Reading this book is like relearning one's history. I learned for the first time, for instance, that a drugstore I used to go to as a child had been a flashpoint of the civil rights struggle, since Hartsough himself was part of a sit-in there. Through his life, we discover new dimensions of our own lives and of our society—some disturbing, some hopeful, all of them true. As much as it's the story of a heroic life, it's an accessible handbook for how the rest of us can make our lives heroic, too."
—Nathan Schneider, editor, *Waging Nonviolence*, and author, *Thank You, Anarchy*

"Despite knowing David personally for years, I had no idea about the breadth of his involvement in nonviolent struggles around the world. His story opens a window into what a life of commitment looks like. From the civil rights movement to Occupy, David has always been involved front and center in ceaseless attempts to transform conditions of oppression and violence through nonviolent means. What he shows in these pages is that engaging in nonviolent struggle, with all its attendant hardship, is a way to live a life of deep joy and integrity. May it inspire many to embrace love and courage and the vision that says that we will prevail."
—Miki Kashtan, author, *Spinning Threads of Radical Aliveness: Transcending the Legacy of Separation in Our Individual Lives*

Foreword

by John Dear

David's been waging peace all his life. In a nation which wages permanent war, where people wage violence and don't even know it, David Hartsough consciously wages active, assertive, militant, public, loving, dangerous, transforming nonviolence. He should be world famous, but David's not that interested in fame and fortune. He's interested in ending war, abolishing nuclear weapons, and leading everyone along the way of nonviolence which he learned firsthand long ago from Martin Luther King Jr. He's so humble, simple, and gentle that no one would know the powerful force that moves within him. This beautiful, inspiring book sets the record straight. I hope it will be widely read, especially by young people, that others, too, might take up the life of nonviolence and discover the power within to help make peace.

David is one of those rare *satyagrahis* who practice what Gandhi called "the nonviolence of the strong." We see that strong nonviolence throughout this story. It's right there at the start, when seven-year-old David suffers the icy snowballs of some bullies in Gilman, Iowa. What to do? He has just heard his father preach on those Sermon on the Mount commandments—"Turn the other cheek," "Offer no violent resistance to one who does evil," "Love your enemies." So he turns around and says, "I'd like to be your friend, and I certainly don't have anything against you guys." The bullying ended, and he walks away transformed. He's been saying those same words with the same transforming effect ever since.

"I suppose that my calling in life was given to me on that cold Iowa day," he writes. "I have tried through the subsequent decades to take Jesus's command to love our enemies just as seriously as I did as a seven-year-old boy. That pursuit has led me to practice active non-violent resistance on behalf of peace at weapons labs and war zones, on train tracks, and in front of bomb-loaded ships. It has pushed me to cross borders and brought me friendships in far-flung corners of the earth where violence has visited, from the Philippines to Nicaragua, from Russia to Gaza and Kosovo. I have had an amazing and wonderful journey."

He met Martin Luther King Jr. in 1956, and from then on took King's example and teachings personally, which led him to take similar risks and organize similar actions. Sitting in at a segregated lunch counter in Arlington, Virginia, in 1960, he was reading that same Gospel text again—"Love your enemies, do good to those who hate you"—when he heard a voice right behind him saying, "Get out of this store in two seconds, or I'm going to stab this through your heart." He turned and saw a hate-filled man holding a switchblade to his chest.

He took a deep breath and said, "Friend, do what you believe is right, and I will still try to love you." The man was shocked and walked away.

We, too, are shocked and disarmed by David's steadfast non-violence. That sit-in helped bring an end to segregation in Arlington. It also revealed a daring nonviolence in the same league as Jesus and Martin Luther King Jr. This is waging peace par excellence.

"That experience . . . confirmed my belief in the power of love, the power of goodness, the power of God working through us to overcome hatred and violence," he writes. "I had a profound sense that nonviolence really works. At that moment, nonviolence became much more to me than a philosophical idea or a tactic that had once made a difference in Gandhi's India. It became the way I wanted to relate to other human beings, a way of life, a way of working for change."

As we journey with David through his life, we too learn the wisdom of nonviolence as a tactic, strategy, and more importantly, a way of life, a way to God.

"I learned the most important lesson in my life up to that point—and maybe still: that a few people with some courage and commitment to nonviolence don't have to just sit and curse and feel powerless when terrible things are happening. We can challenge and transform injustice, violence, and oppression to achieve a more just society. We can change the course of history!"

Unfortunately, there are not enough people who believe that, but those of us who count David as a friend know from his legendary example that it's true. Now with this book, others can see for themselves and be inspired to test that challenge, to go forth and help change history. David is an amazing nonviolent leader in an underground nonviolent army—taking action, giving helpful suggestions, pushing a way forward, upholding a vision, and most of all, leading the way.

For example, he was a college student at Howard University when he was summoned to join a Quaker delegation to meet with President John Kennedy to discuss nuclear disarmament at the White House. Some of us believe that meeting helped push Kennedy toward peace, steps that may have led to his eventual assassination. David was not yet twenty-two at the time.

Talk about making a difference!

In the years that followed, David opposed the Vietnam War and nuclear weapons, worked with the Quakers to promote justice and peace on Capitol Hill, taught nonviolence and organized peace demonstrations, and became one of the movement's best organizers and practitioners.

In the 1980s, we find him traveling through Central America, and then organizing against the U.S. wars and weapons shipments that killed tens of thousands of innocent people. Then on that fateful day, September 1, 1987, he's with our friend Brian Willson, protesting weapons shipments to Central America at the Concord Naval Weapons Station, when Brian was run over by a weapons train and nearly killed in front of David's eyes.

That event and his account here still shake me to the core. In the months afterwards, I was one of thousands who were arrested regularly for blocking those weapons shipments and spent many days with David in jail. Later, I even followed him to the Philippines to meet with legendary Bishop Antonio Fortich and encourage the nonviolent efforts to stop the death squads and support the movement creating zones of peace, and to Cairo with the Gaza Freedom March. I have also supported the groundbreaking Nonviolent Peaceforce which David cofounded and many other projects David has initiated.

But the day Brian was run over is seared in our hearts, and David's eyewitness account teaches us once again about the waging of peace.

"We have assumed the name of peacemakers," Daniel Berrigan famously wrote during the Vietnam War, "but we have been, by and large, unwilling to pay any significant price. And because we want the peace with half a heart and half a life and will, the war, of course, continues, because the waging of war, by its nature, is total—but the waging of peace, by our own cowardice, is partial. So a whole will and a whole heart and a whole national life bent toward war prevail over the velleities of peace."

Here in these pages, we discover another peacemaker, like Daniel Berrigan and Brian Willson, who has been willing to wage peace with his whole will, his whole heart, his whole life. This life, and the telling of it, are a great gift to all of us.

David's story is a shining example of relentless peacemaking and a luminous record of peacemaking efforts in the second half of the twentieth century and the start of the twenty-first. But more, *Waging Peace* proves that every one of us can make a difference, every one of us can practice active nonviolence, every one of us is needed in the movement for justice and disarmament, every one of us has the power to change the world for the better, if we only believe in that power and act on it.

"This is my faith—that we are co-creators with God, helping to build a world of peace, justice, and human dignity for all people," David concludes. "All over the world, people are increasingly embracing nonviolence as the most legitimate and effective way of waging struggle against oppression, injustice, and dictatorship. We are all learning from one another's struggles. My hope is that the rest of the world will realize that violence and war are costly, outmoded, ineffective, and morally tragic means of resolving conflict."

In a world of permanent war, poverty, nuclear weapon, and catastrophic climate change, David Hartsough gives us the story of his peacemaking life and, in doing so, calls us to be wagers of peace. Practice nonviolence, sow the seeds of peace, try to make a difference and believe you can. Take public action for justice and disarmament, speak out publicly, trust the God of peace, take the nonviolent Jesus at his word, experiment with active nonviolence, and walk forward on the road to peace.

That's the lesson we learn from this extraordinary peacemaker. Wage peace, not war. It's the biggest lesson we all need to learn.

John Dear is an internationally known voice for peace and nonviolence. He is a popular speaker, peacemaker, organizer, lecturer, retreat leader, and author/editor of thirty books, most recently, The Nonviolent Life. *John was nominated for the Nobel Peace Prize by Archbishop Desmond Tutu and lives in Northern New Mexico.*

Introduction

by George Lakey

Anna Brinton, a twentieth-century Quaker leader who was legendary for her wry humor, remarked that Quakers like to go about doing good, "especially when it involves going about." David's sharing of his adventures in this book makes him a strong example of Brinton's observation!

Because he's bold enough to present his long life to us, he also invites us to ask what is his *kind* of doing good, and also what has sustained him when there are so many grounds for discouragement and burnout.

The questions are especially pressing when we notice that David's choices are not those of a traditional do-gooder: alleviating the harm that comes from violence and oppression through binding up wounds and supporting individuals to make a fresh start. David aims to stop that violence and upset that oppression, a harder challenge by far and perhaps harder to pursue sustainably.

Unlike his hero Martin Luther King Jr., who was a grown man when he was challenged to take leadership in the Montgomery bus boycott, David volunteered in high school to lead his peers in confrontation. His early adoption of a prophetic role did not endear him to the headmaster.

Even as a teenager David took risks to follow what I call a compelling moral vision. In that way he joined one of the lineages in American history going back to the abolitionists and earlier. In fact, even though David studied in Germany and took pains to immerse himself in other cultures from an early age, the path he describes strikes me as very American.

He has a way of framing an argument that helps to sustain him and has inspired many of those who have worked with him along the way.

The late social scientist Kenneth E. Boulding put the platform supporting David's style this way: "Where there's hypocrisy, there's hope." By holding perpetrators of injustice to the idealistic standard they adopt in public, one gains the energy of moral indignation for oneself and sometimes the political leverage to force the perpetrators to change.

Another way that David sustains his activism for the long run shows up in this book as a set of *reference points* that he cultivates. He might face an immediate situation that is deeply discouraging, but there's a big picture that he returns to again and again. Among these reference points:

- All over the world there are people standing up for themselves and their communities.
- More organizers—and scholars—are recognizing the power of nonviolent action to force change against the will of the unjust.
- Campaigns without short-run success at least provide the space for some participants' remarkable personal growth, or even heroism, and have stirred some perpetrators to break out of their roles and confess a common humanity.

It's often remarked that successful organizers (and entrepreneurs) are temperamentally optimistic, but a virtue of this book is it reveals some tactics that support optimism. One tactic is to push to the edge and experience the stimulation—and often adrenaline—offered by that edge. David shares with other adventurers who don't die young an awareness of the metrics of courage: did he go too far? Did he go far enough? Did he take an easy out on this one? Through David's expression of moral earnestness in this book, the reader gets a sense of his inner dialogue around these important existential questions, questions we also may share.

When reading a book of exploits readers may wonder if they are meeting a character or a real person. I first met David when he was still in high school, at the Nike missile protest he organized and recounts in this book. Our families have been in and out of each other's lives ever since. I can say, therefore, that the man you meet in these pages is the man I've known. For David there's no need to turn on television to watch a reality show—he prefers to live his own, packed with adventures and challenges and shared with his astute and loving partner Jan. I'm glad he put in the work to share this life with us.

George Lakey is a visiting professor of Peace and Conflict Studies at Swarthmore College and was recently named Peace Educator of the Year by the Peace and Justice Studies Association. George cofounded A Quaker Action Group, the Movement for a New Society and Training for Change, and is currently active in Earth Quaker Action Group. He envisioned and manages the Global Nonviolent Action Database of nonviolent campaigns at Swarthmore College, available to the public through its website. Lakey is author of Toward a Living Revolution *and* Facilitating Group Learning: Strategies for Success with Adult Learners. *He has coauthored* Moving Toward a New Society, Manual for Direct Action, and Grassroots *and* Nonprofit Leadership: A Guide for Organizations in Changing Times. *George writes a column, "Living Revolution," in* Waging Nonviolence: People Powered News and Analysis.

Acknowledgments and Thanks

First, I want to thank my mother and father, Ruth and Ray Hartsough, who through their love and nurturing support helped set me on the path of peace and justice-making.

I want to express my profound thanks to all my friends and colleagues through the decades who are and have been an important part of my life and work for a more peaceful and just world.

I feel deeply blessed by all the spiritual giants whose lives and life work have deeply inspired and supported me in my experiments with truth and nonviolence. These include: Mahatma Gandhi, Martin Luther King Jr., Ralph Abernathy, Bayard Rustin, A.J. Muste, Daniel Ellsberg, Steve Cary, George Lakey, Wally and Juanita Nelson, Charlie Walker, Raymond Wilson, Ed Snyder, Senator George McGovern, Lawrence Scott, Dave Ritchie, Randy Kehler, George Houser, Ken Butigan, Medea Benjamin, Kathy Kelly, Dick and Phyllis Taylor, Spahr Hull, Dick Hiler, Mel Duncan, Brian Willson, Howard Zinn, George and Lillian Willoughby, David Swanson and the many other beautiful people who have been part of the nonviolent movements and actions which have been an important part of my life over the past sixty years, and the many others whose names could fill many pages of this book.

I am so grateful to my friends and colleagues around the world—my extended family—who are confronting poverty, injustice, and war courageously and nonviolently and helping create a livable and peaceful world for our children and all future generations. This includes all the people in the Nonviolent Peaceforce who are helping realize Gandhi's vision of a Shanti Sena or nonviolent army protecting civilians in areas of armed conflict and helping create the peace.

I especially want to thank the people without whose help this book would not have been possible. These include my loving wife Jan Hartsough, Monica Dunlap, Sally Davis, Sherri Maurin, Jamie Newton, Ken Butigan, Paul Burks, and the board of Peaceworkers, who have supported me in working with and building nonviolent movements over the past twenty years and my writing and publishing this book. Joyce Hollyday, an excellent writer and friend, was an invaluable help in putting all these stories from my life into a readable book. And my thanks to Ramsey Kanaan and all those at PM Press for publishing *Waging Peace.*

Finally, thank you, Margaret Mead, for reminding us, "Never doubt that a small group of thoughtful, committed citizens can change the world. Indeed, it's the only thing that ever has." I hope this book will help you, the reader, realize the truth of this statement and encourage you to become more actively involved in the global movement of concerned world citizens around the world working for a peaceful, just, and environmentally sustainable future for all the world's children and all future generations.

CHAPTER 1

The Seeds Are Sown: A Childhood Experiment with Nonviolence

I t was 1960, and I was twenty years old. I was sitting on a stool at the lunch counter of the ironically named People's Drug Store in Arlington, Virginia, along with ten African American classmates from Howard University. The voice I heard was laced with venom, and the eyes of the speaker were filled with hatred. He was threatening to thrust his knife—its blade just inches away from me—through my heart. We were both shaking.

How did I come to be here? Why wasn't I safely at some liberal white college, studying for some safe and predictable occupation? More importantly, where could I find the strength and love to match this man's fury?

My first encounter with the power of nonviolence came early. I was seven years old, trudging home from school through a park that I crossed every day on my way to and from the second grade. A bitter wind was blowing that winter day in Gilman, Iowa. The ice balls that landed on my face and chest stung, some fortified with stones to increase the pain on impact.

My face started to bleed. I was mystified by the glee on the faces of the small gang of older boys who were pelting me. A quick mental review told me that I had never done anything to them to merit this treatment.

On a recent Sunday in church, my father had preached a sermon about love, based on Jesus's command: "You have heard that it was said, 'You shall love your neighbor and hate your enemy.' But I say to you, Love your enemies and pray for those who persecute you" (Matthew 5:43–44). I was certainly feeling persecuted.

I hadn't yet lived long enough for the questioning realism that often overtakes adults to have settled on me. It didn't occur to me to ask: did Jesus really mean these tough words? Will loving these guys make a difference? If I don't fight back, aren't I giving in to evil? I just took Jesus's words at face value and asked myself: how *do* I love these guys?

I stood still for a few moments. Then I faced those boys and piped up, "I'd like to be your friend, and I certainly don't have anything against you guys." I wanted them to know that I wasn't afraid of them. They threw a few more ice balls. But eventually the thrill wore off, as I wasn't throwing any back or reacting in any aggressive way to their onslaught.

I walked on home, trying to figure out what else could I do in this challenging situation. The previous summer I had visited several Indian reservations in the Southwest with my family, and my most prized possession at the time was a little copper letter opener inlaid with an Indian precious stone. I decided to give it to the boy who appeared to be the leader of the gang. He received it with surprise and gratitude, and we became good friends after that.

I suppose that my calling in life was given to me on that cold Iowa day. I have tried through the subsequent decades to take Jesus's command to love enemies just as seriously as I did as a seven-year-old boy. That pursuit has led me to practice active nonviolent resistance on behalf of peace at weapons labs and in war zones, on train tracks, and in front of bomb-loaded ships. It has pushed me to cross borders and brought me friendships in far-flung corners of the earth where violence has visited, from the Philippines to Nicaragua, from Russia to Gaza and Kosovo. I have had an amazing and wonderful journey.

It's no mystery to me where my instincts originated. My mother, Ruth Goodell Hartsough, was a teacher who overflowed with kindness and affirmation. She was also an artist, whose paintings of nature and landscapes expressed the beauty in her soul. She had lost her first child soon after birth; she rejoiced when I was born healthy and poured her love into me. Many other people also benefited from the wide embrace of her compassion and adoration. Our home was always open, filled with guests who reveled in her loving, gracious, and joyful hospitality.

My father, Ray Hartsough, was a Congregational minister. During the Second World War, the U.S. government had tried to get him to go into military service as a chaplain, but he had refused to participate in the military in any way, choosing instead to support conscientious objectors. While serving the community church in Gilman, he learned

Parents Ruth and Ray, brother Paul, and the author at age seven (1948).

about Quaker peace projects. He told George Willoughby, head of the regional office of the American Friends Service Committee (AFSC), to call on him if the Quaker service organization ever needed someone like him.

He didn't have to wait long. I will never forget the day before Christmas in 1948. I was eight years old then. My bedroom was the upstairs front room of the parsonage where we lived. We owned a wire recorder, which used tiny wires on spools to make sound. We played music of Christmas chimes at full blast out my open window in the middle of winter. It was our way of sharing the spirit of Christmas. That afternoon, Dad told me we had to go to the post office. He pulled me on a sled, and we picked up a telegram from the AFSC. It was a request for my father to go to work in Gaza, Palestine, with the tens of thousands of refugees created by the war between Israel and the Arab states. He had to be on a plane in two weeks. I didn't know anyone who had ever flown on a plane or worked in a refugee camp, and I remember wondering if he would come back alive.

Dad's work involved getting tents, food, and medicine to refugees on both sides of the conflict. He carried supplies across battle lines into camps in a truck that bore a red-and-black star, an AFSC symbol. It was a signal at Israeli checkpoints that he was not an enemy but someone on a mission of compassion, as he intrepidly crossed the "no man's land" strewn with land mines between enemy soldiers pointing guns at one another. I remember praying for my dad every night. He wrote to my younger brother Paul and me every week, sharing stories of what he was witnessing. We were without a father at home for nine months and we missed him terribly. But I was deeply impressed that he was willing to risk his life day after day to get supplies to thousands of traumatized and hungry people, who owed their lives to the courage of my dad and others like him.

My father was a shining example of what it means to be a caring Christian, and I was very proud of him. When my brother and I were young, family friends used to say, "Paul is cute—and David looks like his dad." I took that as a compliment. I was happy to look like my dad.

While my dad was away, our mom, Paul, and I moved in with my grandmother in North Jackson, Ohio, to finish the school year. In June 1949, we moved to Pendle Hill, a Quaker retreat and study center near Philadelphia. This was my first introduction to Quakers who were not only living their Faith, but trying to put their beliefs into action and help create a more peaceful and just world.

When Dad returned safely from Palestine and Israel in October, we moved into a big, old house in Gwynedd, Pennsylvania, that we shared with another family, the Hoskins. Dad continued working for the American Friends Service Committee, first as College Secretary and later as Peace Education Secretary But it was my mother who participated in our family's first nonviolent direct action. In 1951, the U.S. Congress was considering legislation mandating a peacetime military draft for all young men. I was ten at the time, and Paul was eight. Mom went to Washington, DC, where she fasted for a week and visited many members of Congress. Despite the strong opposition registered by her and many others who wanted peace through peaceful means, the legislation passed.

That same year, I had a fifth-grade teacher who was also the principal of my school. Extremely patriotic and very law-and-order, Mrs. Alexander ran the school like a queen and our class like a general. One day she told us we were all going to go outside and march around the flagpole.

"I don't want to march," I told her.

"You have to," was her brusque reply.

I went outside, and while the other kids marched around the flagpole, I sat and watched. Mrs. Alexander was very upset with me. She threatened, "You have to march, or I'm going to call your mother." Little did she know . . .

I just shrugged my shoulders and refused to march. Mrs. Alexander left and went inside, then came back out and told me she had talked to my mother, who said I had to march around the flagpole. Out of deference to my mom, I very sadly marched with the other kids, trying to hold back my tears.

When I got home, I found out that the principal had never talked to my mom. I lost a lot of respect that day for law and order.

When I was twelve, my dad learned about Tanguy Homesteads, founded after the Second World War by conscientious objectors who had done alternative service, such as fighting forest fires and being guinea pigs for new medicines. Some of them had become good friends in the camps where they had been placed during the war, and they wanted to continue the sense of community they had shared there. So in 1947 they bought a piece of land in Tanguy, Pennsylvania, surrounded by cornfields and orchards, which they owned cooperatively. Families held ninety-nine-year leases on two-acre lots, where they built their homes.

In 1952, my parents bought a house in Tanguy from a family who was moving away. The house was very small, built of cement blocks with a cement floor. It had big windows and a three-foot overhang on the south side—passive solar heating, ahead of its time.

Moving there was one of the best decisions my parents ever made. (I often say that I chose my parents very well.) Paul and I believed that our parents' philosophy was "Keep the boys busy and they'll stay out of trouble." So we had goats and chickens, a big garden, and a nursery.

The chickens were my responsibility. They often laid more than one egg per chicken per day, which the experts said was impossible. I delivered eggs to all the neighbors, and some joked that I must have been taking eggs out of the refrigerator and sticking them back under the chickens.

The nursery was started by our Uncle Charles, my mother's brother, who was well-known for his "green thumb." He had been a nuclear safety engineer during World War II, first in Oak Ridge, Tennessee, and then in Los Alamos, New Mexico. He was involved in top-secret work related to the development of the atomic bomb. He wasn't allowed to leave the research sites for a very long time—not even to attend his father's funeral in 1944.

In 1950, he finally left Los Alamos and his work on nuclear weaponry. He went on a retreat of several months in Death Valley, to "cleanse" himself and search out next directions. Then he drove across the country and showed up at our house in a '36 Oldsmobile with a rumble seat, stacked to the brim with beautiful wooden boxes that he had made, which were filled with sweet dates from the desert.

Uncle Charles had planned to stay a couple of weeks but ended up living with us for the rest of his life—until 1976, when he died of cancer, most likely caused by his exposure to radiation. He was like a second father to Paul and me during those years when Dad traveled so much with AFSC. I shared his love of nature, his friendliness for everyone around him, and his affinity for glazed donuts, which he brought home on a regular basis.

Tanguy was a wonderful place to grow up. We had workdays one or two Saturdays a month, when we all pitched in on community projects. Paul and I learned basic construction and carpentry skills from Uncle Charles, which Paul applied with artistry later in life to the homes he built.

An old farmhouse served as a community house, where we held square dances, potluck meals, and other gatherings. I particularly remember the times when Tanguy member Charlie Walker, who made several trips to India to meet with Gandhi's disciples, regaled us with his adventurous and riveting tales. At Tanguy, we lived like a great big family and were always welcome in one another's homes.

Don and Violet Richman, who were accomplished musicians, taught Paul to play piano and guitar, which he did beautifully. As a teenager, he sang just like Ricky Nelson. During a talent night at the end of a week of camp that we attended, Paul sang and played his guitar. As he was finishing his last song, a throng of adoring girls rushed at him.

Paul's guitar flew up into the air, and I rescued it. I began to regret that I hadn't taken advantage of the free guitar lessons at Tanguy. But I did love to sing. My style, however, was folk music—not quite so popular with the girls.

Another gift of Tanguy was that I encountered and lived with people from a diversity of backgrounds. We were one mile from the very small town of Cheyney, where Cheyney State Teachers College, an African American institution, was located. Most of the faculty at the college had to live twenty miles away in Philadelphia. Blacks could not live in our area because of zoning and discriminatory real estate practices—except at Tanguy.

One of the community members took us children into local prisons to sing to, and with, the inmates. And many of us also participated several times a year in weekend work camps in Philadelphia, where we got to know people who were living in very poor and tragic circumstances. The work camps opened our eyes to a world that the average young person living in the suburbs knew nothing about.

I remember one family, a mother and her four children. I felt sorry for the children because they had no place to play. They lived in a rundown apartment that had been neglected for years by the landlord. It was winter and very cold, especially at night, and they had no heat. In the middle of the day, melting snow came in through a leak in the roof.

We worked with the family, painting the rooms of their apartment. When it came time for lunch, we discovered that their refrigerator was completely empty. We shared our sandwiches with them.

That family and the other people I met through the work camps in Philadelphia had a profound impact on me, enlightening me to the harsh realities of poverty close to home. My experiences there played a key role in helping me feel that I needed to do something with my life to try to challenge and change the terrible injustices in our society.

The leaders of those work camps acted out of compassion and a deep spirituality. Dave Richie, John Ingersol, John and Betty Corry, and Peter Hill were early role models for me, and some became very good friends over the years. It was from them that I first learned about the practice of war tax resistance. Opposed to offering their support to the killing of other people, they were consciously living on an income below the taxable level, so that they didn't have to pay federal taxes that would be used to pay for war.

In high school, I began attending Quaker seminars in Washington, DC, and at the United Nations in New York City. Visiting the embassies of other countries, including Arab nations, Israel, and the Soviet Union, opened my eyes to a variety of perspectives. At the Soviet Embassy in particular, I wondered why our governments didn't seem as committed to talking with one another as we teenagers were. I found it inspiring to meet other high school students who shared an interest in trying to build a more just and peaceful world.

In 1953, my father answered another call to a place of conflict. He agreed to direct a Quaker work camp in Berlin, with volunteers from around the world, to rebuild a community center that had been destroyed during the Second World War. Berlin had been partitioned right after the war, and that year an uprising against the Communist regime in East Germany had been violently repressed. Dad was headed to a hot spot near the border with East Berlin, where the United States and the Soviet Union were threatening a nuclear showdown. Before he left, we held a family worship. I remember Dad quoting the 23rd Psalm:

"Yea, though I walk through the valley of the shadow of death, I will fear no evil, for Thou art with me . . ."

As with his trip to Gaza and Israel, Paul and I had the feeling that he was going off to a war zone where we would contribute our beloved father to the cause of peace. Scared, we wondered again if he would come back alive. Dad was open about his concern that he might not come back, but he felt a deep devotion to that work and to the well-being of all God's children, and that helped us to accept it.

I was attending Westtown, a Quaker school that was two miles from Tanguy. I rode my three-speed bike there for the first few years and then lived on campus the last two. I remember a film that we students saw one day called *Children of the Atomic Bomb*, about the U.S. nuclear attacks on Hiroshima and Nagasaki, Japan.

A young woman who was a survivor of the Hiroshima bombing spoke with us after the film. She had been disfigured by the bomb and was in the United States for plastic surgery. She told us, "We in Hiroshima have experienced the horror of the bomb, and we are committing our lives to make sure this never happens again to anyone else in the world."

People in Japan were still dying from the atomic bomb's effects, and many who survived were severely disfigured or ill from radiation poisoning. I was deeply moved that, rather than pledging revenge or being filled with hatred toward Americans, this woman cared so much about others that she was speaking out so that they wouldn't have to suffer as she had. Seeing that film and meeting her was another key moment in my young life, making me want to commit my life to sharing the story of the people of Hiroshima so that this horror would never happen again.

I found my chance to take a stand against nuclear weapons when I discovered a danger close to home. Philadelphia was ringed with twelve military sites containing Nike missiles, designed for use in the event of an attack by the Soviet Union. One of these sites was in Edgemont, three miles from Tanguy. I saw it as our local manifestation of nuclear madness, lulling people into believing that there was a way to protect ourselves from nuclear war, while governments were madly scrambling to build more bombs.

I talked with several other kids at Tanguy. The youngest was eight, and I was the oldest at fifteen. We decided that instead of having Thanksgiving dinner that year, we would fast—and hold a vigil at the Nike missile site for eight hours each day of our Thanksgiving vacation.

First demonstration I ever organized, at the Nike missile site near my home at Tanguy Homesteads in Pennsylvania in 1958. It earned me an FBI file.

Charlie Walker helped us write a leaflet about what we were doing and why, and he mimeographed it for us. Our parents, who I think were very proud of their children and our Thanksgiving action, drove us to the site, but only we young people kept vigil and passed out leaflets. I remember feeling elated that we got coverage in the local newspaper.

I was surprised to discover many years later, when I received my FBI file under the Freedom of Information Act, that it began with "David Hartsough, son of Ray Hartsough, who organized a vigil at a Nike missile site . . ." It was rather sobering to realize that the FBI had decided that at age fifteen I was already worthy of their attention.

Most of those young friends who participated in the Nike vigil continued to be active in voicing their concerns through peace and justice activities. That first step made us feel like part of an important movement. For many, it led to a lifetime of being involved in one way or another.

The comfort of my life was beginning to feel uncomfortable. I was grateful for my education and experience at Westtown, but it was a privileged place. Many seniors were focused on getting into the very best colleges so that they could get the best jobs and the highest salaries after graduation.

I was more interested in putting Quaker principles into practice, and I felt Westtown should be, too. That's why I decided as I entered my senior year that I was either going to start a nonviolent revolution in the school or I was going to get kicked out. I came close to doing both.

I was on the Religious Life Committee and organized an early-morning meditation time before breakfast several mornings a week. I also launched a Beliefs into Action group. We examined our beliefs as Christians and Quakers in light of the nuclear arms race and the state of the world.

This was the 1950s, during the virulently anticommunist McCarthy era, when the "nuclear scare" was big in the news. Schoolchildren across the country had to hide under their desks during air raid drills. Most people believed that nuclear war could break out at any moment and that we needed to "be prepared."

Our Beliefs into Action group began going to Philadelphia for vigils outside City Hall, protesting air raid drills and nuclear weapons. We went to Morton, Pennsylvania, to hold signs of protest outside a plant that made military helicopters. A few local people didn't like what we were doing in their neighborhood and threw eggs at us.

I recruited other students to go door to door in Washington, DC. We handed out flyers about the dangers of nuclear weapons testing and asked concerned citizens to sign a petition opposing it. We were committed to the cause of peace, but we were also teenagers who preferred talking to people in another city over being back at school studying.

That year, U.S. peace activists planned to sail *The Golden Rule*, a thirty-foot ketch, into the Eniwetok nuclear testing area in the Marshall Islands. They intended to issue a warning that continued nuclear weapons testing was poisoning the environment, endangering the local population and all future generations, and moving us farther along the path to nuclear war. Each of the five people who were on board *The Golden Rule* wrote a letter, explaining why they were risking their lives to try to stop this threat to all of humanity. I can still remember their flyer—nothing but black emptiness on the front page.

Inspired by their action, that spring I joined a Peace Walk from Philadelphia to the United Nations in New York, calling for an end to all nuclear weapons testing. I wrote at the time: "We have a tremendous responsibility as citizens of the country which dropped the first atom bombs on Hiroshima and Nagasaki, and which is now continuing to test and manufacture H-bombs, whose only purpose is to kill and destroy hundreds of thousands of human lives, or even the whole human race. It is not right to endanger other human lives which only God can create."

Walk for Peace from Philadelphia to the United Nations in New York opposing all nuclear weapons testing, carrying sign "Walk for Peace" (1958).

I recruited students at Westtown and other friends to join. Joe Horton, the youngest walker to complete the six-day, hundred-mile walk, was ten years old. I was Joe's adopted "father" for the trip. Each night we stayed in a church or Friends meetinghouse, where local supporters brought us food and listened as we shared what we were doing and why.

We began our walk in Philadelphia with twenty people, and by the time we reached New York the crowd had swelled to a thousand, converging from several directions. Compared to more recent actions, it was small, but it was the biggest peace demonstration I had ever seen— and on a much grander scale than had occurred in this country before then. Our march, together with the hard work of many other people, led to the Partial Nuclear Test Ban Treaty in 1963.

As I prepared to graduate from Westtown, I recognized a deep gratitude for the example of my parents and many others who were my guides when I was young. That feeling remains as strong today. All of the concerns that form the heart of my life now were birthed in those early years. Faith and justice, peacemaking and nonviolence, compassion and community were all lessons whose seeds were planted and nurtured in me long ago. They have borne fruit in ways I never could have imagined when I was young.

Two weeks before my graduation, my parents were in a car accident early on a Sunday morning. I bicycled home to check on them and to help repair their car. I couldn't get back to the Friends Meeting at Westtown in time, so I went with my folks to the Middletown Friends Meeting near Tanguy.

When I got back to school, I explained to the assistant dean what had happened. He accused me of neglecting my spiritual responsibilities. The headmaster called me into his office and warned, "Hartsough, you can either shape up or ship out!"

It seemed clear to me by then that my peace activities, not my spiritual life, were at issue. I was mystified. From my perspective, I was trying to live by my values and principles—which I thought were the same Quaker principles upon which Westtown had been founded.

I was more than ready to "ship out." The world was waiting. And I couldn't wait to get there.

CHAPTER 2

One Common Humanity: Meeting Dr. King and a Lunch Counter Showdown

A number of other experiences and decisions had led me to that moment in June of 1960, when a man with a knife was threatening to put it through my heart.

Part of my dad's job as the American Friends Service Committee's college secretary, and then peace education secretary, was taking speakers around to various college campuses, churches, and summer institutes. As a kid, I sometimes went along and got to meet such spiritual giants as peace activist A.J. Muste and civil rights leaders Bayard Rustin and Ralph Abernathy.

Often when they finished a speaking tour, they would come back to our home on the last night. Just hearing their stories inspired me and made an indelible impression.

Ralph Abernathy told our family after his speaking tour that ours was the first white home in which he had slept. He invited us to visit him in Alabama. During spring vacation in 1956, my dad decided to accept Ralph's invitation. He took Paul and me to Montgomery, where the bus boycott was four months old.

On the way, we stopped overnight at Koinonia Partners, an interracial Christian community in rural Americus, Georgia. I had never before been in the South, and I knew of Koinonia only because we bought pecans by mail order from their farm. We slept in the guest house, which was across the road from the main community houses.

The week before we were there, members of the local Ku Klux Klan had driven by one night and shot a gun through the wall of the guest house. My clearest recollection is of sleeping on a bed with a hole in the wall about a foot above me. It was a little unnerving, especially for a fifteen-year-old.

Koinonia offered quite an introduction to segregation in the South and to the hatred and violence faced by people who were challenging the established order. We met with Clarence Jordan—Koinonia founder, theologian, and author of the "Cotton Patch version" of scripture—as well as other community members. But that bullet through the wall left the biggest impression.

Driving on to Montgomery, we saw the comfortable, often fancy, homes of white people, contrasted with the shacks where African Americans lived. It was very eye-opening to this already wide-eyed high school student from the North.

Ralph Abernathy welcomed us warmly and drove us around Montgomery, so we could see for ourselves the total segregation of neighborhoods and churches, swimming pools and buses. We visited a church that had been bombed less than a month before we arrived. I remember noting that it had not been boarded up or marked with police tape—no sign of any official acknowledgment that this tragedy had happened.

Even more clearly emblazoned in my memory is the image of the cross at the front of the church's sanctuary. Once hanging centered from two chains, it hung from just one, sideways and shattered. The board out front listing the pastor and sermon topic was also destroyed, and the pews were piles of splinters.

I simply could not understand how white Christians could do this to black Christians. I was stunned by the lengths to which some white folks were willing to go to try to destroy the movement for equality.

I was even more stunned that the victims of the violence were persistently saying that they were not going to give up their struggle for justice—and that they were committed to trying to love their enemies. I was deeply moved by so many people choosing to walk with dignity rather than ride the buses as second-class citizens. Seeing them get up an hour early to walk to work and get home an hour later than usual at night—refusing to hate the people who were imposing the hated system of segregation and creating this hardship—was profoundly inspiring and life-changing for me.

We would never have had the Montgomery movement if they had decided to practice "an eye for an eye." Bombing a white church in retaliation would have launched another vicious cycle in the endless pursuit of vengeance. It all would have ended right there with a lot of violence and death, rather than becoming a beacon of hope and the spark that would kindle the civil rights movement.

In Montgomery, we frequently stopped and greeted people on their front stoops. I remember an older black gentleman who said out of earshot of Ralph, "Before King came, things were very peaceful here." He had grown accustomed to being a second-class citizen, and on the surface everything was peaceful. He felt that Martin Luther King Jr. and others challenging the status quo were causing commotion, which was true.

King said that if you have a boil, you have to excise it and get the pus out before you can really be healthy. But some blacks felt it was better to live with the oppression, and rest in the knowledge that their churches wouldn't be bombed and they wouldn't have to walk to work. I understood their fear.

I remember going to Ralph's church after visiting the bombed one and wondering if it would be next. My family ate dinner in his home and then went to a hotel, because Ralph felt it was too dangerous for us to stay there overnight. A few months earlier, Martin Luther King's home had been bombed.

I still have a photograph of Ralph's daughter, Juandalynn, then four years old, and myself. I carried it in my wallet for many years, until it got so full of wrinkles that the picture was barely discernible. Unlike her, I had been brought up to believe that the police are the people who protect us. In Montgomery, police were routinely beating up, arresting, and ticketing people who challenged segregation.

Ralph had been issued a ticket for driving one mile over the speed limit. Montgomery's City Council had declared it illegal for drivers to offer rides in the carpools that had been organized to facilitate the bus boycott—ostensibly for lack of taxi licenses. New ways were always being invented to harass people in the movement. I was heartened to hear that some of the white women picked up their maids so they didn't have to walk to work, even though this upset their husbands.

I realized when we were in Montgomery that we were hearing and witnessing things the rest of the country barely knew were happening. The boycott wasn't yet big news, and "nonviolent direct action" hadn't become a common term in our national lexicon.

My dad, who gave me a copy of Mahatma Gandhi's *All Men Are Brothers* when I was in high school, had studied Gandhi and written papers on nonviolence in his years at seminary. But here was nonviolence being put into practice in a political struggle in the United

States from a Christian faith perspective. Witnessing its power was an important next step in my life journey.

We attended a Montgomery Improvement Association meeting, amid a crowd of black clergy and one white pastor, who worked closely with the black pastors to organize the carpools. Martin Luther King greeted us and warmly welcomed our family to the meeting: "these young people from the North have come to see the freedom struggle." He was young, though twenty-six seemed old to me at fifteen. With serious intent, he conducted the meeting and played a positive role by getting everyone's input and engagement.

I was impressed with King as a human being, and for the key role he was playing in the movement. But I had no idea that he was going to be one of my heroes for life—and a prominent figure in history. He was starting to do some speaking and fundraising away from Montgomery. But we had no sense that this was the beginning of a very historic period in which African Americans were going to rise up and demand justice all over this country, or that the nonviolent methods employed in Montgomery would influence a whole movement.

Bayard Rustin, who had been part of the first Freedom Ride to desegregate public buses back in 1947, told us many stories of his early meetings with King. Bayard was sitting with King one day at his dining room table and saw a gun on one of the chairs. According to Bayard, the two of them had a heart-to-heart conversation. He understood King's desire to defend himself and his family, but he knew that if King used that gun on his enemies, it would be contrary to the spirit of what they were trying to do and would eventually destroy the movement.

Bayard and Glen Smiley, a pastor from the Fellowship of Reconciliation, spent significant time with King, helping him deepen his understanding of, and commitment to, nonviolence, both personally and for the struggle. Later the AFSC's Jim Bristol, a colleague of my dad who was living in India, arranged for King and his wife, Coretta Scott King, to tour that country and learn more about Gandhi and the power of nonviolent direct action to create change. King's conversion was very crucial for the movement.

Perhaps nothing had more of an impact on me as a teenager than my visit to Montgomery and my brief encounter with Martin Luther King. I was moved by the determination and forgiving spirit of the people I had met in the movement and, painful as it was, I wanted to keep opening myself to understanding segregation and other forms of injustice and the struggle to create change. That was very much on my mind as I pondered where I should go to college.

On August 6, 1958, Hiroshima Day, I participated in a peace vigil of silent prayer and fasting at the White House—an all-day plea for an end to nuclear weapons testing and the nuclear arms race on the anniversary of the bombing of Japan. At the end of that day, I went to Washington, DC's Florida Avenue Friends Meeting for a period of silent meditation. There I received the closest thing to a leading that I had ever experienced. I felt a deep clarity, as if the Great Spirit were speaking directly to me: "You should go to Howard University."

The next day I walked across town to Howard to find out how to apply. Bayard Rustin was one of the first people to encourage me to do what my heart was telling me to do and go to Howard. But when I went home to share this news with my parents, my mother was heartbroken. I had already been accepted at prestigious Swarthmore College, and she had her heart set on me going there.

I still had enough in me of the nine-year-old who wanted to please his mother that I agreed to a compromise. I started college at Swarthmore and spent one year there trying to get more people of color admitted. My sophomore year, I transferred to Howard University, with the hope of helping that predominantly African American institution integrate from the other direction.

Five months after I entered Howard, on February 1, 1960, four students from the North Carolina Agricultural and Technical State University in Greensboro sat down at the lunch counter inside a Woolworth's store, and launched the student sit-in movement. By the next weekend, my friends from Howard and I had set up a picket line at the Woolworth's store in Washington, DC. I was convinced that my leading to go to Howard had to do with being part of that struggle and embracing the opportunity to practice active nonviolence in the movement for racial equality.

Most of the restaurants, hotels, and movie theaters in Washington were already integrated, but in Maryland and Virginia almost everything was segregated. Even African ambassadors to the United Nations could not eat in public facilities in Maryland when traveling between DC and New York. So my African American friends and I began going to Maryland on Saturday mornings.

We would show up at a drugstore and try to get something to eat. Invariably, the lunch counter would be closed and we would be arrested. Unlike most of my peers in college, who spent their weekends at parties,

I spent many of my weekends my sophomore year in jail. We sang freedom songs and shared stories to enliven our spirits behind bars. First thing Monday morning, we would be in court, and back in classes not long after that—until the following Saturday morning, when it happened all over again.

We went to Maryland because the American Nazi Party was active in Virginia. George Lincoln Rockwell, the founder and commander of the militant hate group, lived in Arlington. He was threatening to lynch anyone who challenged Virginia's segregation laws, which imposed a $500 fine and a six-month jail sentence on anyone who tried to integrate a public facility. So, we kept going to Maryland.

We finished our college exams in June, and still nobody had challenged Virginia's unjust laws. We felt that we had to. By then there were sit-ins by students all over the South, and lots of young people were going to jail.

We undertook additional nonviolence training, knowing we were going to face far more physical violence and verbal abuse in Virginia than we had in Maryland. We participated in role plays to strengthen our courage and practice nonviolence in response to the expected violence. Several people decided during those exercises in self-discipline not to go to Virginia. We were only nineteen, twenty years old, and some students knew they weren't up for facing the inevitable danger.

On June 10, ten African American students from Howard, a white woman from another college, and I walked into the heart of the hatred and sat down at the lunch counter at the People's Drug Store in Arlington. Within minutes we heard sirens coming from several directions. We steeled ourselves for the worst. But the store owner informed the police he didn't want us arrested; apparently he didn't want the negative publicity. But he put up "Closed" signs on the counter and refused to serve us food.

We stayed until the store closed that night and then went back the next morning. Those two days were probably the most challenging of my life. We grew very hungry as that first sixteen-hour day stretched on. All sorts of racist epithets and chants of "Go back to Russia" were hurled at us. We worked at remaining calm and peaceful, which became more of a challenge as the harassment escalated to physical attacks.

People spat on us. They shoved lit cigarettes down our shirts, and one angry man threw a firecracker at us. They kicked us off the stools and punched us in our chests and stomachs so violently that we fell to the floor. A young African American woman sitting next to me got hit, which

Sit-in at People's Drug Store in Arlington, VA, June 1960. I am on the far right. [Photo: Virginia Historical Society]

I found particularly difficult to watch. American Nazi Party "storm troopers" showed up with their swastikas and pictures of apes, which they waved around, taunting us, shouting, "Is we, or is we ain't equals?"

Late in the evening of the second day, I was reading from a pocket New Testament I had with me. I had turned to Jesus's Sermon on the Mount, to the same passage that I had remembered as a seven-year-old being pelted with ice balls: "Love your enemies . . . Do good to those who hate you."

I was meditating on those words when I heard a voice behind me say, "You nigger lover. Get out of this store in two seconds, or I'm going to stab this through your heart." I glanced behind me at a man with the most terrible look of hatred I had ever seen. His eyes blazed, his jaw quivered, and his shaking hand held a switchblade—about half an inch from my heart.

Loving my enemy was suddenly more than just a discussion in Sunday school or a confrontation among schoolboys over ice balls. For a fleeting moment I doubted that Jesus meant to include a man so hateful among those who deserved to be loved. I had just seconds to respond to him, and I was grateful for those many hours of role playing and practice the previous two days.

I turned around and tried my best to smile. Looking him in the eye, I said to him, "Friend, do what you believe is right, and I will still try to love you." Both his jaw and his hand dropped. Miraculously, he turned away and walked out of the store.

That was the most powerful experience of my twenty years of life. It confirmed my belief in the power of love, the power of goodness, the power of God working through us to overcome hatred and violence. I had a profound sense that nonviolence really works. At that moment, nonviolence became much more to me than a philosophical idea or a tactic that had once made a difference in Gandhi's India. It became the way I wanted to relate to other human beings, a way of life, a way of working for change.

My response had touched something in my accuser. He had seen me as an enemy. But through my response, I believe I became a human being to him. The humanity in each of us touched. If we treat our opponents as human beings, there's a reasonably good chance that they will respond in kind. What better way could there be to disarm the world's violence?

I reflected a lot on that experience later. I came to realize that I had done not only the right thing but also the most effective thing I could have done to protect myself. If I had tried to fight back, I probably would have been stabbed. Even if I had won the fight, my accuser's hatred and anger would only have grown stronger, and we both would have come out of the confrontation wounded. I hoped that by doing what I did, I opened an opportunity for him to rethink whether hating a person with whom he disagrees is better than trying to find common humanity with someone he saw as "other."

That morning the *Northern Virginia Sun* had published a front-page feature about the first day of our sit-in. And that night a mob of five hundred people was waiting outside, jeering at us and spewing death threats. Some had rocks in their hands. I really didn't know if we were going to get out of that drugstore alive.

Scared, hungry, and exhausted, we decided to write a statement appealing to the religious and community leaders of Arlington to use their influence to get public facilities open to everyone. Behind a flimsy barricade of beach chairs, we stood at the front door and read it aloud. We ended our appeal by declaring, "If nothing has changed in a week, we will be back." After all that we had endured, those words were very hard to utter.

Some supportive media people who were covering the story had cars right outside the drugstore. They hustled us out of there and got us safely back into Washington. Then we shook for six days, trying to decide if we had the courage to go back.

We were inspired by students in other parts of the country who were facing even worse dangers. We felt their moral support and took comfort in knowing that we weren't acting alone. But, still, we weren't sure we were strong enough to go through it all again.

On the sixth day, we got a phone call telling us that the restaurants and lunch counters in Arlington would be desegregated by the end of June. It was one of the happiest moments of my life!

We learned that the religious leaders in Arlington had met after our sit-in, and then talked with the business leaders of the community. Twelve students with some courage had touched something in the hearts and consciences of these community leaders. We had called upon them to reflect on what was happening in their community, and to use their influence to try to change things. And they did.

We were part of a much larger movement that was transforming communities all across the South. We were challenging segregation laws head-on. Together we were bringing that issue into the light so that the cities and the entire country had to deal with it.

I learned the most important lesson in my life up to that point—and maybe still: that a few people with some courage and commitment to nonviolence don't have to just sit and curse and feel powerless when terrible things are happening. We can challenge and transform injustice, violence, and oppression to achieve a more just society. We can change the course of history!

Among my fellow students who participated in the sit-ins was Stokely Carmichael, who emerged as a leader of the Nonviolent Action Group at Howard. A year after our sit-in, in June 1961, he was arrested after a Freedom Ride in Jackson, Mississippi, and spent fifty-three days in a six-by-nine-foot cell at Parchman State Prison Farm, where at nineteen years old he was the youngest detainee among the hundreds of other Freedom Riders from all around the country who had come to Mississippi to challenge segregation in the heart of the south.

One night the sheriff ran an air conditioner and fans until the temperature dropped to thirty-eight degrees. When Stokely was being strong-armed by guards, he began singing "I'm gonna tell God how you treat me"; soon other prisoners joined in the song. Stokely was notorious for keeping up morale in the brutal prison by telling jokes.

Stokely was very active in SNCC (Student Nonviolent Coordinating Committee), eventually becoming the group's chair. He spent a year in Mississippi after his release from Parchman, where he witnessed white racists regularly driving by and shooting into the houses where SNCC members were staying. By the time he returned to Howard, he was preaching that the white race was the devil and that hope lay only in total separation of the races, which grieved me greatly. One evening, the two of us had a conversation that went long into the night, about the effectiveness of nonviolence in the struggle for justice and the future of our country.

Many years later, when I was living in San Francisco, I heard that Stokely, by then having taken the name Kwame Ture, was coming to be part of an event at La Peña, a local cultural center. I'll never forget the warm hug this old friend gave me after his talk. The two of us sat for a while in the back row of the auditorium with our arms around each other, listening to live music from the stage.

I will always be grateful for that moment. There's politics, and then there's the human dimension. His knowledge that I had committed my life to the struggle for justice was stronger between us than the political hurt he had suffered from so many other white people.

During college I had the rare blessing of hearing Martin Luther King preach almost every month at the Howard University Chapel. I began to feel King's spirit even more deeply, with hope and tremendous gratitude for his life. In August 1963, I joined the hundreds of thousands of people who converged on the city for the March on Washington. Bayard Rustin was the main organizer. I can still remember exactly where I was standing amid that huge sea of humanity when I heard King's "I Have a Dream" speech—and the tremendous hope I felt for our country turning away from segregation and injustice and living up to its highest ideals of freedom and justice for all.

I was deeply moved when I learned that in 1964, when King came back from accepting the Nobel Peace Prize in Norway, he went directly back to Washington to speak with President Lyndon Johnson about the need for a voting rights bill. Johnson respected King, but he felt that such legislation would be impossible to get through Congress. He counseled King to wait a few years and then bring it up again.

Wasting no time, King went back to the South and organized with others the voting rights campaign in Selma, Alabama. Images of African Americans lined up at the Selma courthouse being beaten and arrested day after day after day for attempting to vote spread out over our newspapers and television screens. Those brave souls aroused the conscience of the nation, and within months Congress passed the Voting Rights Act.

I was heartened when King took the great risk of confronting not only racism and violence at home, but also our nation's militarism and violence around the globe, particularly in Vietnam when on April 4, 1967, he began speaking out clearly and strongly against the war in Vietnam.

In November 1967, King and the Southern Christian Leadership Conference planned the Poor People's Campaign, focused on economic justice, jobs, and housing. Those of us in DC were anticipating with great excitement the thousands of people who would again converge on the city in the spring of 1968, to build a powerful nonviolent movement to demand justice for poor people in this country. The organizers had drawn up an "Economic Bill of Rights," which they hoped would be passed by Congress. I was ready to follow wherever King led, anxious to be a part of transforming America according to his dream.

On April 4, 1968, I was returning from a conference on World Law and Disarmament at Princeton University. My ride stopped to let me out on Connecticut Avenue at the edge of DC, where I planned to catch a bus to the southeast section of the city where I lived. Just before I got out of the car, the news of King's assassination came on the radio.

When King was killed, I was devastated and in a state of shock and depression. Losing that beautiful and powerful spiritual leader was a terrible setback. It felt like the possibility for transformation of our country had been irretrievably shattered.

I got on my bike the next day and rode up Fourteenth Street, where distraught and desperate people had set blocks of buildings on fire. I understood their grief and rage, but I felt that they were killing the dream. People were firebombing stores, throwing rocks and Molotov cocktails, while fire trucks raced up and down the street. Feeling lost amid the chaos and smoke, I tried to figure out what to do.

I eventually realized that I was faced with a choice—to stay in a depression, or to commit myself to continue the work that King had begun. Fortunately, the people closest to King decided to go forward with the Poor People's Campaign, to honor his memory and help realize the dream.

I agreed to help lead nonviolence training workshops in local churches for people who wanted to be involved with the Poor People's Campaign. I also pitched in to build plywood shanties and set them up on Washington's National Mall. It was a very rainy spring and summer, and water sometimes two and three feet deep pooled around the shanties. But despite the downpours and the mud, people stayed for six weeks, until the police arrested them and destroyed their encampment for equality.

One afternoon, five hundred people from the campaign attempted to deliver their petition for economic justice to Congress. They were stopped at the edge of the Capitol grounds, and those who refused to disperse were arrested. In solidarity, a group of Quakers tried to pick up the march where they had left off. We too were stopped by the police. We knelt and held an impromptu worship service until we also were arrested.

We spent two weeks on the top floor of the sweltering DC jail in the middle of summer, without air conditioning or fans. What a group we were—African American, Latino, Native American, and a few of us pale ones—trying to fulfill Martin Luther King's dream. Though we were physically uncomfortable due to the stifling heat and lack of movement, we were animated in our discussions about America's future and our commitments to bring about fundamental change in our society.

Nothing we would do could bring King back. But we understood that his spirit and his dream lived on in our efforts. Death didn't have the final word. The people who endured the rain and the arrests on the mall were right to name their courageous presence "Resurrection City."

CHAPTER 3

Crossing Borders: Citizen Diplomacy in Cuba and Yugoslavia

From the moment that I was a young boy watching my father leave on a train bound for New York City to catch a flight to Gaza, I have had curiosity about other parts of the world. When I was in high school, in addition to hosting U.S. civil rights and peace activists on their speaking tours as part of his work with the American Friends Service Committee, Dad invited leaders in struggles for freedom and justice from around the globe to speak and then stay in our home. I was riveted by their stories.

After graduating from high school, I participated in a Peace Caravan sponsored by AFSC with students from Yugoslavia, Turkey, and the United States. We traveled throughout upstate New York, giving talks about the nuclear threat and trying to convince people of the importance of working toward world peace.

At that point I had done virtually no public speaking in front of people I didn't know, and everyone in our group felt a bit shaky about giving talks to strangers. One of our first visits was to a Lions Club luncheon. The members launched the event with chanting, "Bite, Bite, Bite"—which did nothing to reassure us that we would get a friendly reception!

In 1963, I organized a second Peace Caravan, traveling this time mostly to conservative Quaker churches and meetings in the Midwest, where Cold War fever was strong. I remember seeing billboards as we entered several towns: "Get the U.S. out of the UN and get the UN out of the U.S." At each stop, the Quakers organized a potluck meal, and then we talked about the need to step back from the brink of war and live in peace with the Russians. The challenges of that experience forged

Quaker work camp participants in Cuba (summer 1959).

some lifelong friendships among several of us on the Peace Caravan, including Marge Nelson, David Morris, Lou Wolf, and Walt Blackburn.

My curiosity about other parts of the world led to an interest in seeing some of them. The summer after my first year of college, I participated in a work camp in Cuba from June to August 1959, a few months after the triumph of the revolution that ousted dictator Fulgencio Batista. We lived in the little village of Barajagua in Oriente Province in the eastern part of Cuba, helping to build a medical clinic and to reconstruct homes that had been destroyed by Batista's forces as a warning to those who supported Fidel Castro and the revolution.

We were digging ditches for water and sewage for new homes for the community. It was hard labor that involved throwing dirt and rock up out of the trenches in which we worked onto a pile above us. My Spanish was even worse then than it is now, but I learned two very important words.

The first was *aquatero*, which was what they called the young boy who came around with a can of water with a hole in the bottom for drinking. We sweated all day in blazing sun, and getting a drink of water felt like the difference between life and death. The other word was *cuidado*, which is what someone shouted when a rock he had thrown up on the pile of dirt started rolling back down at us. When we heard "*¡Cuidado!*" we had to get out of the way very fast.

The only electricity in Barajagua was at the store in the middle of the village, so in the evenings people walked there from all directions to watch Fidel Castro, the new prime minister, on TV. He sometimes gave talks in the evenings that lasted up to six hours, and people listened attentively. Overall, the people I met were very supportive of the revolution. They had lived in desperate poverty, and the feeling prevailed that justice was right around the corner and they would no longer have to live the way they had lived all their lives.

On a Sunday—the only day we had time to do anything other than dig trenches and build cement-block homes—I went up in the hills with a local boy named Ramón. We looked out over thousands of acres of sugar cane. Almost everyone in the village cut sugar cane in the summer, with no employment the rest of the year. We saw the laborers putting in long hours in the fields whenever we went to the stream to get sand for making cement. Right in the middle of our view was a huge, gleaming structure with a golden roof. "What is that?" I asked.

"It's the palace of the landowner from the United States," Ramón explained.

The realization that my country had supported a government as unjust as Batista's, with a few people having so much and most having so little, was profoundly disturbing to me. I wondered if it were possible to build a world of more equitable sharing in which the U.S. government did not support dictatorships. The boy at my side had hope that he would see that world. "After we have agrarian reform," he said excitedly, "everyone will have some land—and enough to eat!"

Following the triumph of the revolution, Fidel Castro had come first to the United States for assistance in helping Cuba make the transformation to a more just society through land reform and educational and health care initiatives. The U.S. government thumbed its nose at him.

Despite the many claims here in the United States that Cuba's revolution was part of an "international Communist conspiracy," for the first year and a half after the revolution Cuba had no diplomatic relations with the Soviet Union. Only after our government turned its back, refusing to cooperate when Cuba no longer allowed our wealthy landowners to play "king" in their society, did the Cubans feel pushed to seek support elsewhere.

After the others from the work camp returned home, I stayed a few extra weeks in Barajagua, living with several families. I then said my sad goodbyes to the people of the village, who had welcomed me with their wonderful hearts. They had received me generously in a time of scarcity and shared what little they had. I still cherish the New Testament that a pastor from the local Baptist church gave me.

In Barajagua, children could attend school only up to the sixth grade unless their families had money to send them to a boarding school in another town, which virtually none of them did. I had grown attached to Ramón, whose education was about to end for lack of about $250. Before leaving, I sold my plane ticket to Philadelphia and gave him the money, so that he could attend seventh grade.

I took a bus across Cuba. When I arrived in Havana, I asked in my limited Spanish for directions to "*el puerto*." I was directed to another bus, which took me to "*el aeropuerto*," the airport—instead of to the port from which boats left for Key West.

It was late by the time I finally reached the port. A friendly fellow I had met on the bus asked where I would be staying for the night. When I told him I was going to sleep on a park bench, he expressed concern that someone might take my backpack or hurt me. I told him that I didn't have anything of value and wasn't worried.

He wasn't happy about it, but he said okay. He came back about an hour later and told me he couldn't sleep because of his concern about me. He said, "I think you'd be much safer at the local jail." He had a friend who worked there. So I decided if he felt so strongly about it, I would go with him and spend the rest of the night in the jail.

At the jail he introduced me as a North American who had come down to help rebuild a village in Oriente Province and asked if I could stay for the night. I tried—unsuccessfully—to sleep in a chair in a common room, surrounded by boisterous Havana policemen who were watching a shoot-'em-up American Western on TV.

After a while, one told me that I could sleep in an empty cell and led me there. In the morning, I woke up in time to catch the boat to Florida. I told the guards, "I'm ready to go now."

One said, "What do you mean, you're ready to go?"

I explained that my friend had said that I could sleep there and that I needed to catch the ferry to Key West. They looked at me very suspiciously. They left to go check out my story before letting me out about an hour later. Fortunately, I was released in time to make the boat.

A Cuban news reporter and her family who were on the ferry gave me a ride from Key West to Miami, where I started my long trek north on Highway 1. Florida was the worst place I've ever hitchhiked. The state had a vagrancy law that made sitting or lying down along the road or in the woods near the road a crime, carrying a three-month jail sentence. I had already spent as much time in jail as I wanted to on this trip, so I kept walking.

The only people who gave me rides were police officers, who drove a little way and then dropped me at the northern edges of their jurisdictions. I had spent two days and nights mostly walking, without any sleep, when finally a guy in a fancy car stopped and picked me up. He told me I looked very tired and invited me to spend the night at his home.

He had a wonderfully friendly family and a beautiful home on a lake. We took a boat ride while he fired up the grill for a barbecue. And then he told me that he and his wife drove their children thirty miles each way twice a day so they wouldn't have to go to school with black kids. That's 120 miles a day of driving to keep their kids in segregated schools.

I faced a moral dilemma. Should I tell this family that I was headed back to start school at Howard University? Should I challenge their racism? I pondered it a while. And then I decided to keep quiet, eat some great food, and get a good night's sleep before heading north the next morning.

A year later, after completing my sophomore year at Howard, I was relieved that the officials of Arlington, Virginia, had decided to desegregate their lunch counters. This was true not only because it meant that my friends and I didn't have to ramp up our courage again for more sit-ins. I had received a scholarship to spend the summer in Yugoslavia with the Experiment in International Living, beginning a few days later, and I would have had to give it up if I had been in jail or otherwise occupied in Virginia.

This early experiment in citizen diplomacy gave young people of many countries the opportunity to get to know one another and experience different cultures. The hope was that these encounters would help to lay a foundation for more peaceful relations between peoples and nations all over the world. I was interested in understanding Communism, and Yugoslavia was the only Communist country that welcomed participants in the program.

On June 19, 1960, I went to Canada and got on a boat departing from Montreal, bound for Italy. Our group included ten students—one from the Virgin Islands, one from Puerto Rico, and the rest of us from across the United States. We spent twelve days at sea, getting language lessons and each sharing and leading a discussion about a particular aspect of Yugoslavia that we had studied.

The sea was calm, and we moved slowly. Our first view of Europe was the glow of the lighthouses of Portugal in the distance at night. In the morning, we glimpsed the elegant mountains of Africa on our right and the southern hills of Spain on our left as we headed toward the massive rock at Gibraltar. We sailed on past France, finally making port at Genoa, Italy, a gorgeous city built on a hill.

I truly felt that I had reached the "Old World," appreciating ancient walls and narrow streets—and the beautiful gardens everywhere. We took a train to Milan, standing the whole way, looking out the window and waving to the people in the villages and towns along the way, and then walked about fifteen miles through Milan meeting people. At 3:45 in the morning, we got on a train to Ljubljana, Yugoslavia. We traveled through the Southern Alps and along the Adriatic Sea, meeting some Yugoslav students with whom we enjoyed trying to talk and share ideas.

The Experiment in International Living included living with a family. Before I arrived, I had been paired with a relatively well-to-do Yugoslav family. They were part of the emerging upper class highlighted in *The New Class: An Analysis of the Communist System*, written in 1957 by Milovan Djilas, a former Communist vice president of Yugoslavia, whose class exposé had made him a prominent dissident.

I had corresponded with the young man who was to be my Yugoslav "brother," and I realized that it wasn't the right fit. I wanted to live with an "ordinary" family. So I was placed instead out in Preserje, a rural village nestled in the heart of the mountains, with a family that was quite poor. The Rogeljs were definitely not part of the "new class." They were wonderfully kind, with the most memorable smiles.

The mother was ill and in the hospital. The father was also ill, but he worked when he could as a butcher. My Yugoslav brother, Tone, was a law student who worked on a collective farm, spent his summer as a journalist in a newspaper office, and was planning to work with the Communist Youth Brigades later in the summer. His brother and sister also worked very hard.

The first thing I saw when I entered their living room was their collection of the complete works of Vladimir Lenin, about thirty books in all. They were very curious about my family's possessions—whether we had a car, a refrigerator, a television set. I felt uncomfortable telling them that we had these things and more, and I regretted the clothes I was wearing, which were fancy by their standards. When I talked about peace, they asked if I thought there really could be peace with so many people hungry while others had so many things.

This wonderful family was very generous toward me with the little they had. We usually had bread and coffee for breakfast, lettuce and noodles for lunch, and cornmeal mush for supper. They lent me a bicycle for exploring the countryside. There were about as many bicycles on the streets in Yugoslavia as we had cars in the United States.

Tone and I communicated with a mixture of Slovenian, Scrbo-Croatian, German, Russian, and English. He and I had many fascinating conversations—an idealistic Communist going head to head with an idealistic follower of Mahatma Gandhi, trying to understand each other's point of view and surrender our preconceived prejudices.

The Yugoslav version of Communism was quite different from that of the Soviet bureaucracy, and Tone and his family had great faith in this version of "government by the people," as they described it. Yugoslavs were trying to make their society democratic from the bottom up. Workers' councils were in charge of the factories and farms. The workers owned the economic enterprises and were their own bosses.

One major point of disagreement between us was that Tone and his family felt that religion was unnecessary, believing that science explained everything. I believed—then as now—that there is a spirit at the heart of every person, and that we humans are more than simply material beings.

At the end of the summer, in response to a conversation we had frequently, Tone said to me, "Dave, I hope that you are right and that you can convince the wealthy of the world to share their wealth with the poor people of the world. But I want you to know that if you are not successful, we are going to take it!"

I have always taken that as a challenge. We disagreed about many things, but Tone Rogelj and I became good friends. And that summer I felt that all the people of the world could do the same.

For the second month of the Experiment in International Living, our group—ten Yugoslavs and the ten of us from across the Atlantic—traveled together throughout the country. We were partly sightseeing and partly getting to know the people of Yugoslavia.

The group typically spent about an hour and a half per meal in restaurants. Tone and I were interested in meeting other people, so we asked our leader if she would give us money for bread, which she did. So we ate bread and met people on the streets, often getting invitations into their homes while the others were eating in the restaurants.

We traveled to Zagreb and then to Sarajevo, a fascinating city with a strong Muslim influence. In Belgrade we visited the U.S. Embassy, where the official who met with us gave us a 100 percent State Department version of Yugoslavia. His view of Yugoslavs was that of people living in a Communist prison, longing to break free of their rulers. This was quite different from what we had observed and heard from the Yugoslav people themselves. We wondered if the embassy officials had ever ventured beyond the walls to talk with ordinary people.

We walked the streets of both old and modern Skopje, then traveled forty-eight hours on a bus through the mountains around Albania to Dubrovnik, a resort town on the Adriatic Coast. We recuperated from the long and sleepless bus trip on the small island of Korchula, which gave me time to ponder what I was learning. The greatest gift of my time in Yugoslavia was the warm friendship of the people. I also felt that my understanding of Communism had been greatly deepened. "Communists" were no longer the faceless enemies our government told us we had to fight and kill.

I appreciated the willingness of Yugoslavs to give up some basic freedoms in order to make material progress, sharing resources among all. But I also saw the tragedy of people choosing not to offer any critique of their government, for fear that they would lose out on good jobs or scholarships for education.

I met up with my brother Paul, who had been in Eastern Europe with the Quaker European Travel Seminar, and we participated in the Zadar International Camp with students from all around the world. It was really quite impressive. Young people from all parts of Yugoslavia, who were building a "new Yugoslavia," shared a spirit of community with those of us from other countries. After long days of digging ditches for irrigation, we told stories and sang songs around evening bonfires and got to know one another, building a caring community.

As I walked the streets of Zadar, I saw evidence of the horrible devastation of World War II. I realized sadly that the remnants of buildings and statues also signified destroyed lives. Almost two million people—10 percent of the country's population—died in the war, their only crime being that they lived in Yugoslavia.

In Zadar, most of the families had been imprisoned in concentration camps or had lost one or more family members in the war. Yugoslavs, more than we, understood why war should never happen again. Though they felt strongly about the rightness of their beliefs, they were like people all over the world who wanted to live in peace.

Amid the ruins, I contemplated all the suffering and death and destruction that had taken place all over Europe. I wondered why, with all our collective human intelligence, we have not been able to find a better way to resolve conflicts than bombing the homes and killing the people in countries whose governments we don't like. I imagined what

With Tone Rogelj in Preserje, Slovenia, Yugoslavia (1960).

would happen if young people from all over the world could have the kind of experience I was having in Yugoslavia. Perhaps they would not want to kill one another, and maybe we could throw wars into the trash bins of history.

After the end of the Second World War, under the leadership of Marshal Josip Broz Tito, Yugoslavia initially sided with the Eastern Bloc. But after Tito split with Joseph Stalin of the Soviet Union in 1948, as the Cold War heated up, Yugoslavia pursued a policy of neutrality and became one of the founding members of the Non-Aligned Movement. I found that stance compelling, believing that the future of the world rested in nations being willing to take such a neutralist position.

When I was in Yugoslavia that summer, people in all the republics saw themselves primarily as Yugoslavs—not as Bosnians, or Croats, or Serbs, or Slovenians. Tito was investing profits from the nation's various economic enterprises into a tremendous social welfare program that lifted everyone. People were benefiting from being part of Yugoslavia, rather than competing as citizens of separate republics.

Commerce, friendship, and intermarriage flourished among the various ethnic groups, which was remarkable. Three decades later, when unspeakable horror changed everything, I would carry with gratitude and heartbreak my memories of that unforgettable summer. And I would remember with great fondness the generous warmth of the people of Yugoslavia.

CHAPTER 4

Bridging the Divide: Forging Peace at Checkpoint Charlie

M y brief stays in Cuba and Yugoslavia whetted my appetite for understanding other cultures and pursuing peace by build- ing international friendships. I particularly felt in that era of Cold War fever that I wanted to gain a more in-depth understanding of Communists and Communism.

When I left the United States for Yugoslavia in June 1960, I hadn't planned to spend the next school year in Berlin, a continuing flashpoint in the conflict between East and West. But spending my junior year of college abroad seemed like an important next step and an amazing opportunity. The situation had heated up even more since my father had been there seven years earlier. I was arriving at a moment defined by history as "The Berlin Crisis," with the United States and the Soviet Union threatening nuclear war over the divided German city.

I had studied German in high school and college, and I thought that Berlin might be the perfect place to live, to get to know people on both sides of the "Iron Curtain" and try to understand their realities. I hoped to gain a better understanding of how we could live in peace, rather than continuing the Cold War—which could so easily become a "hot war," with the potential of killing millions of our fellow human beings on the planet.

I left Yugoslavia with great sadness, feeling when I departed from Ljubljana like I was leaving my second family and hometown. I got on a train that carried me through the gorgeous Austrian Alps and then hitchhiked from Salzburg to Germany. I arrived in Munich at midnight without a German *pfennig* and was fortunate to find a kind stranger who helped me get a room.

My first visit was to Hockenheim, where I was pursuing a piece of my family history. In 1871 my great-grandfather left this small village outside of Heidelberg to avoid conscription into the Prussian army. In 1953, during his time in Berlin, my dad had visited some of our relatives who lived there. When I showed up, they embraced me warmly and treated me like their long-lost son. They had kept all of our family's Christmas letters through the years and cherished the connection.

Elizabeth Boehm, a distant cousin, had a son who was killed in Tunis and another in Russia during the Second World War. Her only surviving son, who had also fought in the German army, was covered with war scars. We had long talks about the war, including his very difficult years surviving a Russian prisoner-of-war camp.

During my year in Germany, these generous relatives sent me care packages filled with homemade cakes and cookies, nuts and fruit, cheese and pretzels, treating me like a visiting king. They invited me to come back and visit them at Christmas, and I wanted to take them an appropriate gift. I spent days combing bookstores looking for a book by Gandhi in German and was delighted when I finally found a copy of his autobiography, *My Experiments with Truth*.

I launched my studies with two months of intensive language lessons in Cologne. I was there with students from all over the world, and the only language we shared was German, so we got a good deal of practice.

Cologne had suffered heavy bombardment during the war, and 70 percent of the city had been destroyed. Walking one day through ruins with a student who had fled from East Germany, I realized that our countries had been on opposite sides during the war and that mine had been responsible for the terrible destruction we were witnessing. That such devastation was looming again against this city, many parts of which had been beautifully rebuilt, was very disturbing.

I wondered once more: does humanity have no higher destiny than this? A few German students told me they didn't think humankind was worth much if we couldn't find a way to live without destroying one another. But most Germans, after watching the Soviet Union take over Poland, Hungary, Czechoslovakia, and East Germany, felt that force was necessary to stop the Russians. I felt compelled once more to do all that I could toward fostering friendship instead of hostility between nations and pursuing alternatives to war.

The Friends Meeting in Cologne had only five members. Frau Schierk and her eighteen-year-old daughter, Lisa, "adopted" me.

Sundays after meeting for worship, they invited me to their home for lunch and told me pieces of their story.

Frau Schierk's son was only seventeen when he was forced to sign up to fight in Hitler's army. He felt compelled to "protect the fatherland" and get rid of the Allied invaders who were bombing it. He was severely wounded in battle, and for months his mother did not know if he was alive or dead.

In 1945, he was captured by the Russians and driven on foot, barefoot, across Czechoslovakia. He was then taken by train to a Russian prisoner-of-war camp. After six months, he was allowed to send his mother a twenty-five-word letter. Every month until the middle of 1949, they exchanged twenty-five word letters, until her son came home.

This Quaker mother also told me about her brave husband, who had felt compassion for people whose homes were being destroyed. The train station in Cologne had been reduced to rubble. Masses of displaced people crowded into the cathedral across the plaza, one of the few buildings that had withstood the intensive bombing, until there was no more space. It was wintertime and bitterly cold.

When bombs fell on apartment buildings, a few minutes elapsed between when they came through the roof and when they exploded. Frau Schierk's husband regularly ran into buildings and up to attics to grab the bombs and throw them out onto the street before they exploded. He, his wife, and everyone else knew that this was very dangerous and that he would likely get killed. But he explained that if he didn't do it, many people would have no shelter and would die on the frozen streets of Cologne. One day a bomb did explode in his hands, taking this brave man's life.

Both Frau Schierk and her daughter Lisa were, as a result of their family's suffering, committed pacifists. They believed that Germany and the United States should negotiate with the Russians rather than kill them. I was moved by their strength, especially given what the Russians had done to their son and brother.

Stories of suffering from the war were everywhere in Germany, and many people wanted to share them. Another woman told me about her husband, an army officer who had been badly wounded in 1943. Seeing the truth of what Hitler was up to, he joined a conspiracy that on July 20, 1944, made an unsuccessful assassination attempt on the Fuehrer. Army leadership was purged in response, and her husband was killed.

The stories I heard brought the human side of the conflict home to me. The war wasn't just about "fighting Hitler." In reality, our attacks and bombs had made life virtually unlivable for the entire German population.

About three weeks after I arrived in Germany, as part of our German study program, we students watched the movie *Mein Kampf*, based on Hitler's book about his plan to exterminate the Jews and dominate the world with a pure Aryan race. It was extremely disturbing. What was clear was that Hitler succeeded by whipping up emotion against Germany's enemies and manipulating the masses who were suffering under a severe economic depression.

I couldn't understand why Germans hadn't read the book and refused to support Hitler's diabolic plan. I felt unnerved by the parallels with the United States in 1960. Our fear of Communism was so great that our government was willing to risk everything—even a nuclear world war and the possible extermination of all humankind—to stop the menace. And no one seemed to be asking if there wasn't a better way to achieve the same goal.

I happened to be reading *Uncle Tom's Cabin* in German at that time. The hypocrisy of our own self-righteousness was overwhelming to me. Enslaving millions of African Americans, and then continuing to treat them as subhuman second-class citizens, was a crime on a massive scale in "the land of the free."

I wished for a book as compelling as *Uncle Tom's Cabin* about our global situation. And I wondered why the United States couldn't fight the growth of Communism by sending economic aid and thousands of Peace Corps volunteers to struggling countries instead of continuing to build atomic bombs.

I believed that, in our fight against Communism, if we hated the Communists so much that we failed to live up to the best principles of our democracy—and our faith—then they had already won. Didn't our Christian faith teach us that we all bear the image of God? Couldn't we find a way to listen to one another and strive to live as brothers and sisters? Wasn't living together peacefully a more worthy goal than fighting Communism? And weren't the Communists right in saying that our faith didn't mean much if we were willing to incinerate the world to "defend" it?

I kept trying to understand both sides of the looming conflict over Berlin, but I lived in a sea of propaganda. The newspapers from both

East and West Germany were filled with it. I felt clear that peace would never come if people knew only the worst about each other.

I visited a Catholic and then an Evangelical (Protestant) church in Cologne. The people in both places seemed very serious in their worship, and they prompted me to wonder what it means to be a Christian. Jesus told his followers, "Just as you did it to one of the least of these who are members of my family, you did it to me" (Matthew 25:40) Could we love God and also let millions of our sisters and brothers starve—or prepare to kill them with nuclear weapons?

I had a fascinating conversation with a student from Persia, modern-day Iran. He pointed out that, although he was not against me personally, he felt I needed to understand that almost all the foreign aid given to his country from the United States was for the military, rather than for the machinery and technical assistance so badly needed in underdeveloped countries. Persia, he said, remained as poverty-stricken as it was before it began receiving U.S. aid seven years earlier, when the CIA had overthrown Iran's democratically elected prime minister and restored power to the repressive shah.

This student believed that my country was primarily interested in his country's oil. He also believed that the United States was wrong to label every country that wanted to throw off imperialism as Communist. Persia, he said, was neither capitalist nor Communist, and it was definitely not a democracy, even though the U.S. government used rhetoric about "protecting democracy" there.

He contrasted the Soviet Union's political imperialism with America's economic imperialism: our siphoning off of resources from other nations and then sending troops to defend "our way of life." Though I didn't fully understand it at the time, looking back now more than half a century later, I admire the prophetic ring of truth of this young man's perspective.

I also met a young woman from Indonesia, whose family had fled because of the repressive government there. I was moved by how many people around the globe seemed to be waking up, desiring to be free and to take control of their destinies. Nations were throwing off colonialism and revolting against oppression by the United States, the Soviet Union, and the rich. I hoped that we in the United States would wake up as well, putting our considerable influence on the side of peace and the well-being of all people in the world.

Toward the end of my two months in Cologne, I visited the Netherlands. In Rotterdam I was warned not to speak German while I was in that country. Early in the war, a majority of Rotterdam's population and most of its buildings had been destroyed in one day of bombing that came without warning.

During the war, every Dutch male between eighteen and forty years of age had been forced to work in German factories, to replace the German men who had become soldiers. If a man hid and was found by the German army, he and his entire family were killed. I felt pretty sure that if I had lived in Europe, I would not have survived World War II.

I hitchhiked to the Hague, taking in the Parliament, the International Court of Justice, and the North Sea, then went on to Amsterdam where I attended the Friends meeting. I found the Netherlands, with its flowers, canals, windmills, dikes, and ships—and the beauty of its people and architecture—to be friendly and fascinating.

Back "home" in Cologne, I attended a meeting on "The Jewish Question and the Evangelical Church." The professor who spoke said that Jews are looking for a Messiah, such as a king or military leader, to lead them out of earthly bondage. Christians call Jesus "Christ," or Messiah. Jews understandably have to ask what this Messiah means to Christians, who were responsible for the killing of millions of Jews in Europe, and hundreds of thousands of Japanese with two atomic bombs. If that is what our Christ condones, he could never be their Messiah. I found myself once again asking difficult questions about the meaning of faith.

One morning, I got into an argument with a professor in class. He declared that it was "complete nonsense" for the British Labor Party to talk about unilateral disarmament. I responded that I thought it was even greater nonsense—and both immoral and inhumane—to make bombs for the purpose of killing millions of our fellow human beings, who I believed were too precious to deserve death.

He shot back that I was all wrong. "Of course," he admitted, "disarmament is the moral thing to do. But all the people who think morally should become preachers and stay out of politics." I believed that those with moral consciences were the very people we needed in politics. The exchange between the professor and me led to many discussions around the university for the rest of the day.

I appreciated the view of American psychologist Charles E. Osgood, who advocated unilateral initiatives. He encouraged the United States to take the first step toward disarmament, beginning by destroying a few bombs in our nuclear stockpile in hopes that other nations would destroy some of their weapons, and then taking another step. In a public meeting, I heard U.S. journalist Robert Jung say that our worst enemy is not the bomb but our indifference to the bomb.

I hitchhiked one day to Bilstein, about 150 kilometers away and situated in gorgeous rolling hills. The trees were bright with fall color, which felt renewing to my soul. I participated in a retreat with a dozen Quakers and others in a youth hostel around the theme, "How can we become better Friends?"

We talked a lot about conscientious objection to war. The man who had given me a ride to the Netherlands was a conscientious objector and member of the War Resisters League. He had told me that West Germans could be exempted from the postwar draft if all their relatives had been killed during the war, if they were the only child left in a family, if they had relatives in East Germany, or for reasons of conscience.

Some of the students at the retreat had just come from a meeting with several East German Friends, who didn't have to face a military draft in their country. But to attend college they had to go into the military, and no option for conscientious objection existed.

One East German who was with us said that she believed people in her country were happier than in the West, because they were not obsessed with material goods and were content with their lives. But freedom was extremely limited in East Germany, and speaking against the military meant arrest and imprisonment. Ubiquitous plainclothes police listened all the time for such declarations.

At a War Resisters League meeting I attended in Cologne, a man invited us to form relationships with, and try to understand, East Germans. He said that if we trusted our "enemies" with a "tremendous fearless trust," they might prove worthy of our trust. Otherwise, he said, we remain in a "hate deadlock," returning hatred for hatred. As he spoke, both uniformed and plainclothes police officers around the room listened carefully—not so different in this democracy from the reality in East Germany.

Emotions were running high in Europe, and I was living in the heart of a potential flashpoint for war. I listened one evening to a program on East German radio, which emphasized the peace-loving nature of East Germans and war-loving nature of West Germans. It also repeatedly mocked Christianity and people who attended church, and especially U.S. evangelist Billy Graham. I couldn't understand why Communists felt they needed to fight so hard against the church.

Most West German Christians had a tremendous fear of Communism and therefore backed their own government's military wholeheartedly, which in turn created tremendous fear throughout other parts of Europe. A friend from Poland, a nation that had lost more than six million people during the war, dreaded the remilitarization of Germany and the possibility of its acquiring atomic weapons.

I rode a bike to Bonn alongside an *autobahn* (turnpike) that had been built in the Hitler era, when six million unemployed Germans were put back to work on such projects—perhaps the only "up side" of that time. I enjoyed the beautiful landscape, the homes of the president and of composer Ludwig von Beethoven, and the Rhine River. I saw a stunning sunset on my way home behind a bombed, boarded-up church and thought sadly, "And it was destroyed in God's name."

Having passed my German language exam, I was ready to head for Berlin and the Freie University. I was determined to live as simply as possible in Germany. Located in the Dahlem neighborhood of Berlin was an American shopping mall. I was greatly bothered that in the heart of a foreign country were Americans pretending like they were the kings of the world. I felt strongly that in order not to be a hypocrite, I had to relate to people who had few resources and not be one of the "ugly Americans" who were splurging everywhere with their money.

In West Berlin, I lived in Kreutsberg, the poorest part of the city. I found a very small room to rent in the home of an older woman, who lived on the top floor of a walk-up apartment building. Her husband had died of a stroke the week before I arrived, so she was feeling particularly sad and lonely and glad to have me share her home.

The winters were frigid, and the apartment had no heat. When I came home from the university each night, she would have prepared a hot water bottle to put in my bed so it would be a warm place to crawl into. She also put water in the teakettle every night that winter. In the morning, she turned on the heat under the ice in the teakettle. After it melted, she poured the hot water over the pipes to thaw them. She had lived through World War II, so although this was difficult, she said it was nothing compared to the hardship of the bombing during the war.

The Schwersenskys, the Quaker family that "adopted" me in Berlin, included mother Elsa, father Gerhardt, and grown daughter Roswitha. Most of their relatives had been killed during the war. During the time of Hitler, they had hidden Jews in their home and refused to display the Nazi flag or cooperate with the Nazi government.

Gerhardt was half Jewish. Initially, when all the Jews were rounded up, he was safe because he was married to a non-Jewish person. Later, the Nazis targeted people like him as well, and he had to live in cellars apart from his family, moving from city to city to avoid the Gestapo, until he was discovered and arrested, too.

The Nazis held him and others like him in prison during the war. Elsa and other wives of the men went and demonstrated at the Gestapo office in front of the prison day after day, demanding that their husbands be freed. The street they stood on was Rosenstrasse, and their protest became known as the Rosenstrasse Women's Action.

In order to avoid the bad publicity of having the protest continue, or resort to shooting German women on the street, the Gestapo eventually gave in and let the Jewish husbands of all these women go. This was an early example of "people power." A movie called *Rosenstrasse* about this extraordinary nonviolent action against the Nazis tells the story of these courageous women.

After the war, the generous Schwersensky family established a home for homeless children. They cared for twenty children aged three to fifteen, whose parents had been lost or killed in the war. One-day representatives of the U.S. military told them they had to leave their home within fifteen minutes, so that it could be used as a recreation house for U.S. soldiers.

The Schwersenskys found another home and operated for nine more months, giving everything they had to the children in their care. Then, in December 1945, the Communists told them they had to become Communists if they wanted to continue to run the home. They couldn't in good conscience embrace Communism, so they were put out of the house with nothing but the clothes they were wearing.

A kind family saw them on the street and invited them to live in their cellar. Friends donated a few goods. They had a plate and spoon for each of them, a small table with two chairs, and a triple-decker bed that all of the children shared.

The day before Christmas, someone gave them a loaf of bread, and they were overjoyed to have bread to eat on Christmas Day. On Christmas morning, the mother encountered on the street two former soldiers, who were starving and barefoot, with bloody feet. She took them to the cellar, cleaned and bound their feet, and invited them to share the bread, even though it meant even less for the children.

Later that day the family heard a knock on the door, and the son of a Jewish family, whose lives they had saved during the war, appeared with a fully decorated Christmas tree. A little later there was another knock. The Quakers at the door asked if the Schwersensky family lived there, and then handed over a food parcel that had been sent from some U.S. Quakers.

In five years, the family had not laid eyes on such bounty: soup, sweet potatoes, and fruitcake. The father invited in a few more folks off the street, and the former soldiers welcomed some of their friends. They all sang Christmas carols and shared, as the family told it, "the most wonderful Christmas in our lives."

Walking through Berlin, especially East Berlin, I was moved again by the terrible destruction of the war. Many houses were in ruins, their inhabitants forced to live in the cellars of their homes. Most of the standing houses bore scars from the blasts of bombs or guns. It was especially sad to see so many destroyed churches silhouetted against the sky and remember again that Christians bombed these churches and killed the Christians who worshipped there.

My German professor at Howard, Wolfgang Seifert, had been especially supportive of my effort to study in Berlin. He had told me about his three sisters, who lived in Leipzig, in East Germany. He had not seen them since the outbreak of the war, and he encouraged me to go to Leipzig and meet them. I had to navigate a morass of bureaucratic red tape to obtain permission, but it was well worth the effort.

I discovered when I got to Leipzig that the sisters ran a vegetarian restaurant. When I told them I was a friend of Wolfgang, they spread a delicious feast for me. I enjoyed it thoroughly—I had come a long way from the boy who didn't know the term *vegetarian* and didn't want his food mixed together!

The sisters had owned the restaurant since 1910. Almost fifty years later, they still remembered the group of men who came regularly to have dinner in 1916 and '17. Their talk was very animated, and their discussions went into the wee hours of the night, but the sisters didn't know what they were about.

In 1917, one of the sisters opened up a newspaper and saw a picture of one of the men who had been eating there all those months. It was Vladimir Lenin. He and his friends had been plotting the Russian Revolution in exile in their restaurant!

In Leipzig, I stayed with the family of Herman Ackner, who became a friend with whom I'm still in touch. His maternal grandfather, Emil Fuchs, was one of the "weighty Quakers" in Germany. His uncle was Klaus Fuchs, the nuclear scientist who was accused of turning over the

American tanks facing Soviet tanks at Checkpoint Charlie border crossing between East and West Berlin (1961).

secret of the atomic bomb to Russia. He was a "Most Wanted" man in the West. The authorities hoped to put him in prison for life.

When we had dinner, Klaus was often at the table with us. During grace before meals, I held his hand, along with others in the family. We never talked about who he was. I just remember him as a regular person and member of the family.

In Berlin, I was living just a few blocks from Checkpoint Charlie, the main crossover from the American to the Soviet sector of Berlin. I bicycled through that checkpoint almost every day while I was living there, passing through both U.S. and East German security.

It was there that tanks from both the United States and the Soviet Union were facing each other and threatening war, just a decade and a half after the end of World War II. The threats between the rival super-powers were very real, and I feared that the people in Berlin on both sides would be incinerated if they were carried out.

I began reading the works of Marx and Engels and Lenin, trying to understand their theories and motives. I agreed with their commitment to a redistribution of wealth, but I absolutely disagreed with their means. I could not embrace the ideas of violent revolution and the dictatorship of the proletariat.

I went to a neighborhood meeting with a woman who, along with her husband, had spoken out against the East German government and was sentenced to twenty-five years in prison. After serving five years, they were released and moved to the West, where they wrote about their experience and the lack of freedom in the East. But they discovered that the West was not paradise either, and they criticized the West German bureaucracy, the cultural materialism, and the passivity of the people, who did not, in her opinion, speak out enough about their concerns.

Most of the East Germans I met expressed their desire to live in a socialist society, but not in the form that was being practiced in their country and Russia. They wanted everyone to have work, a home, health care, and enough to eat—but they also wanted freedom.

West German TV, radio, and newspapers took the perspective that East Germany and the Communist world were occupied by an evil regime and that the West's job was to liberate the people from their oppressors. At that time, I observed very little questioning on either side of this mentality being put out by the media and governments. I certainly didn't see it in the universities, the churches, or the newspapers.

I attended a lecture at the Humboldt University in East Berlin, where I talked with several of the students and asked them what they thought could be done to foster international understanding. They were a little bashful but agreed to meet again. They told me that I should not expect students generally to say what they really think.

Half a dozen students from Humboldt eventually came and met with fifty students from West Berlin's Freie University. Although a lot of not-too-friendly words were exchanged, the East Berlin students stayed for almost three hours. I was glad for the opening, seeing it as a first step toward deeper listening and understanding.

I began attending some morning classes at Humboldt at the invitation of some of the students. My education in East and West included the history of Germany and the Soviet Union, the question of blame for the world wars, the political economy of Marx, the Hitler Reich, the role of justice in the state, and developments in Africa. In the mornings, I would challenge the Communist propaganda and be labeled a "capitalist warmonger." In the afternoons, at the university in the West, when I challenged their propaganda I was called a "Communist conspirator." I thought I must have been doing something right if neither side appreciated my questions!

I didn't consider myself any of these things: capitalist, warmonger, Communist, or conspirator. But I learned quickly that challenging the official propaganda was unacceptable behavior in both places. It was very unpopular to question authority and the way people on both sides were supposed to think about the world.

After about a month, a professor at Humboldt asked me, "Herr Hartsough, do you have official permission to be studying at our university?" I told him I didn't. He said in no uncertain terms, "If you are going to study in our university, you have to get official permission from the minister of education for the German Democratic Republic."

I thought, "Well, I guess this is the end of my studying in East Berlin." But I decided I might as well try to get permission. So I got an appointment with the minister of education. His office was a long, red-carpeted room, with pictures on the walls of Lenin, Marx, and Walter Ulbricht, the First Secretary of the Socialist Unity Party in East Germany.

As I walked in, he asked brusquely, "What do you want?"

I told him, "I am asking for permission to study at the Humboldt University. I am an American student."

Using the term I had come to expect, he scolded, "We don't want any capitalist warmongers corrupting the young people at our university."

I responded that I appreciated what he was saying, but that I believed that if we in the United States continued to listen to our propaganda, and to develop nuclear bombs, and the same happened in the Soviet Union, we would have war and all end up dead. "I'm interested in hearing and understanding how you folks in Communist countries think," I told him, "and how we can try to resolve these problems without blowing each other off the map."

His demeanor changed a bit, and he asked, "Would you like to have a conversation?"

We talked for about an hour and a half. I spoke as honestly as I could about my time in Cuba, my peace activities, and my participation in the civil rights movement. Most of what he said seemed like Communist propaganda, hardline stuff. But at the end of the hour and a half, he asked, "How long do you want to study at our university?" Speaking truth to power worked even with a Communist bureaucrat!

Probably my most unsettling moment in East Germany came when I lost my passport on the subway. When I reported the loss at a police station, an officer grilled me intensely. A U.S. passport was of great value in East Germany, and apparently Americans were known to sell theirs to make money. I was very relieved when, about an hour and a half later, someone called the police station to report finding mine.

During spring vacation, I hitchhiked and then caught the boat across the Channel to Great Britain. I stayed with a friend, Dan Elwyn Jones, whose father was a Member of Parliament. Dan was one of the key organizers of the Aldermaston Peace March in 1961, calling for an end to all nuclear weapons testing and for global nuclear disarmament. I joined him and helped organize the international contingent. It turned into the largest peace march in the world up to that time.

One of our jobs was to go out in a truck with a loudspeaker, inviting people to join the march. One day there were just two of us—one person to drive and the other to speak on the microphone. It was a bit challenging for an American to do either of those things—to drive on the "wrong" side of the road, or to speak over a loudspeaker in the streets of London with an American drawl. I tried the microphone, but then ended up driving—my first experience of navigating the challenges of driving on the left side of the road.

My friend Dan was very politically informed, and he expressed his belief that the U.S. military bases around the world and our occupation of Europe indicated that the United States wanted to be an empire. I said quickly in response, "No, no, the United States is a democratic society that wants to live in peace with the rest of the world." I thought his assertion was really far out. Turns out he was actually much more astute than I was.

After the Aldermaston March, I returned to Germany to participate in a two-week international work camp. We planted trees, both for private companies and for the German government. Instead of receiving compensation, our pay was sent to the State of Israel, as reparations from the German people for the crimes committed against Jews during World War II.

At the camp I met a young man from Algeria named Tahar. He spoke only Arabic and French, and I spoke only English and German, but we became close friends over time as we planted trees together. The only French I learned was *Mon bon ami*—"My good friend"—to which Tahar always responded, "*Mon bon David.*"

Through a translator, Tahar told me horror stories of the desperate effort by the French to maintain control of Algeria. Brutal torture was used against anyone who questioned French authority. That included Tahar and many members of his family on an ongoing basis. The horror and pain of torture were made real to me in Tahar's stories, and years later I remembered them and felt compassion for the victims when I learned of my own country's torture of perceived enemies.

Tahar had escaped from Algeria without documentation papers or passport, and I didn't know what would happen to him. I assumed after the work camp that I would never see him again. But one day, at the student house in Berlin where I was staying, I received a message that Tahar was at the airport.

I was concerned and rushed right there, since no option existed at that time to call on the phone. As I approached Tahar, he smiled and exclaimed, "*Mon bon ami.*" He came home with me and stayed for a few days while he figured out his next steps.

Our connection showed me how deep feeling can grow among friends who lack even a common language. The capacity to cross the many chasms that divide humanity—nationality, politics, language, age, experience—was the enduring gift of my time in Europe.

Ten years after my year in Berlin, the FBI put out a warrant for my arrest. It was signed by J. Edgar Hoover himself. Two FBI agents came to visit me, asking if I had known a Herr Franz Ultze when I lived in Berlin. I told them, truthfully, that I didn't remember him.

The agents proceeded to tell me for forty-five minutes everything I had done in Berlin—the weekly international student gatherings, my attending the universities in East and West Berlin, the courses I took. After reading me all this from their files, they asked me, "Now, do you remember Herr Ultze?"

By that time, I did remember. He was an East German pastor who had come to my apartment one evening in West Berlin, after I had met his daughter at *Freundshaftheim* (Friendship House) in West Germany. I was interested in learning what it was like to be a Christian minister in a Communist country. That's what we had talked about that evening.

But the FBI officials believed he was an agent of the KGB, the Soviet Secret Service, who was trying to enlist me to do espionage for the Soviet Union. They thought I'd been a spy for the KGB for the previous decade. That was why they had tracked me down. Fortunately, I was able to set the record straight.

That was the only thing they had wrong in their files about me—the rest was all accurate. The fact that they had been following a college student and knew my every move was amazing to me. Since then, whenever people say before a peace demonstration something like "Let's not tell the police what we are going to do," I respond, "We don't need to worry about that. They already know."

But even if my year in Berlin did peak the interest of the FBI in my peacemaking work, I am eternally grateful for the experience of living

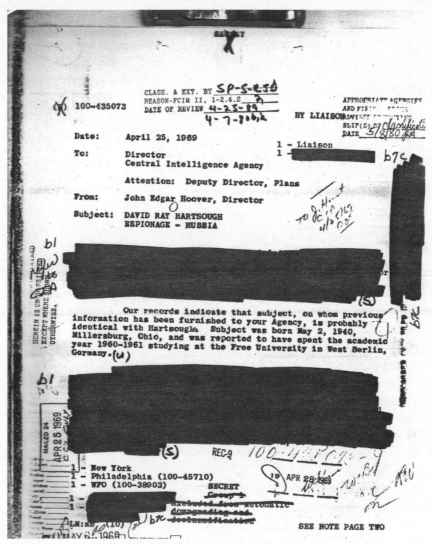

A page of my FBI file, which begins in 1956, signed by J. Edgar Hoover.

in Berlin. I was extremely grateful for the opportunity to make many friends and gain a better understanding of the Cold War and the danger and tragedy of the nuclear arms race. During my time in Germany, my commitment deepened to help move our world from one of enemies and nuclear confrontation to one of peaceful relations and friendship among all of us in the world family.

CHAPTER 5

Meeting the "Enemy": Making Friends with Russians During the Cold War

L iving in Berlin for a year had plunged me into facing up to the massive division that was plaguing our world and the extreme danger of the United States and the Soviet Union threatening one another with nuclear destruction.

In the late 1950s and early '60s, the globe was in the grip of a Cold War mentality. In the West, the belief was widely held that Communists were the epitome of evil. They were viewed as the "new Hitlers," trying to take over the world by force, with the Soviet Union (USSR) as command central. The response in the United States was to race ahead in the development of nuclear bombs, widely believed by government officials and citizens alike to be the only choice in dealing with "the Soviet threat."

I wanted to see for myself what was true. At the international work camp in Germany, I had met a British man, Mervyn Taggart, who told me that he was going to go camping in the Soviet Union that summer. I was amazed. "Camping in the Soviet Union?"

"Yeah," he said. "Two dollars per person per day, and you get your visa and permission to camp!"

This seemed like another small opening in the "Iron Curtain" that should be walked through. As far as I know, our conversation that day marked the launch of citizen diplomacy with Russia. When it turned out that Mervyn was unable to make the trip, I recruited some other traveling companions.

I soon found more than enough students to fill a Volkswagen Bug, which my parents had lent me $1,200 to buy. After lengthy consideration of backgrounds and abilities, our group of five was selected. Three of us—Ruth Turner, Margie Wolfe, and I—were from the United States, and two—Edith Questor and Gustav Tanski—were from Germany. We were four Caucasians and one African American: two Quakers, two Protestants, and one unaffiliated.

Through the spring and early summer of 1961, we did a great deal of preparatory work, mapping our route and filing applications for our camping visas. We were committed to keeping expenses low; the total cost of our five-thousand-mile, thirty-one-day trip came to $110 per person. With food, kettles, and dishes in the back compartment, our luggage in the front, and tents, sleeping bags, and air mattresses strapped on top of the VW Bug, we left Berlin at four o'clock in the morning on August 4, 1961, and arrived in Warsaw, Poland, at five that evening.

We immediately noticed a great difference in the standard of living. We saw few cars on the roads, and the houses were older than those in West Germany. The activity in the fields was not that of tractors and machines but of simply clad people farming by hand. We stopped and chatted with a few. They talked openly with us; in contrast to East Germany, people seemed to experience more freedom and less fear in Poland.

We squeezed in a hitchhiker, whose entire family had been killed by a bomb dropped on their home during the Second World War. His desire for peace hardly needed to be expressed. We visited the area where the Warsaw Ghetto had once been, where eight hundred thousand Polish Jews had been killed during the war. Through tears, a family of three told us about their personal experience of this enormous tragedy.

We crossed into the Soviet Union on August 6, Hiroshima Day, and voiced our hope that such a terrible catastrophe as that Japanese city had suffered would never again visit humankind. Once there, I had trouble believing that I was actually in the Soviet Union. I had been told for so long that this country was our number-one enemy, and our whole society at that time was geared toward fighting the Soviet menace and preparing to carpet the USSR with nuclear weapons to wipe out all the Communists.

The main goal of our trip was to get to know the Russian people and their ideas, and to give them a chance to know us and our ideas. I had taken some classes in Russian, but I was very grateful that one of the Germans with us was fluent, enabling us to have many good conversations with Russian people—in parks, on the streets, and in their homes and backyards.

With a group of Russians on first camping trip to Soviet Union (1961).

Near Minsk, we realized that our car was low on gas and a hundred kilometers from a gas station. We turned off the main road into a small village, where people in old clothes were arriving at the market on horseback and in carriages. A policeman immediately directed us back to the main road, causing us to wonder if there was a military base nearby.

Back on the road, another policeman gave us gasoline from a collective farm truck. When we offered to pay for it, he smiled and said, "*Nyet*. You can't pay for it. It belongs to the people."

Minsk had been almost entirely destroyed by the war, but apart from some old shacks on side streets, the city appeared to be completely rebuilt. Our first evening there, we attracted a crowd of about sixty people, who asked us questions about our universities, our families, and our lives. We, in turn, plied them with similar questions.

What impressed me most was the tremendous pride the Russians had in their country—its beauty, its culture, and its achievements. Just the day before, the cosmonaut Titov had circled the earth seventeen times in *Vostok II*, and they wanted to know what we had to say about that. Police officers eventually tried to break up our discussion, but the people refused to leave and told them they had no right to interfere.

We continued on to Smolensk. Our campsite there seemed luxurious, with a kitchen, electric lights, and showers—hot, if you paid the equivalent of a dime. I talked for several hours with a couple from Moscow, who were camping with their two large bulldogs, their pride and joy.

They expressed their hope that American and Russian soldiers would refuse to shoot each other if war broke out again. "The Russian people, as probably all the people in the world," the woman said, "would just like to live their simple lives, have their small homes and families, and make their living." Referring to the leaders of our respective countries, her husband added, "They are not concerned about all these Khrushchev-Kennedy problems."

The couple told us that they had met all kinds of people at the camp—British, French, Polish, Czech—and got along well with all of them. "Why should we be forced to fight against one another?" they wanted to know.

My companions and I were on the two-lane road to Moscow on August 10, 1961, without much traffic. Suddenly, lines of tanks and trucks, filled with thousands of Soviet soldiers, were coming toward us from the opposite direction. We didn't learn until we got to Moscow where all those troops were headed and why.

The banner headline in *Pravda*, the Soviet newspaper that was posted a few days later in kiosks on the street, read "Wall Built between East and West Berlin as Tensions Mount between USSR and USA." Those thousands of soldiers were headed to Germany to build the Berlin Wall! They completed the initial version of it in only one night on August 13, 1961. I could not imagine how it would feel to go to sleep in Germany and wake up the next morning completely separated from family members and neighbors by a wall and armed soldiers—a separation that would last for twenty-eight years.

And there we were in Moscow, the heart of the Soviet empire, a likely target of U.S. bombs if war broke out over Berlin. Luckily for us—and for all the Soviet, German, and American people, as well as the rest of the world—nuclear war did not break out that summer. But our uneasiness mounted daily.

The next day, my traveling companions and I appeared at the Soviet Peace Council office in Moscow, and were soon meeting with the director and the editor of the *Young Communist* newspaper. They asserted that the Soviet Union was doing all it could for disarmament, having unilaterally halted nuclear testing in 1958, proposing to cut its military forces by two million troops, and abolishing all military bases outside its own borders.

They had received little response, the men said, with the United States completely surrounding Russia with bases and racing ahead with the development of nuclear weapons. They claimed, sadly, that the Soviet Union needed to build up its military power "for defense," so that never again would they be unable to fight off an attack such as Germany's in 1941.

The following day we talked with the chair of the Student Council of the USSR, learning about youth organizations and discussing setting up some work camps and international seminars, like the one in which my brother Paul had participated the summer before. We urged the chair to push for unilateral disarmament, or at least unilateral initiatives from the Soviet Union, as we promised to do with our own government back home. It seemed the only course to avoid a suicidal arms race between our two nations.

We acknowledged the damage done by propaganda and the need to know one another better. A Russian guide had said to us, "I know about the unemployment in the United States, about its slums and about the practice of discrimination against the Negroes. I know all there is to know about America." A few people we met registered their surprise that our group included an African American, and that we all got along well.

Similarly, we in the United States were getting less than the whole picture of life in the USSR. Many people expressed to us how deeply they desired peace, and the heartfelt thanks with which they would greet any move by the United States to show that we did, too.

We met a Czech, a tall, friendly fellow who told us that he felt it was necessary for his country to ally itself with the Soviet Union, to avoid being the target again of a rearmed Germany. I understood the fear. But I felt more concern about a world in which everyone identified enemies and took sides.

We learned that the Soviet Union had fifty million Russian Orthodox Christians and half a million Baptists, as well as fifteen million Muslims. Pockets of Jews, Roman Catholics, Methodists, Lutherans, and Seventh Day Adventists also worshipped throughout the country.

My friends and I wanted to attend church in Moscow but were informed that the downtown churches were so crowded that worshippers had to arrive a couple of hours early to get a space. So we chose a Russian Orthodox Church in the suburbs. As we approached, we heard the organ playing and saw people crowded around the entrance.

Except for some very elderly people, who took turns resting themselves for a few minutes on a small bench by a pillar, everyone stood for the two-hour service. Many times throughout it, they got on their knees, bowed down, and touched their foreheads to the floor. I had never witnessed such humility and devout reverence in my own self-proclaimed "Christian nation."

After the service, thirty children were baptized. We were told that about this number were baptized every Sunday. Many people expressed to us their great joy that we had come as fellow Christians to visit and worship with them.

We traveled one day to Zagorsk, south of Moscow. There we visited the Russian Orthodox theological seminary and monastery. These fine institutions served approximately 230 students and ninety monks, the latter of which struck me as a fascinating blend of piety and high spirit.

The archbishop of the Russian Orthodox Church told us that in the Soviet Union the main job of the church was "to counteract the antireligious propaganda of the state." He admitted that morality was being taught in the schools, saying, "Good morality and education prepare the child for the seed of Christianity better than Christian teaching and bad morality."

The archbishop told us that he felt that the United States suffered from "gangsterism" and from teaching children to expect rewards. "The West has quiet atheism; the East has warlike atheism," he declared. He continued, "The moral aims of Communism and Christianity are about the same. A heathen who loves [humanity] is better than a Christian who does not."

In the city of Kharkov, a tour guide explained that the government was so insistent on atheistic propaganda because Communism wanted people to concentrate on trying to make a better world and a better life. She felt that, in contrast, Christians were so busy thinking about the next world that they could easily be made content with a bad life in this one. We did our best to expand her understanding.

A student in that city had quite a different perspective from our tour guide's. He told us that the government policy of not allowing Christians in high government positions was foolish, because often Christians were the most active in helping to create a just and socialistic society. He believed that Christians were motivated by deep concern for their sisters and brothers.

This student wanted to know if we thought that capitalism was compatible with Christianity. We pondered the question and discussed it at length. Ultimately, we had to admit that the fact that the United States comprised 6 percent of the world's population and consumed almost half of its resources was not very Christian.

When we did finally attend a Baptist Church in Moscow, we spent time with two very sincere and dedicated Christian men—one young and the other seventy-five years old. They told us that being a Christian in the Soviet Union required standing up courageously for faith and ideals. Sunday schools and formal religious training for youth were forbidden, so most spiritual formation had to happen privately at home.

The church service ended with a prayer for peace. The congregation made such a heartfelt and sustained murmur in response that I felt that I had never heard or seen people with a greater longing for peace. I prayed that we in the United States would do our part to see their hope and prayer realized.

One afternoon we visited a mammoth fairground, which showcased the Soviet Union's achievements in the arts, sciences, and agriculture. Each of sixteen sections highlighted the beauty, resources, and growth of one of the Soviet republics. The place was filled with elegant statues, fountains, and floral arrangements. I had never seen anything so outrageously luxurious or gorgeous.

We also made a visit to Moscow's Lumumba University, founded in 1960 as People's Friendship University and renamed in 1961 after Congolese independence leader President Patrice Lumumba, who had been killed by the CIA. This impressive institution served students from Africa, Asia, and Latin America.

One evening at the Hotel of the Youth, we met students participating in a World Youth Forum. An African student stated his belief that socialism was the best economic system for the countries on the African continent emerging from colonialism. He felt that they had insufficient private wealth to make private enterprise work, which he believed enriched the few at the expense of the many.

A student from Ecuador similarly felt that the nations of Latin America needed revolutions like Cuba's, in which the economy served the interests of the majority rather than landowners and foreigners. An Estonian expressed his belief that good and bad existed in the economic systems of both East and West, a balanced opinion that seemed rare. I noticed that many Russian students simply parroted official state doctrine. I wondered if they had ever heard other political perspectives, or if it entered their minds to think anything else.

My companions and I were anxious to spend as much time as possible with ordinary Russians. In a poor, old part of Moscow, we visited a family playing dominoes and ping pong with a homemade table and paddles. Evcryone, especially the children, welcomed us with warmth and joy.

We had a similar experience when we visited a construction site. Though their monthly pay was just 100 rubles—the equivalent of about $100—people expressed contentment with their lives and their work. All Soviet citizens received subsidized housing and free medical care. Free childcare was provided for the young children of working parents, and free education for all students, as well as benefits similar to our Social Security for the elderly.

Most students in Russia who were not studying medicine or technical sciences worked for two years before entering the university. This gave them experience in their chosen field and helped them decide if they were making the right decision for their life's work. They had to pass examinations to be accepted for university study. Those who didn't pass could work another year and have a second chance. All university students received scholarships, so that family income was never a deterrent to education.

We visited a clothes factory, where the workers—mostly women—labored on small sewing machines six days a week. They received a paid day off each week to further their education if they so chose, two to four weeks of paid vacation per year, and four months off with pay after giving birth. They attended weekly political information meetings, where they discussed international events.

At a collective farm outside Moscow, the people tended a thousand pigs and many acres of cabbages and potatoes, but we observed a very low standard of living. They worked hard for little pay to meet a plan handed down by the government. We visited the center where young children from infancy to five years of age stayed during the day so that their parents could work the farm. The Komsomol (Communist Youth Organization) organized activities for young people.

On the way to Kharkov, in the town of Orjol, we saw people living in conditions much as they had two hundred years before. The small houses topped with mud-and-straw roofs had no running water, and more horses and carts than cars were on the streets. Kiev, where people were better dressed and the houses were sturdy and attractive, was a dramatic contrast from much of the rest of Russia. I loved walking the streets of Kiev—the old houses with music drifting out of open windows, the grandmas sitting on park benches, the children playing everywhere.

We stopped one day at a Pioneer Camp, run by Komsomol, the Communist children's organization, and beautifully situated in the middle of a vast green forest. About twenty such camps existed around Moscow, and children could attend them without cost for a month during summer vacation. As in the United States, the schedule was mostly recreation—hikes, games, sports, movies—and it also included nationalistic indoctrination, not unlike the patriotism instilled by such organizations as the Boy Scouts and Girl Scouts at home.

I walked one evening through the streets of Moscow to Gorki Park. There, clusters of people played dominoes, checkers, and chess—as well as a game that resembled our baseball. I enjoyed conversations with the young people, who shared their taste in music, movies, and sports.

One morning, our group walked past an apartment building near our campsite that held fifteen families. Some of the residents greeted us like old friends and beckoned us into their backyard. A group of men who had been playing dominoes around a table quickly got up to make room for us.

Each family had just one or two rooms, sharing bathrooms and kitchens, but they had made their small spaces cozy with curtains and flowers. A widow invited us into her room, and soon her neighbors began parading in with food to share with us: pancakes, bread, cucumbers, watermelons, cookies, candy, tea. Several mothers approached us, carrying their babies, each saying with great emotion words along the lines of "There must be peace and friendship in the world. There can be no more wars."

Several people told us that during the Stalin era, everyone was afraid to say anything critical about the Soviet Union or positive about another country, for fear of being charged with treason and shipped off to a prison camp in Siberia. But, they explained, things had changed and people were able to say anything they wanted—as long as they didn't organize a group to do something about it. "Now we are living in heaven," one man said.

Some young people invited us to a dance one night. I wrote in my journal about that unforgettable evening: "Some of our group did the rock 'n' roll, and all the people just stared because they had never seen it before. Rock 'n' roll is supposed to be a Western sickness and unsocialistic, so it is officially looked down upon. One of the soldiers there said, 'Don't keep doing that dance, or tomorrow the whole crowd will be doing it.'"

Later, a journalist at an independent press agency expressed his hope for more cooperation between the United States and the Soviet Union. He felt that there was much that we could learn from one another—except in one area. He admired American industry, science, and technology, but said that Russians were less interested in American culture. Russians, he explained, did not like "modern art, rock and roll, and the Twist."

We met a man who was an American citizen but had chosen to live in Russia. He felt that relationships were superficial in the United States and that our country lacked culture. He also felt that Americans didn't want to admit that socialism was the best system and hindered the Soviet Union and other countries that were trying to improve the lives of their citizens. He earned the equivalent of a hundred dollars a month and lived with his wife and child in a two-room apartment. "I couldn't ask for anything more," he told us.

At four fifteen in the morning on September 2, our group drove from the town of Lvov toward the Czech border. We passed through beautiful mountains above the clouds—a nice break from the Soviet Union's mostly flat land we had experienced. Suspected of "doing some spy work and stealing gold," we were stopped and detained at the border.

Informing us that they had received telegrams from police saying we were in places we shouldn't have been, the Soviet border officials searched every paper and piece of luggage, and me, down to the skin. After two and a half hours of my explaining the purpose of our trip and the reasons I felt it was necessary to work for peace, they were finally convinced that I wasn't a spy after all. We departed, shaking hands with all six officials.

We drove on to Germany, and I said goodbye to my friends in Berlin, then went on to Hamburg. I didn't have much money for getting myself and my VW Bug back to the States. I eventually found a freight company that would take both me and the car for a reasonable price.

We encountered a few hurricanes on our trip across the Atlantic, which made most of the other ten passengers on the boat very sick. I just stayed calm, enjoyed the beauty of the sea, and read *Dr. Zhivago* in German until we caught sight of the United States.

As I reflected on all that we had seen and heard during our five-thousand-mile journey, I was extremely grateful for all the people who had welcomed us so warmly. I felt sadness about the lack of freedom and protest I had observed. It seemed to me that the will of individuals was being ignored in the name of ideology, and that the Russian people existed to serve the state, rather than the state existing to serve them.

But I also realized that we in the United States couldn't too smugly criticize their lack of freedom as long as we ourselves didn't fully use the freedom available to us. And, we couldn't speak too loudly about defending democracy around the world as long as we deprived our own citizens of their rights because of their skin color.

I felt more deeply than ever after this trip that our country's possession of almost half the world's wealth, while two-thirds of the world's people lived hand-to-mouth, was a crime against humanity. What should a mother in India think when her tiny child went without food while Americans got sick from overeating? How could we blame people in Asia, Africa, and Latin America for choosing Communism as the best system if we refused to share and work to alleviate their poverty?

An engineer we met in Kharkov, who was very familiar with life in the United States, had stated what seemed very clear to me on this trip: the world would work much better if wealth were more equally divided among people. He believed that countries in the so-called developing world wouldn't "resort to Communism" if they could experience a "human standard of living" in the capitalist world. He also expressed his opinion that the controlling financial interests in United States government and media, and the lack of tolerance for nonconformity in American society, amounted to dictatorship.

I came away from that trip feeling that peace could never be built on a foundation of prejudice and mistrust based in propaganda. Although I saw many differences between East and West, my fervent desire was that we would make the effort to get to know one another as people and work toward peace. The irony didn't escape me that while I was in the Soviet Union trying to break down walls and barriers, the world's most famous political wall was being constructed in Berlin.

After I returned home, someone affiliated with Radio Free Europe offered me a hundred dollars to talk about the "bad things" I had seen in Russia for a worldwide broadcast, which I found very upsetting. I refused, telling him that I would be happy to share my experiences—both positive and negative—from my time in the Soviet Union. He was not interested.

Instead, I wrote a booklet called *Discovering Another Russia*, in which I related the stories and conversations I shared with people I had met that summer. I spent a lot of my free time speaking, presenting slide shows, and trying to help Americans see Russians as human beings, not as nameless enemies in a "godless Communist empire" who were trying to blow us up.

In the audience at one of the places where I presented a slideshow of my trip was Dick Hiler. He served as high school secretary for the American Friends Service Committee and had organized the

Washington seminars that had been so important to me. Afterward, he approached me and said excitedly, "David, we have to take another group to Russia next summer!"

So I returned to the Soviet Union in the summer of 1962 with eighteen more students, fifteen of whom were in high school. In two months we traveled seven thousand miles in two Volkswagen microbuses, in reverse order of my first trip—from West Germany through Czechoslovakia to the Ukraine and then north to Moscow, back via Smolensk and Minsk, through Poland to Berlin.

When we arrived at the Russian border to enter at Lvov—my point of departure from the previous trip—a border guard looked into our van and said to me, "Weren't you here last year?" It was the same man who had accused me of being an imperialist spy and detained me for two and a half hours. He again rifled through all of our luggage, perused the booklet I had written about the previous year's trip, and then let us pass with a handshake.

As in the first trip, we met and conversed with as many people as we could. Textile workers shared with us about their lives, and kindergartners accompanied by an accordion sang us songs. We observed farms and factories, attended concerts and suppers conjured on our behalf, visited a Pioneer Camp and churches. I was particularly struck on this visit by the beautiful icons and paintings in the Russian Orthodox churches, depictions of the creation, crucifixion, and parables of Jesus.

In Moscow we visited the home of the fifteen families that had received my friends and me so warmly the year before. Their hospitality had not dimmed. We talked animatedly and took turns singing Russian and American folk songs.

Their street had been transformed by towering, new apartment buildings. Soon, they told us, their home would be torn down and they too would move into larger, more modern apartments. In Moscow alone, 390 apartments were being constructed each day, and in the previous four years fifty million Russians had been moved into new housing. The pace would have been even quicker, our friends said, had there not been an arms race. Money that had been slated for housing, they explained, was being redirected to nuclear weapons development.

Our group made visits to the U.S. and Chinese Embassies, the Soviet Peace Council, and Moscow University. We browsed in bookstores and the 22-million-volume Lenin Library. We saw Lenin's body lying in state at the Kremlin, prompting this comment in my journal: "It was not very inspiring to look at him."

I encountered this sentence in an edition of the magazine *Soviet Union*: "The dynamo that powers the policies of the imperialist governments of the West is their constant striving to sustain and aggravate international tensions in order to justify the arms race." I felt the painful element of truth in this propaganda piece. While both the United States and the USSR were supplying arms and soldiers to many nations around the globe, the Soviet Union was usually on the side of liberation movements, while the United States was too often supporting tottering, brutal dictatorships to safeguard its own interests.

As on my first visit, rarely did we encounter anyone who was critical of Soviet policy. About our questions regarding nuclear arms, typical responses included, "Our bombs are peaceful bombs." And, "In World War Two we weren't powerful enough, so we lost twenty million people. You have to understand it is not our choice, but we have to defend ourselves."

A few months before I made this second visit, I had participated in a protest against nuclear weapons in Washington, DC, in front of the White House. On our last afternoon in Moscow, Paul Rhodes, a high school student and trip participant from Boston, and I decided that someone needed to protest nuclear armaments in the Soviet Union. We made signs that read in Russian "Bomb Tests Kill People."

We decided to keep vigil in silence with our signs for two hours in front of the Kremlin, next to the Lenin Mausoleum, in Red Square. Because I had helped to organize the San Francisco-to-Moscow Peace March the year before, I had leaflets in Russian and five other languages about why we were opposed to nuclear weapons testing. We began handing them out to people.

"Why are you demonstrating against Russia's 'peaceful bombs'?" someone wanted to know.

"Your country had the bomb first and forced us into an arms race," retorted another.

"Why don't you go back and demonstrate in the United States?" still another suggested.

We broke our silence to explain that we had already demonstrated in the United States—and that our fellow citizens had told us to "go to Russia"! We also said that we heard similar perspectives about "peaceful bombs" from the U.S. side, and that somebody needed to take a first step back from the brink of nuclear war.

Some police officers in red caps approached us. One threatened, "Don't you know that you can be charged with criminal conspiracy for

Demonstrating in Red Square, Moscow, opposing Soviet nuclear weapons testing. Police threatened us with twenty years in prison for the protest (1962).

protesting?" He warned us that if we didn't stop immediately, we would get twenty years in prison. That was a bit shocking to Paul and me.

We conferred and decided that, despite the risk, we needed to continue our vigil. I thanked the police officer for alerting us and then said something along the lines of "If this nuclear arms race continues, then none of us are going to be alive. Twenty years in prison would be better than that." I explained that I had been arrested a couple of months before in Washington, DC, for doing exactly the same thing.

He said, "Well, we have to talk to our superiors and decide what to do with you." The police officers all went off, and we never saw them again. So, Paul and I stayed for two hours and then went back to our campsite.

On the way home from Russia, we traveled through Poland and stopped at Auschwitz. The former Nazi concentration camp was a terrifying place. Seventeen years after the end of the war, the gas chambers, which resembled showers, were still filled with piles of clothes and human bones. Those images are seared in my mind. The horror and pain of that place had a particularly strong impact on Paul. I hoped that this remnant of brutal truth had been preserved in the hope that such barbaric cruelty would never again take place.

When I got back home to Pennsylvania, I was again contacted by a person in radio—this time an old family friend who was sympathetic to my concerns and wanted to interview me about my trip. Ed Randall hosted a national radio program called *This Is a Friendly World*, which I had listened to every evening at Tanguy while I was milking the cows. Through my dad's contacts, Ed was able to interview people from the civil rights movement and peace leaders from all over the world. I was happy to give him an interview about my trip to the Soviet Union.

Ed was developing a new show called *Yankee in the Heart of Dixie*, and that summer he asked me to visit every radio station in Alabama to see if they would like to air the weekly program. So I drove my parents' VW Bug around Alabama to eighty radio stations, playing a sample tape at each. About half agreed to air the show, which presented Ed's travels and encounters with interesting people in the South—and also carried subtle messages about racism, opening people's minds to promote understanding across the racial divide.

The project was very low-budget, so I slept in fields next to the car and ate peanut butter sandwiches for several weeks. My big splurge on that trip was a half-gallon of ice cream that I bought for thirty-nine cents in a grocery store in Montgomery. I sat down on a bench in the city square across from Martin Luther King's first church and ate the entire half gallon, as I remembered back to my life-changing visit to Montgomery in 1956.

A few years after my visits to the Soviet Union, while I was working in Washington against the Vietnam War, I got to know a man from the Soviet Embassy quite well. In 1968, just before the U.S. presidential election, he told me that he had an invitation for me "from the people of the Soviet Union." He said they were inviting ten American peace leaders to come to Russia the day after the election to talk about the U.S. peace movement and how to create peace between our countries. I was thrilled.

But a few days before I was supposed to go, he came to my office and told me that, though everyone else on the delegation had been granted visas, the Soviet government had denied my application. Through tears, he said, "David, I can't understand what happened. First we invade Czechoslovakia, and now we don't allow you—a great American peace leader—into our country!" I was touched that he placed the denial of my visa on an emotional par with the three-month-old Soviet invasion of Czechoslovakia, which had undermined the hopeful liberalization and reform efforts of that country's "Prague Spring."

My friend's worldview in which the Soviet Union could do no wrong was beginning to crumble. He had telegrammed Moscow to see why his government had refused to allow me in. He received a telegram back, which read, "David Hartsough's behavior in the Soviet Union has not been becoming of a guest of the Soviet people. He demonstrated in Red Square, and even went to Dubna."

Dubna was a city outside Moscow where the Joint Institute for Nuclear Research was located. I had a friend there whom I had met while I was living in Berlin. He was a very impressive Polish physicist, who had informed me of his refusal to do any work on nuclear weapons for the Soviet or any government. He had invited me to come visit him at his home, so I jumped on a train and went to Dubna.

The most radical thing I did with him was swim across the very wide Volga River, which had a current so strong that by the time we made it to the opposite shore, we were about a mile downstream. But the Soviet government had apparently been aware of that visit. I didn't know until I tried to go with the peace delegation in 1968 that I had been banned from Russia. I wasn't allowed back in until 1991.

Despite that slight, I still believed strongly in what I had written in *Backyard Russia: Getting to Know the Russian People*, the booklet I produced after my second trip to the Soviet Union. I ended my reflections on that journey with these words:

> This trip has confirmed my belief in that of goodness, that of joy and kindness, and that of God in all [people], no matter where they might live in the world. It has also helped me see that there are real differences in ideology between East and West, but that none of these differences is great enough to be worth fighting World War III about. We could solve these differences peacefully, if we really put our minds to it. Finally, it has made me feel the tremendous responsibility I have—and I think all of us have. If we are really concerned about peace, we must speak out with our lives to help bring this peace about.

CHAPTER 6

Taking a Stand: Life as a Conscientious Objector

My experiences in Berlin and in the Soviet Union underlined the commitment I had made several years earlier that participating in war and killing people was not only tragic for the future of humanity, but against everything I believed.

In the months leading up to my eighteenth birthday, I had been embroiled in intense soul searching. The decision with which I grappled was whether I should register with the Selective Service and apply to do alternative service—or refuse to register and go to prison. Behind this was the question, How can I most effectively say to my government that the military system that forces young men to kill others is wrong?

I saw the answer as a decision I was making not just for the required two-year stint, but for the rest of my life. I considered mass slaughter an absurd, immoral, and tragic way of trying to solve problems. I wanted to devote my life to experimenting with the power of nonviolence and helping to end militarism and injustice in the world.

I talked with some of my dad's friends who had been imprisoned for refusing to fight in World War II and the Korean War. My heart was settling on refusing to register, to make it clear that I wouldn't kill and also that I wouldn't cooperate with a system that forced others to do so. But my mother didn't like the idea of her son spending years in prison.

I finally decided to register as a conscientious objector. I had to at least entertain the possibility that this had to do with cowardice, but I don't really believe that it did. I remembered Bayard Rustin, a CO who had served time in prison during the Second World War and then became a leader in the civil rights movement, saying that being a pacifist is one-tenth conscientious objection and nine-tenths working to do away with the things that make for war. I felt that for two years I could do something positive to help take away the causes of war and then continue that commitment for the rest of my life.

So on May 10, 1958, I wrote this letter to the Selective Service Board in Media, Pennsylvania:

> I am registering as a conscientious objector because I do not feel that it is right to take any human life. God has given life, and we don't have the right to decide that other human beings, like ourselves, no longer have a right to live.
>
> I believe that our whole draft system, which forces young men to kill others, is immoral and wrong. The only reason that I have registered at all is that I have a very strong affection and concern for our country and its democracy, and I hope that through love and kindness I can appeal to the good in our government to abolish this law which forces young men to kill other human beings. I hope that in my alternative service, I can do those things which will truly help create an atmosphere of peace in the world. I believe that those things which do help toward peace can only be done in a spirit of love and kindness toward all people.
>
> How can we expect to gain peace by war? We cannot reap figs from thorns or grapes from thistles. The ends do not justify the means. We cannot use evil means to achieve good ends. Force subdues, but love gains. We cannot get peace through war.
>
> In our effort to stop Communism by force, we are tending more and more to use the means of the very enemy which we are fighting against. In our military forces, the individual conscience no longer has any say as to what should be done or what is right. Each man is forced to kill mass numbers of men (and now also innocent women and children), thinking of them not as human beings, but as targets which must be shot and killed. In the army a man must obey the order of the man above him, or he is liable to the severest of punishments. This is a country of democracy. Why are we resorting to these dictatorial means to protect it?
>
> I have chosen the conscientious objector position because I want to give the most of myself that I can for the furthering of peace and good will among [hu]mankind. I am refusing to go into the army, not because I don't want to be killed, but because I cannot kill another person.

I am choosing the alternative service position, rather than the non-registrant position, because I want to make my protest in as positive and loving a way as possible. I hope and pray that our government will realize and take into consideration that I, one U.S. citizen, feel that this law is wrong and am willing to spend my whole life in trying to win friends by love instead of hate, killing, and the H-bomb.

When I showed up for my sophomore year at Howard University, I discovered that, because it was a land grant school that received federal money, ROTC (Reserve Officers Training Corps) was compulsory for all male students. Just the sight of all those young men marching around campus in uniform made me feel ill. I found it particularly tragic that when the civil rights sit-ins started, most of the male students after several months in ROTC refused to participate in the demonstrations because of what they were learning in ROTC: allegiance to country, obedience to orders and all laws, and avoidance of all "un-American activities."

Initially, I was told by university officials that I had to join ROTC or leave Howard. Both the president and the vice president of the university were friends of Gandhi, and my dad introduced me to them. Vice President William Stuart Nelson, who taught the first class I took on nonviolence, offered a solution. He said that if I received recognition as a CO by my draft board within ten days, I could stay at Howard without participating in ROTC.

Mike Ingerman, a friend in Washington who was doing alternative service at the Friends Committee on National Legislation, helped me file the extensive papers—with many, many questions to answer—before the deadline. In my responses I elaborated on my letter to the Selective Service Board:

> I believe that there is that of God in every [person] regardless of race, creed, or nationality. Therefore, killing or even hating any [person] is injuring part of God himself. Just as I could not kill my brother, neither can I kill another human being (who is also my brother) on the other side of the world. Both are human beings created by God and given life by God. Who can give us the right to put an end to this wonderful creation of God, human life? Who can give us the right to cause suffering to the family of the man or men we kill?

Noting the dangerous era we had entered with the advent of nuclear weapons, I made the point that not just individuals or nations, but the entire human race, was endangered by war. I felt that we needed to uphold the humanity of all people and get past thinking of others as targets, as Communists or capitalists, as enemies. I stated my belief that if we put one-tenth of the effort we spent on learning to kill others into trying to build understanding between nations, peace could be reached. "I must follow this conviction and try to live it," I wrote, "even though, at present, my government does not agree with me." I continued:

> I believe in the power of love as the strongest force in the world. It is the ability to accept suffering rather than inflict suffering that can win over the world. Hatred breeds hatred, while love and understanding try to bring friendship and conciliation with the so-called enemy.
>
> We call ourselves a Christian nation, our coins state "In God we trust." What has happened to our age-old teachings of "Thou shalt not kill," "Love your enemies, do good unto them that hate you"? Jesus said, "You have heard that it was said, 'You shall love your neighbor and hate your enemy.' But I say to you, "Love your enemies and pray for those who persecute you." . . .
>
> I must ask myself the question, To whom do I owe my highest loyalty? Do I owe it to my school, or to my local community, or to my country, and in the meantime ignore all the other people in the world? I feel that I owe my allegiance to the whole human race and to God. However, I feel that while my highest loyalty is to God and to the whole human race, it is at the same time the greatest loyalty I can give to my country.

Fortunately, the draft board in Media, Pennsylvania, recognized me at a conscientious objector within the ten-day limit, and I was allowed to stay at Howard. During my time there, I worked evenings and weekends in the university library to make a little money. Working for the school required signing an oath of loyalty to the United States. I had pangs of conscience about whether or not to sign it. I ended up writing in, "I would defend my country nonviolently," which was apparently good enough.

I remembered that during one of the Quaker seminars I had attended as a high school student, a woman took a dollar bill, held it up, and began cutting it into pieces with scissors. She told us that it represented the federal budget. Over half of it was in one piece, and that represented the amount of money that went for the military and wars. She held up tiny pieces that stood for the amounts spent on education, health care, and all foreign aid. I was moved that she cared so much about this issue, she was willing to destroy a dollar bill to help us students realize where our tax dollars really go!

I recalled the leaders of the Philadelphia work camps who had been early role models for me, and I decided while I was at Howard to live on $600 a year, to keep my earnings below the federal taxable level and avoid paying taxes for war, as they had done. This was one more thing that set me apart from the other students. I'm sure they thought I was quite strange.

I survived by buying thirty cents' worth of three different vegetables in the college cafeteria for lunch and dinner every day, supplemented with peanut butter sandwiches. I kept a stash of peanut butter, bread, and apples from home in my room for breakfast. I had become, by default, a vegetarian!

I was particularly grateful for my friend Jim Lancaster, whom I had first met at a vigil against germ warfare at Fort Detrick, Maryland. He lived at home while attending Howard. Once a week, I bicycled there for a great home-cooked meal that he prepared for me.

During my first year at Howard, my friend Bill Martin and I launched a project out of the Florida Avenue Friends Meetinghouse. We acquired the names and addresses of all the high school students in the Washington area. Then we wrote a letter, making a case that they had a choice about whether or not to go to war as soldiers, and mimeographed thousands of copies of it.

It took us many weeks, but we hand-addressed twenty-two thousand envelopes and sent out the letters with information about conscientious objection and a copy of my letter to the draft board. When news about the mailing appeared in *The Washington Post* the next day, Bill—who supervised all the pages serving Republicans in the U.S. Senate—was fired from his job.

A few weeks before my graduation from Howard, on May 1, 1962, Ed Snyder, executive secretary of the Friends Committee on National Legislation, invited me to join a delegation of six Quakers to meet with President John Kennedy in the White House. I was the "token young guy." Our primary message was a plea for Kennedy to unilaterally stop nuclear bomb tests and work much harder toward peace with the Soviets. I suggested that he might challenge them to a "peace race" rather than continuing the escalating arms race.

We also expressed our concern about a new, nuclear-powered aircraft carrier that was going to be christened the *William Penn*. We pointed out the irony and affront of naming a battleship after a Quaker who had refused to take up arms and had established Pennsylvania as an American sanctuary for freedom of conscience. Kennedy chuckled and told us he would make sure that didn't happen.

At that time, the people of China were suffering under a severe famine. The U.S. government was spending hundreds of millions of dollars each year storing excess food in silos in Kansas. We appealed to the president to take some of that food that the taxpayers were paying to store and give it to the Chinese.

"You mean we should feed the enemy?" he asked us.

We said, "Yeah. That's what we mean."

The president had just finished reading *The Guns of August*, a military history that describes in great detail the events leading up to the First World War. President Kennedy found "scary" the similarities between what was happening in 1914, when the world's nations were "arming to the teeth to avoid war" and what was happening in 1962. We didn't know then that his words were an ominous foreshadowing of the Cuban Missile Crisis, which we would face less than six months later, in mid-October. Before that year ended, the world would come the closest it ever has to a full-scale nuclear war.

Our delegation was a group of very ordinary folks. We were all impressed that the president of the United States sat in his rocking chair in the Oval Office talking with us for forty minutes. We felt that he really listened and treated us as friends who had some truth he needed to hear. When his secretary came in to tell him that his next appointment had arrived, he said, "Tell him to wait. I am learning something from these Quakers."

When we encouraged Kennedy to take more leadership in moving us away from the potentiality of nuclear confrontation with the Soviets to a more peaceful coexistence, he responded, in essence, "If you are serious about this, you are going to have to get out there and build a much more powerful movement to enable me to do that. The military-industrial complex is very strong." He had his marching orders, and so did we.

A month and a half later, I was back at the president's house, but on the other side of the fence. Quaker peace activists Larry Scott and Wilmer Young—who had helped to organize the sailing of *The Golden Rule* into Pacific nuclear test waters when I was in high school—were holding a silent prayer vigil in front of the White House. Calling for an

Quaker delegation reports on a visit with President Kennedy outside the White House (May 1962).

end to nuclear weapons testing, they had decided to vigil and fast for forty days. A friend and I rode our bicycles from Howard almost every day to give them moral support.

On the twenty-seventh day of their fast, a third person joined them. A federal ordinance made it illegal to assemble in front of the White House—and apparently three's a crowd—so the police arrested them and put them in jail. They were charged with being a "public nuisance."

A fellow named Cecil Thomas and I decided to continue their vigil in front of the White House. We held a sign, like the one I would hold in Red Square in Moscow a few months later, which read "Bomb Tests Kill People." After a few days, Helen Corson, a ninety-two-year-old Quaker woman, joined us, and so we too were arrested for illegal assembly and being a nuisance. Opposing wars and militarism is indeed a nuisance for the military-industrial complex!

Helen was an amazing woman. In court the judge scolded her, "You shouldn't be here. You're too old to do this kind of stuff." The essence of her response was: "Judge, I don't know how I look, but if I don't have much longer to live, I want to make sure I spend what little time I've got making sure the world is still here for my children and grandchildren." It was a very touching moment.

We were arrested on a Friday afternoon, and Friday night was a bad time to be in lockup. Dinner was a piece of baloney on moldy white bread. Men who had imbibed a bit too much were being thrown in with Cecil and me throughout the night. Eventually sixteen of us were crowded into a cell designed for two people.

Cecil and I alternated, one of us sitting on the steel bench, the other lying down on the concrete floor with the cockroaches, all night long. At one point he rolled over and said, "Dave, there must be a better way to work for peace."

I was allowed my one phone call, which I used to contact Vice President William Stuart Nelson at Howard. I alerted him that I might not make it to commencement the next day because I was in jail. I said, "Please tell everyone I'm sorry I can't be there." He said he would be sure to pick up my diploma and make an announcement about where I was and why.

Unexpectedly, I was released at noon the following day. I rushed back to Howard to get my cap and gown, just in time to walk across the stage and receive the diploma myself.

After graduating from Howard, I was faced with a multitude of possibilities for alternative service. I could have taught English in Poland. I could have worked on community development in India or Mexico, or one of a few nations in Africa. I could have volunteered to be a guinea pig in the search for a cure for diseases. I weighed all the options.

Ultimately, I decided to stay in Washington, DC, and work with the Friends Committee on National Legislation (FCNL). This Quaker lobbying organization tried to influence policies related to war, hunger, and poverty that affected millions of people around the world.

I worked as the college secretary, getting paid, at my request, fifty dollars a month, so that I could continue to keep my earnings below the level at which I would have to pay federal taxes to fund war and nuclear weapons. I lived for the first year at the Peace Action Center, a cooperative household founded by Larry Scott, which accepted whatever I could afford to pay—which, given my salary, wasn't much. It was a wonderful place, hosting peace people from all over the world. My second year with FCNL I lived in the basement of friends, in a tiny room with a hot plate, where I heated the pea soup I ate pretty much every night, paying ten dollars a month in rent and providing some childcare for their young children.

FCNL certainly got its money's worth. I spoke all over the country on college campuses and in churches, trying to raise interest in what was going on in the world and FCNL's work to change it. A few weeks after I started, I was driving home on October 22 from a speaking event in North Carolina with Ed Snyder, my mentor, who had a very humane way about him that he tried to bring to bear on international relations.

We were in my VW Bug, listening to the big, clunky radio that I had taken out of my brother Paul's old Hudson when he junked that car and that I had jerry-rigged into the glove compartment of mine. We were coming up the Blue Ridge Parkway, straining to hear President Kennedy's ultimatum that if the Soviet ships loaded with missiles heading toward Cuba's missile silos didn't turn around, he would unleash nuclear missiles on Moscow.

Washington, DC, felt like the scariest place to be living in the country at that time. I could literally see the fear and feeling that "This day may be our last" on people's faces every day the following week as I rode my bike the five miles between home and the FCNL office on Capitol Hill every day.

I was deeply relieved when Soviet President Nikita Khrushchev blinked and the crisis passed. And I was heartened the following summer when Kennedy gave an address at American University. He publicly challenged the Soviets to a peace race—just as our Quaker delegation had asked him to do a year before. He also proposed a ban on nuclear testing. Within five months, Kennedy was killed, another victim of an assassin's bullet. I felt like I had lost a friend, seeing the hope for change draining away once again.

Another crisis followed a year and a half later. During the Gulf of Tonkin incident in August 1964, my job included calling the Pentagon to try to substantiate the Johnson administration's charge that the North Vietnamese navy had launched torpedo attacks on our ships in the gulf. History has shown that the administration's accusation was unfounded, but the lie became the justification for the congressional Gulf of Tonkin Resolution, which gave President Lyndon Johnson the authority to intervene militarily in any Southeast Asian country that was vulnerable to "communist aggression." It opened the way for an escalation in the deployment of U.S. forces in Vietnam and essentially launched the full-scale war there.

Before the congressional vote took place, I made numerous calls to the Pentagon over several days and was always referred to someone else, getting no real answers. Finally, I was handed off to a general, who apparently thought he had put me on hold. I overheard him say to a fellow officer, "This guy Hartsough has made close to a hundred calls to the Pentagon over the last several days, and his questions are of more than just passing interest. If I had anything to say about it, I'd draft him and send him over to Nam."

Fortunately, I had only two weeks left before completing my alternative service and was not shipped off to Vietnam. But after my time at FCNL, the federal authorities decided not to allow conscientious objectors to do alternative service there anymore. It was not in the Pentagon's best interests to have COs working against their wars and exposing their lies to Congress and the American people. If I had been successful in getting truthful answers to my questions to the Pentagon that August, I am confident Congress would not have voted for the Gulf of Tonkin Resolution and two million lives would not have been lost in that war and hundreds of billions of dollars could have been available for a real War on Poverty in the United States.

That fall, I decided to enter graduate school in international relations at Columbia University in New York City. I was accepted into the prestigious International Fellows Program, which I thought would deepen my cross-cultural understanding and offer new insights in how to resolve differences among nations peacefully and end the Cold War. But "international relations" there was with the Cold-War mindset and the need to continue developing massive military might, threatening the use of nuclear weapons, conducting covert CIA operations around the globe, and getting the upper hand to "win" the Cold War and maintain U.S. control of the world.

Most of the other students were headed toward high-powered government jobs with the State Department or the CIA. They wrote papers on how to win the Cold War, which Columbia regularly published. I wrote papers on improving relations with Cuba and ending the war in Vietnam. Neither of these got published—except by the American Friends Service Committee. Needless to say, I found the mentality at the university and my fellow students rather depressing. I felt quite lonely and unappreciated for challenging their way of thinking. None of them joined me when I went to the first draft card burning in Greenwich Village—which was a powerful moment for me.

I was still living very simply. Entertainment for me consisted of spending fifteen cents to ride the Staten Island Ferry. And I went to one movie that year—because it cost a dollar. The theater was so crowded that the only space available was sitting in the aisle. I thought *The Sound of Music* was profoundly beautiful, and for many nights I drifted off to sleep singing its songs.

We students had an appointment one afternoon with Vice President Hubert Humphrey in the White House. When we arrived, a staff person told us, "The vice president is in a very important meeting and will be here as soon as he can." He was meeting in the room next to us with President Johnson and his full cabinet.

Humphrey showed up about two hours late. He greeted us, "Hello, boys. We've just made a momentous decision. I'm not at liberty to share what it is, but by this evening, you'll know." That night the president announced that U.S. armed forces were invading the Dominican Republic.

Humphrey asked us if we had any questions. Not yet aware that we were about to invade the Dominican Republic, I asked about what most concerned me. I mentioned that we were getting more deeply involved in the war in Vietnam, that lots of people were being killed, both Vietnamese and American. I asked him why the United States had refused to allow free elections to take place in Vietnam in 1956, as was called for in the Geneva Accords, which likely would have prevented the horrendous war there.

Humphrey went into a harangue for an hour and a half about how we can't trust the Communists and they'll take over the world if we give them an inch. I guess he did answer my question—you can't support elections if people are going to vote for Communists! At the end of his answer, he announced, "I have another meeting to go to." My question was the only one that got asked that afternoon.

On November 9, 1965, the biggest power failure in U.S. history took out all of New York City and portions of seven states, plunging us all into darkness. During the "Great Northeast Blackout," in the class with Zbigniew Brzezinski, my fellow students flicked their cigarette lighters as we took lecture notes in the dark. I was very discouraged and sick of academia, feeling that they were in the dark both literally and metaphorically.

I turned in my thesis comparing attitudes toward wars of liberation in the Soviet Union, China, and the United States, and received my master's degree in January. In February 1966, I hitchhiked out of New York holding a sign that read "Frisco or Freeze." When I finally got to California, looking forward to a break and a visit with my brother, I found a message from Ed Snyder, asking me to call FCNL's DC office "any time of day or night." He made a job offer I couldn't turn down.

I returned to FCNL later in February, to direct a "three-month emergency campaign" to end the Vietnam War. I stayed for five years. I

worked as a lobbyist to end the war and change the government's priorities, urging the redirection of the billions of dollars going into the war
effort toward programs to alleviate the massive hunger and poverty in
the United States and around the globe.

I was growing increasingly uncomfortable with carrying a draft
card in my wallet. That year I finally sent it back to the Selective Service
Board, with a letter explaining to the authorities why I could not cooperate with the war system in any way. Though they could have imprisoned me for that action, they didn't pursue me, and I was grateful.

When I arrived back in Washington, the Friends Committee on
National Legislation was the only church-based lobbying group in town,
and only two members of Congress had voted against supporting the
Vietnam War. We organized "Wednesdays in Washington," hosting
people from all over the country, briefing them to visit with their
members of Congress and urge a cutoff of funding for the war. Barry
Commoner, who would run for president in 1980 on the Citizens Party
ticket, brought a group every month from Washington University in
St. Louis.

We also organized lunch meetings at William Penn House on
Capitol Hill, inviting twenty to twenty-five staffers of members of
Congress to hear reports from people just returned from Vietnam. I
accompanied around the Hill former peace and development workers
who had served in Vietnam, trying to help members of Congress see
the truth about the war, in contrast to all the propaganda they were
receiving from the Pentagon, the State Department, the White House,
and the news media.

I'm grateful for people such as Don Luce and Gene Stoltzfus, who
were concerned about being used by the U.S. government as the war
escalated and left International Voluntary Service in Vietnam to spend
their time talking with members of Congress and the American people.
And for David Schoenbrun, a war correspondent who had been fired
from CBS because of his open truth-telling about the war, who met
with twenty-five members of Congress in a very powerful session in the
Capitol Building that I organized.

One of the legislators who was most receptive to their stories and
perspective was Ted Kennedy. He always had an open-door policy
toward FCNL. He was genuinely interested in what we were doing and
the reports we had from on the ground in Vietnam.

Getting meetings with his brother Robert Kennedy was more difficult, but I succeeded a few times. Both he, and later Senators Eugene

McCarthy and George McGovern, asked my opinion about whether they should run for president. I encouraged them all. They were responsive to my reports about the quagmire in Vietnam and were strong antiwar candidates. I later joined the staff of the McGovern for President Campaign in 1972 after I moved to Philadelphia.

I happened to be riding to the ground floor in an elevator in the Senate Office Building with Robert Kennedy the day he declared that he would not run against Lyndon Johnson for the Democratic nomination for president. As I walked with him to his car, I really wanted to say to him that he should read his brother John's book, *Profiles in Courage*. As it turned out, Johnson declined to run again, and Kennedy stepped into the race, which tragically ended with his assassination in June 1968. It was another huge loss in the effort to transform the country, and another deeply personal grief for me.

FCNL worked closely with the Vietnam Moratorium, which was a sustained, and very powerful, nationwide movement against the war. At noon on October 15, 1968, all across the United States, in houses of worship, workplaces, and communities, people rang church bells, participated in vigils, and stopped work to indicate that they were fed up with the war and to demand that it end. Each month we added another day—two days of resistance in November, three in December, and so on.

I also worked closely with CALC (Clergy and Laity Concerned), thankful for that group's commitment to the struggle to end the war. CALC organized five hundred constituents to come to Washington from all over the country to lobby, and I felt honored to offer the briefing for members of the clergy before they went to visit their Members of Congress.

I helped to organize a talkathon on the floor of the U.S. House of Representatives, which went on for fourteen hours, during which many members of Congress spoke out powerfully about the need to end the war. With A Quaker Action Group (AQAG), I also took part in a silent worship service in the gallery of the U.S. Senate, while the legislators below us debated and voted for more funding for the war. When the vote was over, we were arrested on a charge of "praying without a permit," which I found particularly fascinating.

Later, we had a very moving public reading on the steps of the Capitol of all the names of those who had been killed in the war. We began doing the reading at the Capitol every Wednesday at noon. We usually made it through only the first fifty to a hundred names before the Capitol Police arrested us.

Quakers reading the names of those who died in the Vietnam War on the Capitol steps, joined by three members of Congress (1969). [Photo: Bob Burchette, *Washington Post*]

A few weeks into it, on a Tuesday afternoon, I went to see George Brown, a member of the U.S. House of Representatives from California. I explained what we were doing and asked if there was any way he could help. He leaned back in his swivel chair, took a puff on his cigar, and said, "Sure." He joined us the next day on the Capitol steps.

And not only that, he wrote a letter to every member of Congress, urging them to lend their support. The following Wednesday, he and three other members of Congress showed up. Because they had congressional immunity, they were not subject to arrest, so they continued reading the names of the war dead after the rest of us were hauled off to jail. They made it through all forty thousand of the names of U.S. soldiers who had been killed to that point.

That made the news. It was a very beautiful and powerful action and was reported widely in the local and national press. Soon afterward, *Life* magazine devoted an entire issue to picturing every American who had died in the war, with their birthdate, hometown, branch of service, and date of death. Within weeks, people were reading the names of the war dead in front of federal buildings, courthouses and post offices all over the country. We learned of at least a thousand communities that participated.

Later, I asked George Brown, who was running for the U.S. Senate that year, whether he was worried that his action would hurt his chances for getting elected. His answer was, "Dave, I decided a long time ago that if I did only what I felt was politically safe, I wouldn't do very much." I wished for many more such courageous politicians.

Soon after that, Stewart Meacham of American Friends Service Committee had an idea for a witness at the White House. Tens of thousands of us gathered one evening in Arlington Cemetery, each of us carrying a candle and wearing around our neck the name of an American or Vietnamese person who had been killed in the war. We made a long funeral procession by candlelight across the bridge over the Potomac, marching solemnly all night long.

As we arrived in front of the White House, each of us in turn read out the name we carried. Someone with a large drum beat it for every name. The reading went on for more than twenty-four hours. It was a deeply moving witness, a reminder of the enormity of the loss of human life in the war on both sides.

Another action related to the war was a Quaker project to send medical supplies through the Vietnamese Red Cross to North Vietnam and the parts of South Vietnam controlled by the National Liberation Front. First we tried mailing them through the U.S. Postal Service to Hanoi. But the postmaster general deemed this "aiding the enemy" and issued a regulation making it illegal for post offices to accept packages addressed to the Red Cross in Hanoi.

So we started mailing the supplies to the Canadian Friends Service Committee (CFSC), which forwarded them to Vietnam. The postmaster general caught on to this as well and issued a directive to post offices, informing them they could not accept anything for CFSC, either. We decided to make a public witness.

We carried the medical supplies we'd collected to the Central Post Office next to Union Station, Washington's train terminal on Capitol Hill, and tried to mail them to the Red Cross in Hanoi. When they were refused, we readdressed them to the CFSC, and they were refused again. So we held a press conference on the spot, asking, "Don't we have a right to send medical supplies to Canadian Quakers?"

Subsequently, the ACLU (American Civil Liberties Union) in DC filed a lawsuit—"David Hartsough et al. versus the Postmaster General, the Secretary of Defense, the Secretary of State et al."—which lasted several years, and was eventually dropped. We later launched an "underground railroad" for the medical supplies, carrying them to

Philadelphia, then Buffalo, and then on into Canada, where the CFSC sent them on to Vietnam.

We also raised funds to send the *Phoenix*, a fifty-foot yacht loaded with $10,000 in medical supplies, to Hải Phòng—a very risky venture for the Quaker crew, as the United States was bombing the Vietnamese harbor at the time. Though bullets were flying through the air over the boat, they managed to successfully deliver the supplies. A subsequent effort was thwarted when the South Vietnamese government turned the *Phoenix* away.

A huge antiwar demonstration took place at the White House in November 1969. President Nixon claimed to be watching a football game on TV, but he was actually paying close attention to what was going on beyond his front lawn and at smaller demonstrations all around the country. We learned later that Nixon delayed bombing North Vietnamese cities for a couple years and decided against using nuclear weapons because of his fear of a revolution in the streets of America.

While Presidents Johnson and Nixon wanted the peace movement to believe that our actions had no impact on U.S. policy, author Tom Wells arrived at a different conclusion. After interviewing many of the key players in the government and the peace movement, he wrote *The War Within*. The book concluded that nonviolent resistance to the war by the American people—on college campuses, in the religious community, within the ranks of the military, and in towns and cities across the country—had played a crucial role in ending the war. Certainly the determination of the Vietnamese people to rid themselves of outside domination was critical, but so was massive U.S. protest and refusal to cooperate with the war effort by the American people.

On the Hill, I worked most closely with Wes Michaelson of Senator Mark Hatfield's staff and John Holum from Senator McGovern's office. FCNL helped to write the Senate bill proposing a cut-off of funding for the war, which Hatfield and McGovern cosponsored. I visited other senators to add cosponsors and also members of the House of Representatives, to encourage similar legislation there. Though getting it passed would take some years, that bill eventually played a key role in ending U.S. involvement in the war.

I also worked very closely with Senator William Fulbright, who was the chair of the Senate Foreign Relations Committee. His book *The Arrogance of Power* was life-changing for me and for many others. His insightful analysis feels even more profound now, in this era of American Empire.

Toward the end of those exhausting five years as a lobbyist on the Hill, I arranged for three Maryknoll missionaries who had been kicked out of Guatemala—accused unjustly of supporting the guerillas there—to come to Washington and speak to members of Congress about their experience. It was discouraging to realize that, even then, our nation was sowing the seeds for its future wars in Central America.

One of the last and most powerful actions in which I was involved in Washington, DC, was the People's Lobby in the spring of 1971. Thousands of people came from all around the country and participated in demonstrations at the White House, the Capitol Building, and at the Selective Service and Internal Revenue Service offices. More than seven thousand people were arrested for demonstrations of conscience against the war that week.

About a thousand of us were at the Selective Service headquarters. Many of us decided to stay all night and block the entrance in the morning, so that the employees couldn't carry on the business-as-usual of drafting young men to go to war. Early in the morning we bowed in prayer so the workers would have to walk on our backs to get to work. But the police cleared us away before the employees arrived and charged us with disturbing the peace—ironic, since we were there trying to disturb the war.

The court judge offered us a choice of paying a low fine—fifty dollars—or spending up to three months in jail. He strongly encouraged us to pay the fine. A few of us refused to pay, asserting our belief that we had done nothing wrong. The judge lectured us sternly, threatening to give us the maximum sentence. We persisted, and he finally declared, "One day in the county jail."

We were very relieved. As it turned out, we had barely changed into our jail clothes when a prison guard came and told us to get ready to be released. Apparently it wasn't legal to sentence someone to one day in jail—a minimum of two was needed to process prisoners in and then process them back out. So we were set free after a couple of hours.

I was learning that the powers-that-be would do virtually anything to scare people into submission—short of calling our mothers, as Mrs. Alexander had claimed to do. But over and over I watched the grip of the system crumble when people refused to give in to their fears or grant the government power over them, withholding their cooperation from its unjust orders and demands. It's a lesson I would need to cling to tightly as I decided to escalate my opposition to the deadly and relentless war in Vietnam.

CHAPTER 7

Blockade: Standing in the Way of Bombs Headed for Nam

My five years as a Capitol Hill lobbyist were extremely stressful. An encounter a year after I arrived made that time survivable and changed my life for the better. I was helping to serve food for a Quaker Leadership Seminar at William Penn House. Among those who received a dollop of the apple cobbler I was doling out was Jan Talcott, a graduate student teaching high school social studies in the Anacostia section of Washington, DC.

Our conversation that night led to walks through the National Arboretum and canoeing adventures on the Potomac River. I was living and breathing the Vietnam War in those days, giving every ounce of my energy trying to end it, so our talks, our forays into nature, and Jan's loving presence were a great gift and antidote to the stresses I was encountering on a daily basis.

I invited Jan over for dinner at the apartment near Union Station where I was living then. My roommate Stan cooked that night—chicken gizzard soup or some such culinary calamity. Jan wasn't exactly impressed. And it didn't help that on one of our early canoeing escapades, when we capsized in the Potomac, I put my rescue efforts toward the canoe while Jan floated down the river.

I think Jan got the idea that being part of my life would involve excitement and some risk. But she was used to that. She had been in the Peace Corps in Pakistan, and she liked adventure. When she went to Vermont for the final quarter of her graduate program, I made many long-distance calls to her to stay in touch over the summer—a rare extravagance for me.

When she finished her program in Vermont, I convinced Jan to travel with me to Wyoming's Grand Teton Mountains, which I considered my spiritual home. Ever since my family visited them when I was a teenager, I have loved those snowcapped mountains rising out of the plains, with their gorgeous lakes and stunning waterfalls. Jan and I camped by Jenny Lake and hiked my favorite trails.

When I proposed near the top of a mountain on the Indian Paint Brush Trail, to my delight, Jan said yes—though later she would wonder if she had been affected by the high altitude and its low oxygen level. We drove on to Seattle where I met her family. All of our parents blessed our marriage in October 1967.

Our son Peter was born on January 16, 1969, a day after the birthday of my hero. I wanted to name him Martin Luther King Hartsough, but Jan objected. Wise woman. We had trouble bringing Peter home from the hospital because of all the roadblocks set up for President Nixon's inauguration. Once again, politics got in our way.

I was very busy in those days, and our friends were amused that among Peter's first words were "Daddy gone to meeting." In fact, when he was in the fourth grade, his schoolmates were all talking about how there was going to be a nuclear war, and Peter piped up, "I don't think there's going to be a nuclear war, because my dad is going to meetings to make sure it doesn't happen." He occasionally answered the question "What does your father do?" with "He goes to jail."

Our daughter Heidi was born on October 12, 1970. We drove directly from the hospital to spend a sabbatical year at Pendle Hill, a Quaker study and retreat center near Philadelphia. It was a perfect place for recovering from the exhaustion of my Washington years.

Our year at Pendle Hill offered me the opportunity for spiritual and physical renewal, as well as more time with my family, which I cherished. While there, I participated in a weekly economics seminar in which we did a lot of reading and studying, trying to understand the deeper causes of U.S. war-making around the world and the increasing gap between rich and poor at home. Many of us also began laying the foundation for what was to become the Movement for a New Society.

Our children had their first experience of nonviolent witness when Peter was two and Heidi was six months old. Our family participated in a Quaker Meeting for Worship in front of the White House in the spring of 1971, trying to encourage Nixon to end the Vietnam War. About 250 Quakers converged on DC for the witness from all over the Eastern United States.

With my wife Jan and children Peter and Heidi before being arrested at a White House Quaker protest against the Vietnam War (1971). [Photo: UPI]

Over a bullhorn, a police officer warned us that we had to leave, but nobody did. We just continued our silent worship, so the police started arresting people. They arrested everybody except Jan and me and the children.

So we were left sitting there on the sidewalk, while everybody else was loaded onto buses and hauled off to jail. The police chief approached and crouched down in front of us, trying to "reason with" us. He told us that Peter and Heidi would be taken away from us and put into Juvenile Hall, where "God knows what could happen to them."

"Don't you love your children?" he asked us.

We tried to explain as best we could that we appreciated his genuine concern for our children, but that we were also concerned about the children in Vietnam, who were dying and were going to continue to die. "We're here, and we're going to keep praying for an end to this tragic war," I said. "We've done exactly the same thing as all these other people, so if you have to arrest us, we'll take the consequences."

The police roped off the area so nobody else could come anywhere near us, except some media people who were there with their cameras.

For half an hour the chief pleaded with us to just go home. When he saw that we weren't going to leave, he asked us to go to his police car. I said that if he put us under arrest, we would walk to the car, which is what happened. He then drove us to Georgetown and let us out behind the police station.

A photograph of us went out over the UPI (United Press International) wire service and appeared in the *Washington Post*, showing the police officer crouching in front of Jan, with Heidi in her lap, and me, with Peter standing by my side. Friends from all over the country sent us copies that appeared in their local newspapers. One went into each of our children's baby books: their first arrest.

I am eternally grateful that—as we watched so many of our friends embrace different values when they had children—Jan and I were together in our resolve to continue living out our commitments to nonviolent witness as a family and our belief in the unity of the human family worldwide. And also that we shared a commitment to living simply.

We had bought our first house in Washington, DC, in 1969 for $13,000. I had accepted a yearly salary of $3,000 from the Friends Committee on National Legislation when I returned in 1966—half of what they offered but enough to put our family over the taxable level. I requested that FCNL honor my conscience and not withhold from my salary and turn over to the federal government the approximately 50 percent of my taxes that would go for the Vietnam War and preparations for future wars.

Both FCNL and the American Friends Service Committee had employees who took this position, and both Quaker organizations wanted to honor our consciences, but the law required that employers withhold taxes. So together the two organizations filed a lawsuit to get exemption from that law, so they would not have to take the war portion of our taxes against our consciences and give it to the government. In the meantime, they took the money out of their own resources to pay our taxes, rather than take it from us. They held our resisted tax money.

Jan and I have written a letter to the IRS (Internal Revenue Service) every April since then, explaining why we won't pay the portion of our taxes that funds wars and preparations for killing. I've written about Jesus's command to love our enemies. I've quoted the Nuremberg Principles, developed out of the trials of members of the Nazi Third Reich after World War II and later adopted as both U.S. and international law, which declared that individuals must not obey the laws of their government if they involve crimes against humanity. The Vietnam War, I asserted, was a crime against humanity.

In 1969, exactly three months before the launch of Apollo 11, I wrote, "We are almost at the point of landing a man on the moon. But we have not yet learned how to live together peacefully and resolve our problems by other means than war." I registered my dismay and sorrow that individuals "in the prime of their youth" were being sent to Vietnam to become "corpses to be gathered up and buried."

In 1972, I included quotes from Vietnamese refugees who had fled to the Plain of Jars in Laos: "Our village was filled with bomb craters, the land made barren. I grieved very much to see my village in ruins, my animals vanished, my crops destroyed, more and more dead and wounded." . . . "There wasn't a night when we thought we'd live until morning . . . never a morning we thought we'd survive until night. Did our children cry? O, yes, and we did also. I just stayed in my cave. I didn't see the sunlight for two years. . . . I used to repeat 'Please don't let the planes come, please don't let the planes come, please don't let the planes come.'"

Before we had moved from DC, an IRS agent had paid me a visit at the FCNL office. We had a most interesting conversation. He told me that he agreed with my position on the war and that he supported my decision to follow my conscience. But, he explained, it was his job and responsibility to collect the money for my unpaid taxes.

He expressed concern about my family's safety in the neighborhood in which we chose to live, and I assured him that we were fine. He had many questions about the work of FCNL, and he asked for some of our newsletters and other literature. He insisted on paying for them. He gave me a dollar for about forty cents' worth of material and told me to keep the rest as a contribution to FCNL. It seemed ironic to me that this man who had come to collect my money ended up giving me some instead.

He told me that our interaction was "off the record." Then he returned to the subject of my taxes and said, "It's my job to get this money from you in any way I can. I don't like to do this kind of thing, but I can take any property you have—your car, or your house . . ."

I told him, "Well, I do have a bicycle downstairs."

"Oh no, no," he insisted. "I wouldn't take your bicycle."

"I have this suit that I have on," I said.

"Oh, no, no, we wouldn't take your suit." He left without accomplishing his mission.

While our family was living at Pendle Hill, an IRS agent came out almost every week to harass us. The IRS had repossessed the car of someone else at Pendle Hill for unpaid war taxes, so we parked our car far from our little home.

One day the couple who were living in our house in Washington, DC, came home to find a notice on the front door: "WARNING—U.S. GOVERNMENT SEIZURE. This property has been seized for nonpayment of Internal Revenue taxes, by virtue of levy issued by the District Director of Internal Revenue. All persons are warned not to remove or tamper with this property in any manner, under severe penalty of law."

I made a trip back to DC with Quaker friends Colin Bell and Vint Deming, to meet with two IRS agents and discuss the lien they had put on the house Jan and I owned, for nonpayment of $31.90 in taxes. I had explained our position in a letter to the IRS, and also made clear that FCNL had already handed over the money for my refused taxes from the organization's own funds. One of the agents explained that the IRS does all its business by computer, and "the computer does not read letters."

The agents also insisted that we owed $15 in "phone tax," an excise tax that had been added by Congress to all U.S. long-distance telephone communications specifically to fund the Vietnam War. I refused to pay it, and I also refused to give the name and address of our bank, which they demanded. They told me that I needed to call my wife to make sure she was aware of the jeopardy I was putting us in.

I called Jan back in Philadelphia. She, of course, agreed with my position. One of the agents joked that he would add the excise tax from that phone call to our bill. Eventually, after meeting for almost three hours, he signed a release on our house. But he warned, "This does not mean we will not come back and seize your house again in the near future." We shook hands as we parted.

We never again heard from the IRS about those taxes. And Jan and I have continued our war tax resistance for more than forty years. Our most recent letters reflect the same concerns and commitments we raised in our earliest ones—with Iraq, Afghanistan, and Pakistan mentioned in place of Vietnam.

The IRS usually succeeds in getting the money eventually—often through liens on the accounts we have had with Oikocredit, which offers microcredit loans in the poorest parts of the world, and Chicago's South Shore Bank, whose mission before closing in 2009 was to support America's poorest neighborhoods. But Jan and I take comfort in knowing that we have not voluntarily given our money to support war.

If someone appeared at the door asking for a $5,000 contribution for the war in Vietnam or Iraq or whatever war comes next, I believe that most of us would not hand over the money. But the wars continue because the vast majority of Americans continue to pay their taxes without question. As former Secretary of State Alexander Haig said so famously when he looked out over a sea of war protesters at the White House, "Let them march all they want, as long as they pay their taxes."

Jan and I contribute the war portion of our taxes to humanitarian causes that we believe in. The amount that we submit to the federal government we send by check written out to the Department of Health and Human Services, explaining that we want our taxes to support education, low-income housing, and other critical needs. Sometimes the government returns our check marked "Wrong Addressee," and then we resend it with another letter explaining our position.

After our year at Pendle Hill, our family helped to found the Life Center Community in Philadelphia, which was part of the Movement for a New Society. Several of us in the community had ties to A Quaker Action Group, and two had worked closely with Martin Luther King through the Poor People's Campaign and the Southern Christian Leadership Conference. We realized, as King had expressed so eloquently, that tinkering with this or that problem in the system was not enough; that we were facing a problem that was much bigger than racism and civil rights.

We came together out of a shared desire to go deeper in challenging our society and building a new one. We were particularly moved by Martin Luther King's naming of the scourges of militarism and materialism alongside racism. He declared that the triple menace of racism, militarism, and extreme materialism was not only devastating other countries and our nation's international reputation, they were "destroying the soul of America."

The United States was devouring the world to perpetuate a lifestyle of comfort and greed, and we had become, according to King, "the greatest purveyor of violence in the world" in our efforts to protect it. Those of us in the Life Center Community wanted to experiment with ways to bring about nonviolent transformation of our society, continuing the work of building a movement that King had begun.

We knew that lowering our cost of living would free up time to work on justice and peace issues and be consistent with our beliefs about just sharing of the world's resources. So we moved into shared households in the same neighborhood in west Philadelphia. Our household included six adults and four children. We shared the cooking and the cleaning and kept our expenses to a minimum. Our family of four was able to live on less than $200 per month.

We started a food co-op and worked on local issues such as community safety and neighborhood policing. We also held seminars on the overseas impact of the American Way of Life and our nation's global domination. Our community became a training center, where people came from all over the world, spending from a weekend to several months learning about nonviolence and social change.

We had what we called a "floating Quaker meeting." Once a month, we went to be in solidarity with someone taking a stand—for example, a young person who had refused to become a soldier and go to Vietnam and was taking sanctuary in a Quaker meetinghouse, or a doctor who was receiving death threats for his work among vulnerable patients. We would go and spend a weekend offering presence and support.

The horrible news about the war was relentless. Just before Christmas in 1971, U.S. forces began bombing Hanoi and Hải Phòng and the surrounding communities in North Vietnam. Up until that point, our military had been bombing mostly the Ho Chi Minh trail, supposedly cutting off the movement of arms along it. The bombing of cities with large concentrations of civilians was a massive escalation of the war, leading to the death, wounding, or displacement of three million Vietnamese in Nixon's first three years in office.

When this bombing started, we called the community together for a meeting for worship in the Quaker tradition. We tried to comprehend the pain of the families in Vietnam that were underneath our bombs, contrasting that with the spirit of Christmas that was enveloping our own nation. As we grappled with the scriptural challenge to overcome evil with good, we acknowledged that the Vietnamese people were our neighbors and children of God, and we tried to discern how to respond to their suffering and do something to stop this madness.

The meeting lasted for more than four hours. It remains the most powerful worship experience of my life. Hearts were heavy, and a lot of tears were shed. We knew we had to do more than wring our hands and send another letter to the president.

We had heard of a few instances in the early 1940s of Europeans lying down on railroad tracks to try to block trains and prevent the Nazis from shipping Jews to concentration camps. We imagined the impact if thousands had taken such action. Out of our silence and prayer, we began to feel that we needed to put our bodies between the bombs and the people of Vietnam who were getting killed.

We decided to act together, as a community, offering concrete mutual support to one another, particularly to those who were willing and able to take the most risk. We realized that not everyone could participate in the same way. Jan and I had two young children, and others had similar responsibilities. We began working out the details of who would care for the kids, help to pay rent if breadwinners were hurt or detained for a long time, and visit people in jail if needed. And who would care for loved ones left behind if someone got killed.

A committee researched where we might physically place ourselves. We considered going to Hanoi and Hải Phòng, to live in those cities with the Vietnamese people, or perhaps on a boat just offshore. But the logistics and expense of such an action were daunting. We turned our sights to U.S. military bases involved in shipping bombs.

We discovered that the Earle Naval Ammunition Depot was about an hour and a half by car from Philadelphia, in Leonardo, New Jersey. A few of us went on an exploratory mission. We parked our cars, adorned with bumper stickers advocating peace, on a street by a beach near the base. We walked to a place where we could see a very long pier, with tracks that carried trains filled with arms for loading onto ships. We knew we had our answer.

When we returned to our cars, we found that we had been issued traffic tickets, and some of our tires had been punctured. We took these actions as signs that the surrounding community didn't view our bumper stickers or our commitments favorably. They certainly weren't going to be happy about what we were going to do next.

When we got home, we called everyone we knew who had a canoe, a kayak, a rowboat, or anything else that floated. By April we had twenty-six canoes lined up, with at least two people for each, and the news that a ship named the USS *Nitro* was on its way to the base.

We left from the beach early in the morning and paddled in a flotilla out to the pier, where crates of munitions were stacked. We got close enough to read cartons labeled "Napalm" and "Anti-personnel weapons." Seeing those really tore me apart. They meant sure death for people in Vietnam, and I felt even more strongly that we had to do everything we could to stop them from reaching their destination.

The deck of the *Nitro* was being loaded very high with munitions, in addition to the arms that were already in the hold. We paddled our canoes within a hundred feet of the ship, trying to get in front to block it. Military Police yelled at us from the pier over bullhorns, threatening us with a charge of criminal conspiracy and sentences of up to twenty years in prison if we didn't leave the restricted area. It didn't escape me that the police in Moscow's Red Square had issued an identical warning in response to our protest there.

The badges and Navy uniforms made it clear that these weren't just idle threats. I sensed that the police were going to do whatever it took to stop us. That felt very scary. It gave me pause to realize that if their warning came true, my children would be in their early twenties before I would be out of prison.

But I also felt deeply at peace, and that peace outweighed the fear. When we had considered going to Hanoi or Hải Phòng and making ourselves vulnerable to our nation's bombs, we knew such an action could well have meant the end of our lives. This was less of a risk. I remember shouting to the police, "Thank you for warning us, but if these bombs reach their destination, the people in Vietnam will suffer far worse."

We knew we had the support of our whole community behind us. And the feeling deepened during that action that we are all brothers and sisters around the world; that not just our blood relatives, but the whole human race, is our family, and we have a responsibility for the well-being and safety of one another. We were clear then, as I am now, that this madness of wars and killing each other because people happen to speak a different language, or are of a different color or nationality, or embrace a different religion, is totally against everything we believe and completely contrary to the kind of world in which we want to live.

The spirit of mutual support and determination, and the feeling that we were putting our love for our fellow human beings into practice, was powerful. It was one of the strongest feelings I have had in my life that I was in the right place at the right time. The other people who were part of that blockade were, and still are, some of my best friends. Doing that action together bonded us in life-long friendships.

For six days we paddled around in our boats, as the mountain of weapons on the *Nitro* grew and grew. One canoe was sunk when a police boat revved its engine nearby to flood it with water, and another when an MP pushed its prow underwater with a grappling hook. Not much else happened. We did some singing to pass the time, because a lot of the time it was actually pretty boring. But we were learning the truth that in peace work in risky situations, a boring day is a good day.

Police often harassed us at the end of the day as we put our canoes back on our cars. We discovered more punctured tires, and sugar in some of our gas tanks. The parking tickets mounted, and a few times our cars were towed away from legal parking spots.

One night a few in our group ran into some of the sailors in a bar. They were young guys who had been drafted—eighteen and nineteen years old—and they weren't in the Navy because they liked the idea of dropping bombs on people. They shared that they weren't happy being on the ship, which had been rushed out of a repair dock in Rhode Island for the trip to Vietnam's Tonkin Gulf. They believed it was very unsafe and in violation of regulations limiting munitions on the deck.

Our group invited the sailors to a potluck dinner one evening at a nearby Quaker meetinghouse, where we had a good sharing of concerns. That was one of my first interactions with active-duty military personnel, and hearing their questions about what they were being ordered to do really opened my eyes. I realized, perhaps for the first time, that it was possible to have a heart and a conscience underneath a uniform.

That night the sailors told us that the *Nitro* was going to be leaving for Vietnam at six o'clock the following morning. We thanked them for this critical information. Taking a circuitous route suggested by a sympathetic local resident in order to avoid police blockades on the roads, we showed up at the pier at 5:00 a.m. We shared the harbor that morning with a launch full of CBS cameramen and reporters, while an NBC helicopter and a small airplane from *The New York Times* hovered overhead.

Members of the Coast Guard also showed up that morning. They had orders to grab our canoes with grappling hooks and were instructed to haul us away from the ship. We had gotten to know some of them on a first-name basis, and we felt like we had some secret supporters. They dragged our canoes only about fifty feet away—technically following orders but making it easy for us to go back and reposition ourselves in front of the ship while they went after someone else.

As the *Nitro* lifted anchor and began to depart, we paddled frantically trying to block it. I looked up on the deck and saw a crowd of sailors cheering and giving us the supportive "V" sign of peace with their hands. Then, to our utter amazement, seven of the sailors jumped off the ship into the ocean and began swimming toward us. That moment made the whole effort more than worth it.

We clapped and beamed very big smiles and then paddled toward them. We were trying to hoist them into our canoes when the Navy police zoomed over, picked them up, and took them back out to the *Nitro*, which was by then moving out toward open sea.

The sailors who jumped ship spent some time in the *Nitro*'s brig. The story of our protest—and theirs—was widely covered in the media in the United States and around the world. We learned later that when

Twenty-two canoes in a People's Blockade action block the departure of the USS *Nitro* loaded with munitions headed for Vietnam from Leonardo, NJ. Seven sailors jump ship into the ocean to join the protest (1972). [Photo: William E. Sauro, *New York Times*]

the *Nitro* went through the Panama Canal on its way to Vietnam, sailors on other Navy ships flashed fists of solidarity in honor of those seven sailors. One of those who jumped, William Monks, later wrote his testimony about his action:

> I jumped from my ship because of my beliefs against the war and the killing in Vietnam. I also jumped to support the antiwar protestors who valiantly tried to keep *Nitro* from leaving for Vietnam. I also jumped for the many oppressed people in the military that think like myself . . .
>
> I see no reason why I should have to fight in Vietnam. I didn't start this war. I have nothing against the Vietnamese people. They never hurt me or my family. Why should I have to bomb them?

Monks spoke of the military as a "huge machine whose purpose is to kill people for something they call peace." He saw himself as an unwilling and unnecessary cog in that machine, who like others who tried to resist, was hammered into obedience.

Though the Navy threatened the resisting sailors with courts-martial, they were instead tried on their ship by the *Nitro*'s captain. Denied the opportunity to speak on their own behalf, call witnesses, or have legal representation, they were found guilty of unauthorized absence and protesting in uniform, with charges of conspiracy dropped. They were fined and reduced one pay grade.

"Our beliefs remain the same, if not strengthened," Monks continued. "But still we are being dragged onward to Vietnam—despite the fact that we've made known that we would take no part in the mission of this ship. I hope and pray that soon someone will listen to us, and accept the fact that we are no longer a part of this ship."

Navy police confiscated our family's canoe, presumably as evidence of my crime. One evening a few months later, on a visit to Washington, DC, our family was driving down North Capital Street toward the Capitol Building, which was brightly lit. I commented to Peter, then three years old, "That's where our government is." He asked, "Are they the ones who have our canoe?"

When our family relocated to California a year later, we had to go without the canoe. When it was finally released from federal custody, friends on the East Coast picked it up for us. They drove it to the mountains of Colorado, where we met up with them and camped for a week, and then we carried the canoe on top of our VW Bug to our new home in San Francisco. The Navy had kept it for more than a year, and it appeared that they had used it while they had it.

Walter Cronkite of *CBS News* called our witness at Leonardo "a nonviolent blockade of an ammunition ship by land and sea." Our actions in the water were augmented by a parallel witness on the train tracks over which the weapons were shipped to the *Nitro* and other ships. Singing "Praise the Lord and Block the Ammunition"—a popular World War II song with a nonviolent twist—a group was kneeling one day on the pier tracks to stop the train carrying weapons.

My good friend Richard Taylor of the Life Center Community was praying for the strength to do God's will when he heard a police officer shout, "Douse 'em!" A blast of water from the hose on the front of the train caught him full in the face. Then he felt a thud as the train hit him in the chest and rolled him over on his back. He grabbed the hose, slid underneath the locomotive, and was dragged along for a few yards before the train stopped. Thankfully uninjured, he joined his fellow blockaders in a police bus headed for jail.

The idea of a People's Blockade of arms ships and trains began picking up steam. Actions were launched at military bases and shipping points on both coasts of the U.S. While the blockades continued at Leonardo, some of us went to Norfolk, Virginia, to block the aircraft carrier USS *America*.

The *America* was a massive ship, and we had only a nine-foot sailboat, a raft, and a few canoes. Our protest felt very much like a biblical David-and-Goliath encounter. As it was leaving for Vietnam, we paddled underneath the *America*'s deck, which was laden with F4 Phantom jets and other warplanes, as well as blue missiles pointed toward the sky.

To our amazement, we also saw hundreds of sailors up on the deck. When eight Navy tugboats appeared to escort the *America* out to sea, some of the sailors began pelting them and their crews with eggs. One of the tugs unfurled a water cannon, and those of us in canoes braced ourselves to be the targets. But instead it was aimed at the sailors, in an effort to clear them all off the deck.

The Navy wanted to avoid the kind of publicity that involves sailors appreciating and supporting peace protesters. We learned later that nearly fifty sailors went AWOL (Absent Without Leave) from the *America* before it left port, including two that abandoned ship just ten minutes before it sailed. These two surfaced at a press conference three days later, asserting their refusal to participate in the *America*'s mission of death.

The response of the authorities at Norfolk was definitely a step up from our experience in Leonardo. When large Navy and Coast Guard boats filled with armed guards pursued us and turned over all our boats with grappling hooks, we knew just how serious and angry they were about our determination to get in the way of their war effort.

After dumping us in the water, they sent frogmen to capture us. They dragged us to a Navy boat, handcuffed us, and forced us to lie face down on the deck, where the Navy men held their guns at the ready. We didn't know how trigger-happy these guys were, and it was a frightening scene.

We tried to engage our captors in conversation, asking them how they felt about the ship and the bombs and the people who would be on the receiving end, wondering aloud how they would feel if it were their families in the bombers' sights. The Navy men remained silent. They kept us in their custody until the *America* was on its way and out of sight. The next day's headline read, "America Defeats Peace Flotilla." So, America was still standing tall!

In Bangor, Washington, protesters camped out at a strategic spot along the Hood Canal, where they could see ships leaving for Vietnam laden with bombs. Stationed there day and night, they were able to paddle quickly out to blockade whenever a ship was sighted. One fellow

People's Blockade with canoes blocking the aircraft carrier USS *America* headed to Vietnam. Sailors on ship supporting the protest were fire-hosed. Norfolk, VA (1972). [Charles Meads, *Virginian Pilot*]

in a small boat was hit by a large arms ship and pushed a quarter mile before the ship stopped. He survived and continued to blockade other ships. Other blockade actions took place at bases near San Francisco and at Seal Beach in Southern California.

This all began because we felt the horror and pain of the war, and our hearts were breaking over what our government was doing to the people of Vietnam. By following the leadings of our consciences, we tried to speak truth to power and say clearly that this could not continue in our name and with our consent. We were speaking out as powerfully as we knew how, and we felt a deep peace about following what we believed was right.

Our actions touched other peace people, who began to blockade in other places. And our witness also moved people in the military to feel more deeply the consequences of what they were doing. I like to believe that we helped to free those sailors who jumped ship to do what they really wanted to do in their hearts as a result of listening to their consciences. And that their courage inspired many others in the armed forces to refuse to participate in the war without questioning, and to openly resist.

The abiding lesson for me from the People's Blockade is that courage is contagious. When we do what we feel is right, other people will be touched. And what they do in response can touch potentially thousands—even millions—of others.

Individually we can feel powerless, and small, and overwhelmed. It's easy to believe that there's nothing we can do to stand up to war and weapons of destruction. But together we can support one another—emotionally, spiritually, and physically. And the bonds that we forge can last a lifetime.

Soldiers in the military develop a deep sense of comradeship that is necessary for survival in war. We learned through the People's Blockade that when we do that in the peace community, the results are powerful. I find great hope in believing that if we are willing to apply the same kind of discipline and determination to do risky and sustained nonviolent actions for peace as soldiers do to fighting wars, we might see remarkable transformation in our society and world.

I have had to remind myself of this truth again and again through the years. It was especially difficult to remember a decade and a half later, when another dear friend had a confrontation with an arms-carrying train that ended far more tragically than the encounter at Leonardo. I'm grateful that several years of nonviolent resistance helped to prepare me for that day.

CHAPTER 8

Reversing the Blueprint: Saying No to Nukes

We loved our years in Philadelphia, but Jan and I began to realize that the city lacked the natural beauty we were craving. I regularly took Peter and Heidi, then toddlers, on walks on the streets around our home, past all the abandoned cars and broken glass, feeling sad for my children—and for myself. Every summer Jan and I drove our young family two thousand miles to the beautiful Grand Tetons, just to refresh our souls.

We decided we wanted to continue the kind of work and community living we had found in Philadelphia, but we were ready for a change of scenery. We spent the summer of 1973 traveling in the West, visiting kindred souls in Colorado, California, Oregon, and Washington. California especially called to us. We spent several days in La Paz with César Chávez and members of the United Farm Workers union, who were getting up at four o'clock every morning to picket in the fields for fair hours and wages, valiantly facing violent men hired by ranch owners determined to beat them into submission.

When a job opened up with the American Friends Service Committee in San Francisco in their Simple Living Program, Jan and I jumped at the offer and happily moved our family to the West Coast. We shared the position, conducting many weekend workshops, leading participants in confronting out-of-control consumerism and embracing simpler lifestyles.

We discovered that, similar to other twelve-step programs, many Americans could benefit from Consumers Anonymous groups, to support one another in making radical lifestyle changes. Most of us who enter the world as middle-class Americans are essentially handed

a blueprint at birth. Cultural expectations about becoming patriotic, self-sufficient consumers are drilled into us from an early age.
Reversing the blueprint takes intentional effort over a lifetime.

At the end of our workshops, we invited people to consider what
they could give, barter, or share with others. Some amazing things happened during those sessions. People agreed to share lawnmowers, tools,
even cars, in order to cut down on their possessions. Some decided to
get together for a vegetarian potluck meal once a month, to learn new
patterns of eating that were less damaging to the planet. One person
owned a cabin in the Sierra Mountains and offered to make it available,
an invitation that our family and others joyfully accepted.

A dentist at one of our workshops offered to take care of my teeth
for a few years at no cost to me. I shared with him the nonviolent
campaign we were launching to try to stop construction of the Diablo
Canyon nuclear power plant, and he joined our protest and got arrested,
which he told me was a high point of his life. I think I got the better deal,
but he felt that we had shared something very important that benefited
both of us.

In San Francisco, Jan and I were part of a simple living collective
of ten people, who together wrote a book called *Taking Charge*. The
chapters covered such topics as food, energy, work, and community. It
included an "Energy Addict's Calorie Counter"—what today we would
call a measure of our ecological "footprint."

We mimeographed the first version. Then it was printed on the
press of San Francisco's weekly newspaper, the *Bay Guardian*. Bantam
Paperbacks eventually picked it up, and later Harper & Row published
a reworked and expanded version titled *Taking Charge of Our Lives:
Living Responsibly in Today's World*.

Our protest movement at Diablo Canyon, which began in 1976, was
a direct outgrowth of the Simple Living Program and the commitments
outlined in the book. According to the energy "experts," if we wanted
to grow in energy consumption at the prevailing exponential rate, we
needed more than windmills and the sun. We had to have nuclear power,
touted by those in the industry as producing an endless supply of energy
"too cheap to meter."

Our campaign at Diablo Canyon was questioning that mentality.
We were confronting our nation's superconsumption and raising questions about safety and the choice to mortgage the future of coming generations—which would be forced to deal with nuclear waste that would
be radioactive and dangerous for thousands of years.

We were opposed to nuclear power in general, but Diablo Canyon had a particular set of compelling issues. Pacific Gas & Electric (PG&E) was building the plant's two nuclear reactors on California's pristine coastline, near San Luis Obispo, over a Chumash Indian burial site. The local Native American tribes were the first to put up a fight against the plant, asserting that the spirits of their ancestors were being violated.

The plant's site is located along the well-known San Andreas Fault, which increases its susceptibility to earthquakes and the potentiality of the surrounding population's exposure to massive and lethal radiation. In 1972, a Los Angeles reporter discovered a report by Shell Oil Company geologists about the existence of a second fault, the Hosgri Fault, just two and a half miles offshore of the site.

During the Nuclear Regulatory Commission's licensing process for the plant, which was constructed despite our protests, PG&E bought up Shell's geological survey, perhaps in hopes of keeping the public from knowing about the Hosgri Fault. The fault had already produced an earthquake of 7.1 magnitude early in the twentieth century—more than Diablo Canyon was designed to withstand. As a result of the discovery of Hosgri and our ongoing efforts to bring this information to light, nuclear regulators made PG&E redesign and reinforce the plant.

In addition to its other problems, Diablo Canyon uses seawater to cool its reactors. On several occasions, masses of jellyfish, marine animals, and kelp have obstructed operations, compromising safety and efficiency, and forcing a shutdown.

In late 1976, members of Mothers for Peace had come to AFSC and asked if we could help them build a nonviolent movement to stop construction of the Diablo Canyon plant. They had heard of farmers in Germany who had successfully stopped the construction of a nuclear power plant in Wyhl by nonviolently blocking it for nine months, and they hoped that we could offer similar sustained resistance.

We launched the Abalone Alliance in 1977, in honor of the tens of thousands of wild California red abalone that were killed in 1974 in Diablo Cove when the reactor's plumbing had its first hot flush. We were aware of the Clamshell Alliance in New England, which was protesting the Seabrook Nuclear Power Plant on the coast of New Hampshire. We modeled our affinity group–based organizational structure on theirs. Everyone who participated in the Abalone Alliance participated in an eight-hour nonviolent training and we made our decisions in spokes councils made up of one representative of each affinity group or support group of eight to ten people.

As one of the organizers of the Abalone Alliance, I climb over the fence protesting the Diablo Canyon Nuclear Power Plant (1977). [Photo: Jon Katz]

On August 6, 1977, the anniversary of the U.S. atomic bombing of Hiroshima, forty-seven of us crossed over the fence at Diablo Canyon using homemade ladders and began walking toward the plant. We were arrested, taken to the county jail, and told that if we didn't pay a $100 fine, we would spend six months in jail. But the judge threw our case out of court when it was revealed that two police informers had infiltrated our group.

The next year we increased our resistance tenfold. On Hiroshima Day in 1978, 487 people entered the plant site. Some tried to blockade the front entrance, others tried to convert the plant into a "Museum of Inappropriate Technology," and still others set up information tables about alternative energy. One group tried to erect a windmill. We spent a few nights in what we dubbed "The Diablo Hilton," which was an old gymnasium that had been converted into a county prison.

At our court hearing, I began my statement with these words: "I participated in the nonviolent occupation at Diablo Canyon because I love my children, Peter and Heidi. I am concerned that they and their children and future generations should have a chance to live without the dangers from this and other nuclear power plants. I do not want my children to die from cancer or my grandchildren to be deformed because of the carelessness, ego-centeredness, or profit of my generation."

I presented the judge with a book written by survivors of the Hiroshima and Nagasaki atomic bombings, expressing my concern about the connection between nuclear power plants and nuclear weapons proliferation. I ended my statement with these words: "Future generations have no other spokespeople. . . . We will do our best to represent them."

Visiting Superior Court Judge Robert D. Carter sentenced thirty-three of us—the repeat offenders—to ninety days in jail and a $300 fine. The next morning, in a startling reversal, he delivered a dramatic apology to a crowded courtroom in the San Luis Obispo Veterans Memorial Building: "This is the first time I have handled a municipal court case, and I must say I handled it badly." He reduced our sentences to fifteen days in jail. None of us ever paid our fines. The members of the Abalone Alliance breathed a sigh of relief at the judge's change of heart, and we continued our campaign.

The Abalone Alliance was the target of one of the first known SLAPPs (Strategic Lawsuit Against Public Participation) in U.S. history. The plaintiffs were San Luis Obispo County and the Pacific Legal Foundation, the oldest conservative public-interest law firm in the country, whose motto is "Rescuing liberty from coast to coast." The goal of a SLAPP—intended to intimidate and silence critics by burdening them with the high cost of a legal defense—is generally not for the plaintiffs to win but to wear down defendants. The lawsuit against the Abalone Alliance lasted five years and was withdrawn just before going before the U.S. Supreme Court.

The Natural Resources Defense Council responded with a countersuit around harassment of antinuclear activists. That's when I petitioned to get my FBI file under the Freedom of Information Act. About two-thirds of it was blacked out and couldn't be read. But there was that first sentence: "David Hartsough, son of Ray Hartsough, organized a vigil at the Nike missile site." That moment seemed like ancient history by then. I was amazed to learn how closely the federal authorities had watched all my activities since 1955.

Many celebrities joined our movement to shut down the country's most controversial nuclear power plant. Actors Harrison Ford, Jane Fonda, Robin Williams, Lily Tomlin, Martin Sheen, John Belushi, and others lent their weight to the Diablo Canyon effort. Performers including Jackson Browne, Joan Baez, Stevie Wonder, Bonnie Raitt, Bruce

Springsteen, and James Taylor held antinuclear benefit concerts on our behalf, including a "Peace Sunday" in the Rose Bowl with more than a hundred thousand people in attendance. A number of these high-profile individuals got arrested at Diablo Canyon, raising the level of public awareness of our efforts.

We staged blockades and occupations at Diablo Canyon from 1977 until 1984, and also organized protests at PG&E offices across California. Support for our cause was building throughout the nation. On April 7, 1979, twenty-five thousand people marched in San Francisco to demand that construction on the plant be halted. On June 28 of that year, forty thousand people attended a protest rally at Diablo Canyon.

On September 10, 1981, thirty thousand people marched along the Coastal Highway toward the plant. More than 1,960 of us were arrested—the largest number arrested at an antinuclear protest in the United States These included all the members of the San Luis Obispo City Council.

Our spirits were high, and musician Wavy Gravy and I organized and acted as emcees for a variety show each evening that we called "The Tornado of Talent." Among other arrestees/performers, it featured Jackson Browne, who had been arrested with us. We convinced our guards to allow in an acoustic guitar, on the condition that Jackson would leave it there when we left.

We knew that Diablo Canyon was bad, but it turned out that things were a lot worse than even we had suspected. A third seismic fault, the Shoreline Fault, was discovered running directly under the plant. Even more stunning was the revelation that came to us in a note snuck into the jail after our large September 10 protest. A twenty-five-year-old engineer had blown the whistle on a serious construction error at the plant: the blueprints had been reversed during construction!

Pacific Gas & Electric eventually disclosed to the public this potentially cataclysmic error. The blueprints for the installation of mandatory seismic safety supports, designed to protect the cooling systems of Diablo Canyon's two reactors from earthquakes, were on a single transparency. One side was for the first reactor, and the reverse side was for the second. But someone forgot to provide instructions to flip it over. Because construction workers failed to reverse the blueprint, some areas in the second reactor were overly reinforced, while others were left without any reinforcement at all.

It was a costly mistake, requiring a $2.2 billion repair. The original price tag for the plant had been estimated at $300 million. When it finally opened in 1985, construction costs were $5.8 billion, with an additional $7 billion in financing costs. Hardly "too cheap to meter."

Unfortunately, the Abalone Alliance was not successful in preventing the Diablo Canyon nuclear plant from going into operation, but we were successful in shutting down the Humboldt and Rancho Seco plants and later the San Onofre plant. And due to our efforts and others in the antinuclear movement across the country, no new licenses to build nuclear power plants in the United States were issued for over thirty years.

During those years, I also became involved with nonviolent efforts to stop further development of nuclear weapons. I participated in non-violent actions organized by the Nevada Desert Experience, a resistance campaign born from the Franciscan and Catholic Worker traditions and the American Peace Test. During Lent, on Hiroshima Day, and at other meaningful times throughout the year, gatherings were held at the Nevada Test Site in the desert north of Las Vegas, protesting decades of nuclear weapons tests there.

During one of these protests, I brought along a carload of people from San Francisco. Among them was a young Palestinian-American woman, who had been part of the musical *The Children of War*. This production, which toured the United Sates and the Soviet Union, was written and performed by young people from countries whose governments had labeled them enemies: Russians and Americans, Palestinians and Israelis, among others.

It was a very moving and powerful play. Their message was, "We are young people, and we want to live." They even met with the presidents of their respective countries to convey their convictions about peace among the nations and their deep concern to stop the madness of the nuclear arms race, so that they and all humanity could have a future.

This young woman decided to cross the line at the test site and was arrested. Those of us who were adults were processed and released. But because she was seventeen, she was taken to Juvenile Hall. The authorities there told me that she could be released only to one of her parents, who were almost six hundred miles away back in San Francisco.

Our carload stayed in a simple motel in the little desert town of Beatty, Nevada, trying to secure her release. One of the local authorities called on the phone and told me, "There's a warrant out for your arrest, for bringing a minor across state lines with the intent to commit a crime." That was a stunning statement coming from an official in a state where prostitution is legal, and testing nuclear bombs is legal, and stealing land from Native Americans is legal—but bringing someone across the state border who believes nuclear weapons are immoral and illegal under international law and wants to follow her conscience is illegal.

I didn't relish facing a felony charge, and I was very torn about what to do. The next morning we woke up, looked out the motel window, and saw a small army of police cars lined up along the street. So the dilemma was: Do I go out the front door with the rest of the group and face the police officers who are going to take me to jail—and if so, what will happen to all these people I brought, including the young woman? Or should I slip out the back door, cross the field, and meet up later with the group? I chose to duck out the back door, an act I had never done before, and never have since.

When we met up again, we faced the question of whether to cross over into Death Valley in California, where we would avoid the Nevada police, or drive the more convenient route through Nevada to Reno. Hoping we could still retrieve our brave young Palestinian friend, we decided to head north toward Reno, calling back regularly to Beatty to get updates and try to secure her release.

Later, we discovered that our stealthy plan had been unnecessary. We found out that some of the police officers lived close to the motel, and their cars had simply been parked out on the street. They had nothing to do with me. The young woman's father eventually had to fly to Beatty to get her released.

One year, early in the 1980s, my brother Paul came and was arrested with me at the test site, along with hundreds of others. At our arraignment in the court in Beatty, we were each sentenced to fifteen days in jail. So many people had been arrested that the local jails were beyond capacity. So the authorities put us on buses and stopped at every little town going north, dropping some of us off at each local jail and then heading on to the next jail to unload more.

Paul, our friend Russ Jorgensen, and I were still on the bus at daybreak, and we saw a beautiful sunrise over Walker Lake. Finally, the last of us ended up in Fallon, Nevada, almost three hundred miles from the nuclear test site. The jail was so small that it had no kitchen, and the warden brought in TV dinners for us three times a day.

We got to know him quite well, and he eventually told us he had served in Vietnam, most of the time on an aircraft carrier loading bombs onto planes. I asked him, "Did you ever think about what happened to those bombs you loaded?" He answered, "Nope, never thought about it."

Paul considered my question insensitive. But a couple of days later, when we were sitting on our bunks having a Quaker meeting for worship, the warden came in. He didn't know what we were doing, and he spoke up: "Actually, I wanted you to know that . . . yes, I did think about it." I thought that was a brave thing to admit to us.

At Bangor Submarine Base near Tacoma, Washington, a civil disobedience campaign grew up in resistance to the Trident Submarine. My dear friends Jim and Shelley Douglass were among the faithful who protested with persistence for many years. Loaded with 408 independently targeted warheads, each Trident missile is capable of destroying that many cities, with devastation far beyond what was rained down on Hiroshima and Nagasaki. Hundreds of us were arrested as we crossed a fence onto the base. We were immediately released—it seemed there were many more of us than the county jail could hold.

Another small campaign that I helped to organize was on behalf of D-Q University, a tribal community college committed to the celebration and preservation of Native American culture and religion. The college was founded near Davis, California, on the site of a decommissioned U.S. Army communications facility. Citing a federal law that requires surplus federal land to be returned to Native Americans, organizers and future students jumped the fence and claimed the unused property for their school. After lengthy negotiations, the federal government granted D-Q University title to the land in 1971.

That same year, federal officials forcibly ended the nineteen-month occupation of Alcatraz Island by Native Americans, who had appealed to the same federal law and claimed title to the island off San Francisco after the infamous federal penitentiary there closed. Two years later, in 1973, members of the American Indian Movement and federal law enforcement officials were embroiled in an armed standoff at Wounded Knee—site of an 1890 massacre on South Dakota's Pine Ridge Indian Reservation—over tribal leadership and the U.S. government's failure to fulfill its treaties with Native Americans. In the wake of this rising Indian activism, the U.S. government threatened to close down D-Q University.

I had gotten to know several Native American activists, including Russell Means and John Trudell, through various campaigns in California and throughout the Southwest. When federal officials threatened to take over D-Q by force if the university didn't shut its doors, I had a meeting with several of the school's leaders, whom I had met on previous visits to the campus.

We mobilized some of the Abalone Alliance activists and others to go up and encircle the campus. The message was, "Over our bodies will you attack this university." Native Americans had had so much stolen from them that it seemed that the least we could do was nonviolently try to help them keep their university. At the very last minute, the FBI and federal marshals backed down, averting a confrontation and allowing the university to stay open.

In 1981, several of us involved in the Abalone Alliance turned our attention to the nearby University of California's Lawrence Livermore National Laboratory, the country's largest research and development center for nuclear and space-launched weaponry. Within its walls, nuclear weapons are brought through the stages of conception, design, and computer simulation. The neutron bomb, which has the capacity to kill massive numbers of people with high doses of radiation while leaving buildings intact, was born at Livermore. So were the warheads for Poseidon, Polaris, and Minuteman III missiles.

My parents had moved to a retirement center in Santa Rosa, California, by then. Among the highlights for me of our sustained witness at Livermore was my mother's arrest with me on a Good Friday. Both of my parents in their own ways had spent their lives caring for others and working for justice and peace, but neither of them had ever been arrested. My mother and I were kneeling with about a hundred others in front of the main gate to the weapons lab, praying for the end of nuclear weapons work at Livermore, when we were surrounded by police and handcuffed.

The police separated the men from the women for processing, and after they fingerprinted Mom, they released her on a street corner. She couldn't find me, so she got a ride with someone from the demonstration into the town of Livermore. There she was, with no ID and no money—and no buses running to Santa Rosa. She ended up finding someone to lend her money for a bus ticket to San Francisco, and someone else on the bus walked her to my home.

I was very worried about her. I had called the security office at Livermore Lab, as well as the local police. After a few hours, when I didn't know what else I could do, I went on home. I was extremely relieved when, after a few more hours, my mom rang the doorbell and we were reunited.

On Easter morning, I got a call from the chief of security at Livermore Lab. He was concerned and wanted to know if I had found my mother. It was quite an act of kindness from an officer who regularly arrested us. I often accompanied older people at our demonstrations,

People kneeling in prayer protesting the development of nuclear weapons at Livermore nuclear weapons laboratory before their arrest (1982).

and from that time on, the police never let me get separated from whomever I was accompanying.

Among the thousand protesters arrested at Livermore Lab in June of 1983 was Daniel Ellsberg. A former military analyst with the RAND Corporation, Dan was most renowned for releasing the top-secret Pentagon Papers, outlining military decision-making during the Vietnam War. He knew the inside story of nuclear weapons development and had firsthand knowledge that every U.S. president since Harry Truman had made serious threats to use them.

While Dan and I were in jail together for a couple of weeks with the five hundred other men who had been arrested (an equal number of women were being held in a separate facility), we convened teach-ins and workshops every day, all day long. Other protesters with us held strategy sessions and yoga classes. It was a rich time. We shared our life stories as a way of deepening our sense of community and appreciation of one another.

Among the efforts of our Livermore Action Group was the Livermore Conversion Project, which I coordinated for a year. The goal was not only to shut down Livermore as it was but to put the lab to work on projects that enhance life. We set up opportunities for dialogue between protesters and the scientists developing the bombs inside the lab. Unfortunately, our efforts didn't help two of the local clergy who were in jail with us. Both had congregation members who worked at the lab, and both lost their positions at their churches after their release as a result of their arrests.

A few years later, resurrecting our Peace Navy from the Vietnam War era—and still a strong believer in having fun and being out in nature while being politically relevant—I invited Daniel Ellsberg to join me in a sailboat in the Suisan Bay. Located on the bay is Port Chicago, the shipping point of the Concord Naval Weapons Station—yet another vital center of the war-making effort in our neighborhood.

During the Vietnam War, 80 percent of the bombs dropped on Vietnam began their journey at the massive thirteen-thousand-acre weapons station, the largest nuclear-weapons storage area in the West and the largest munitions depot in the country. During the People's Blockade in the early 1970s, a friend and I had paddled our kayaks to Port Chicago, in pursuit of ships being loaded with bombs headed for Vietnam. We got close enough to see the ships, but the seas were too rough to try to block them.

A decade later, a friend in the U.S. Navy called to say that a ship was leaving Port Chicago for El Salvador, "with enough ammunition to kill twenty thousand people." Friends and I decided to launch another peace flotilla of canoes, kayaks, and small sailboats. We had to cover two miles of rough sea to reach the ship.

Dan had never been in a sailboat before, and mine was small—only nine feet long—more like a rowboat with a sail. As we were being pitched about in the strong, ten-foot-high waves, I realized that it had perhaps been a bad idea to invite him. One picture of us in a trough of water showed only the top of my boat's mast.

Fortunately, we were wearing life preservers. We were closing in on the ship when a wave overturned us. A boat carrying reporters was close by, and the pilot gunned the engine to back up and get the perfect picture of Daniel Ellsberg bobbing in the water.

Gunning the engine created a wake that pulled Dan underwater. I fished him out of the bay while the media got their photos. The next day's headline was "Media Boat Saves Daniel Ellsberg's life." From my perspective, it was the media boat that had almost drowned my dear friend!

My little boat was picked up by the Coast Guard. However, this time they gave it right back—apparently this one wasn't worth anything to them. The Peace Navy went on to do many actions, including trying to block the aircraft carrier the USS *Enterprise*. I eventually bought a seventeen-foot sailboat and christened it the *Oscar Romero*, in honor of El Salvador's intrepid archbishop.

A decade before, the Vietnam War had finally ground to a halt. But other wars had begun. El Salvador, and the other nations of Central America, were engulfed in violence. Their conflicts were being fanned into blazing flames by U.S. funds and weapons.

I decided that I needed to go and see for myself the impact of U.S. policy on our embattled neighbors to the south.

CHAPTER 9

Accompaniment: Into the Central American War Zones

At a Lutheran orphanage called Fe y Esperanza—"Faith and Hope"—at the foot of the Guazapa volcano outside El Salvador's capital city of San Salvador, small children flocked around me, smiling and wrapping their arms around my legs and waist. A chorus of "Papa, papa" rose from their lips. They had not seen a man in a very long time.

Eighty children lived in the orphanage. They subsisted on rice, beans, and tortillas cooked in a kitchen that consisted of a pile of wood burning under stones and a piece of metal for frying the tortillas. The children made their own clothes, on a loom that they had constructed, and built their own rudimentary school.

One after another, these precious young ones related how El Salvador's civil war had claimed their mothers and fathers, brothers and sisters, aunts and uncles, and how a U.S.-supplied bomb had been dropped on the orphanage a year before. As tears streamed down their cheeks, they pooled in my eyes as well. I realized that these children belong to all of us; they are *our* children. Their pain and loss are our pain and loss.

I spent six weeks in Central America in February and March of 1985, as part of a U.S. peace delegation sponsored by the Fellowship of Reconciliation and Witness for Peace. In San Salvador we were the guests of Emmanuel Baptist Church. Its members had invited U.S. Christians to come to El Salvador to offer a protective, nonviolent presence as they carried out their Christian service.

Two heavy-duty wars were raging in Central America. One was the economic war being waged against the majority of the people through exploitation. The second was the war of violence used against them to enforce the injustice. U.S. financial and military support was escalating the suffering and devastation to unfathomable levels.

I spent my first night in El Salvador in a home near the military airport of San Salvador. All night long, I heard helicopters taking off on their bombing missions. It was impossible to sleep, partly because of the noise, and partly because of knowing deep within me what those bombing missions would mean that night for the people who lived beneath them. The bombs were made in the United States. Paid for with U.S. tax money, they were being dropped in my name—and in the name of "democracy."

On this trip, and another in 1988, I observed firsthand the realities on the ground in El Salvador, as well as Guatemala, Nicaragua, and Costa Rica. El Salvador was a nation of negative superlatives, both the smallest and most densely populated in Central America. The concentration of El Salvador's land and wealth in the hands of a small elite—known as the "fourteen families"—had created massive poverty throughout the tiny country.

Malnutrition, inadequate housing, and lack of health care and education were the norm for the vast majority of El Salvador's people. According to the head of the nongovernmental Human Rights Commission, children under six in El Salvador had the lowest caloric intake in Latin America; 70 percent were malnourished.

A union leader told us that 52 percent of Salvadoran workers were unemployed, and another 30 percent were subemployed. The typical wage from U.S.-based corporations was inadequate to feed a family. Texas Instruments, for example, paid the equivalent of two dollars per day to its laborers in El Salvador; the company's workers in the United States made twenty to forty times that much. People working in the fields picking coffee or bananas for United Fruit made even less than factory workers, about a dollar a day. Salvadoran workers who tried to organize labor unions to demand better wages and working conditions became prime targets of persecution, fueled by economic interests in their own country and the United States.

Educators were targeted as well. A representative of the Association of Salvadoran Teachers told us that more than 360 teachers had been recently seized out of their homes or schools and murdered. Just the week before we arrived, soldiers had entered the campus of the University of San Salvador and began shooting people, killing several students.

The Human Rights Commission leader said, "To ask for better conditions of life is not a crime, [but] anyone who criticizes the government or works for peace and justice—their lives are endangered. The government and the army kidnap, torture, 'disappear,' imprison, and assassinate people they consider subversive—whether they are in the church, the schools, the unions, the universities, or are peasants in the countryside."

Both previous leaders of the Human Rights Commission had been assassinated, one while dropping his children off at nursery school. The man who met with us slept in a different home every night, trying to stay ahead of his persecutors and continue the work a bit longer. But for him, as for many people we met, he felt that the question was when, not if, he would be killed.

The government of El Salvador, supported by the United States and aided by right-wing death squads, was carrying out brutal and unprecedented repression. A union leader told us, "The government in El Salvador assassinates anyone who struggles for bread, land, and liberty."

Among the many victims it had claimed were an archbishop, a dozen priests, and thousands of catechists, union organizers, students, teachers, and peasants. Between 1980 and 1988, seventy-four thousand people were murdered in El Salvador, and eight thousand were "disappeared."

On the third day of my first trip to El Salvador, our group traveled to the eastern end of the country, where I counted more than a hundred fires burning up mountains and across the countryside, all of which had been started by firebombs. A representative of Tutela Legal, the human rights office of the Catholic Archdiocese, told us, "The Salvadoran military makes bombing operations and undertakes military offensives, destroying people's crops and burning their houses, as if everyone were combatants."

The military was attempting to kill or scare away the people living in those areas, defoliating trees and bushes so that they had no place to hide. One-sixth of the country's inhabitants—a million people out of a population of six million—had been displaced, fleeing their homes to escape the persecution. Many of these refugees barely survived on a minimal supply of corn and beans.

Residents from one village had fled to a refugee camp called Calle Real, where two of my friends from San Francisco, Ines Betancourt Ascencio and Francisco Herrera, were working. The refugees told us the story of the military's attack on their village the previous January. Soldiers surrounded them and began shooting. For several hours the people huddled on the ground, praying the Catholic rosary over and over as bullets flew over their heads.

The soldiers carried a list of people they had labeled "subversives" and tried to remove them from Calle Real. But Ines, Francisco, and others surrounded those who were targeted, so that the military could not take them. When I mentioned that I was a friend of Ines and Francisco, many individuals professed their profound love and deep appreciation for them and all that they had done to save people's lives.

While we spoke with the refugees, a U.S. bomber plane flew over the camp. It came so close that we could see the bombs, visible on the bottom of the plane. One of the refugees said, "That kind of plane can't even land unless it drops its bombs."

Our delegation met with several human rights organizations throughout El Salvador. At one of our gatherings, a man from a small, indigenous village where people were being killed weekly, pleaded with me, "Could you come to our village and just walk down the main street? This will save lives, because the death squads will know the world is watching."

Our group made the arduous fifty-mile journey to his remote village and walked down its dusty main street. We heard later that the attacks of the death squads did indeed stop. Apparently, as the man had foreseen, knowing that internationals were watching was enough for them to back off of killing civilians in that village. Learning that merely our presence made a difference—that international accompaniment made it safer for people on the ground to live and work and care for their families—was a lesson I wouldn't forget.

Some church groups in El Salvador had started programs to channel food and medical supplies to refugees in various parts of the country, in addition to founding orphanages for the many children who had lost their parents in the war. For this service, many were targeted with death threats. The woman in charge of the Lutheran orphanage had received a summons to go to the police headquarters for questioning just before we arrived.

One of the three Lutheran ministers in El Salvador had been killed shortly before our visit. A second one—along with a doctor who treated the sick in a Lutheran refugee camp—had been kidnapped and tortured. Only after great international pressure was applied were they released. The minister of Emmanuel Baptist Church had been kidnapped the previous fall, choosing after his release to live in exile outside the country.

In El Salvador, to feed the hungry and house the homeless were "subversive" activities. Many of the Christians I met felt that, to follow Jesus and his teachings of love for brothers and sisters in need, they had to be willing to follow his example and risk being crucified. To live out their faith in the midst of war and poverty meant to risk being killed themselves.

Monsignor Ricardo Urioste of the Catholic Archdiocese in San Salvador had been a colleague and close friend of Archbishop Oscar Romero, who was gunned down on March 24, 1980, while saying Mass in a hospice chapel. According to Urioste, when Romero found the poor, he found the church. The monsignor said that the archbishop, who did not hesitate to speak truth to power, "was the most loved and most hated man in this country—loved by the poor and hated by the powerful." He added, "Just like Jesus."

Urioste continued, "If you go and spend time with, and work with, the poor, you will be called a subversive." He suggested that we needed to look at El Salvador with human and Christian eyes, to see the institutionalized violence behind a system in which the rich got richer and the poor poorer. He quoted beloved pastor Dom Helder Camara of Brazil, who said, "When I give food to the poor, they call me a saint. When I ask why the poor have no food, they call me a communist."

A member of the National Association of Indigenous People of El Salvador told us, "They call us communists, but we do not know what communism is. We do know that we are not paid enough for our work to feed our families, and we have no land, no education, and no health clinics." Another person added, "We have not seen one Russian, Cuban, or Nicaraguan here in El Salvador"—reported by the government to be fomenting communism in the country. "The problem," he declared, "is social injustice."

"We don't like going out on strike," a union leader told us. "We don't like marching in the streets—it is dangerous. We don't like tear gas, assassination, and torture. . . . [But] the people have decided to organize themselves and demand their rights. We will continue this struggle until we achieve our rights."

The situation in Guatemala was tragically similar to El Salvador's. A coup d'état in 1954 had been covertly engineered in the United States by the CIA. It targeted Guatemala's democratically elected president, Jacobo Árbenz Guzmán, whose policy of redistributing land back to

Guatemalan refugees on the Chiapas border in Mexico, having fled their homes and the genocidal violence in Guatemala (1982). [Photo: David Hartsough]

Guatemalan peasants was viewed as a threat to U.S. corporate interests. The CIA denounced the land reform as a communist plot.

A generation later, the cycle of repression was repeating itself. In the decade before I visited, more than 160,000 people had been murdered. An additional estimated 40,000 had been "disappeared" when armed soldiers or death squads seized them out of their homes, off the streets, or from places of work, never to be seen again. Four hundred indigenous villages had been wiped off the map. The bodies were piling up in ravines, dumped on roadsides, and buried in mass graves, and the Guatemalan people were traumatized by fear and terror.

I had first seen evidence of the horror in December 1982, when I visited Chiapas, on Mexico's border with Guatemala. Thousands of refugees, carrying their children and whatever else they could on their backs, were streaming into Chiapas from Guatemala after their homes had been destroyed and their villages burned down. One group had received a visit from survivors of a massacre in a neighboring village, who carried the news, "You are next."

The villagers fled at night, knowing that if they were detected, they would be killed. They lived in huts hastily constructed in the dense, rainy jungle out of palm leaves and bark from banana trees. Small fires sputtered, started by the refugees in a near-futile effort to keep warm and cook a little food. No refugee agencies came to their aid.

In Guatemala in 1985, our delegation met with members of the Grupo de Apoyo Mutuo (Group for Mutual Support of the Families of the Disappeared). The group, also known by its acronym GAM, had been founded in June 1984 by Montenegro de García, a fifth-grade teacher and mother of a one-year-old. After her husband was "disappeared"—and her visits to hospitals and morgues and government offices revealed no trace of him—García met other women suffering the same loss and organized a memorial mass for their loved ones. She formed the GAM to help families give one another support in their time of sorrow and distress, and to press the government for the return of their loved ones alive.

Families of more than five hundred of the disappeared had joined. One family I met had suffered the disappearance of nineteen of its members—daughters, sons, grandparents, brothers, sisters, aunts, uncles, cousins. Only a nineteen-year-old sister, a four-year-old brother, and an eighty-year-old grandmother were still alive. Their grief, and that of the thousands of other families of the disappeared, was overwhelming.

Members of the Grupo had petitioned government officials, taken out ads in newspapers, held weekly nonviolent demonstrations for months, and even talked with Guatemala's president, pleading for the return of their loved ones. In mid-March of 1985, while we were there, President Oscar Humberto Mejía Victores went on national television and denounced the Grupo as "terrorists" and "communists" who were being used by "international subversives." In Guatemala, that was an invitation to the military and the death squads to begin their work.

At the Grupo's weekly Friday march, I joined with more than a thousand members—mostly women—as they walked peacefully along one of Guatemala City's main boulevards, carrying photographs of their loved ones and asking "Where are they?" They were dressed in their colorful indigenous clothing, and most were barefoot. Many were in tears, feeling the pain of the loss of their husbands, brothers, and sisters. Never have I felt so vulnerable, fearful that the death squads would open fire at any moment.

I was part of a small team from Peace Brigades International (PBI), offering witness and accompaniment to the Guatemalans. The only "weapons" we had were our cameras, our notebooks, and some coins that we could use to make a phone call if something horrible happened to these brave people.

The next day at the meeting of GAM, the members discussed what to do in the face of the death threats. In spite of the grave personal risks, one after another declared their unswerving commitment to continue to seek release for their family members. I was moved to tears by the love, faith, beauty, courage, and determination of these people.

I shared with them some of the experiences of the Mothers of the Disappeared in El Salvador, whom I had visited the week before. I related some of the history of nonviolent struggles in the United States and other countries in the face of violence and repression. We talked together about strategies and group process.

The GAM members appealed for any support we in the United States could give to their movement. With the help of the PBI team, I was also trying to drum up support for them in Guatemala—especially among church people. But most people felt that to give any support after the president's remarks would be to risk death themselves.

Within two and a half weeks of my leaving Guatemala, two of the six leaders of the Grupo had been murdered. Hector Gomez had been brutally tortured and burned on his stomach and other parts of his body with a blowtorch. María Rosario Godoy de Cuevas was found dead with bite marks on her breasts, her two-year-old son dead beside her with his fingernails pulled out. A third leader fled the country after heavily armed men, spewing threats, showed up at his workplace.

One of the remaining leaders of the GAM appealed to the PBI members, "We don't want to die, but we cannot remain silent. Can you accompany us twenty-four hours a day?" The PBI members gulped and responded, "We will try."

That was the beginning of the PBI team's continual presence with the leaders of GAM. They were with them when they went to church, or took their children to nursery care, or met for demonstrations. For five years, they accompanied the Grupo leaders day and night, and, thankfully, with PBI accompaniment, none of the other GAM leaders was killed. GAM founder Montenegro de Garcia credited PBI with her survival in a 1994 interview: "Thanks to their presence, I am alive. That is an indisputable truth. If it had not been for them, I would not be here telling you this today."

During that same time period, U.S. President Ronald Reagan asked Congress for an additional $35 million in military assistance for Guatemala. While the Grupo members struggled to survive and carry on their work, the death squads were well financed and assured of survival by the United States.

The courage of the women of the Grupo began to break the dictator-ship's reign of terror, empowering others in the religious community, human rights organizations, and the labor movement. Many others all across Guatemala began organizing and speaking out against the outrages.

Young indigenous men, who were being dragged from their villages and forced to fight for the Guatemalan army, began to resist. My friend Amílcar Méndez, and Rigoberta Menchú, who was awarded the Nobel Peace Prize in 1992, began advocating for indigenous rights and educating the Indian peasant population in resistance to massive military oppression. Both Mendez and Menchú received many death threats for their work, but they carried on courageously, along with many other Guatemalans.

Neighboring Nicaragua was living a different reality, but its people were suffering similar pain. U.S. Marines had occupied Nicaragua from 1912 to 1933. When they left, the U.S. government installed as president the first member of the brutal Somoza dynasty, which would keep a stranglehold on the country, with U.S. support, for more than four decades.

In July 1979, a popular, broad-based revolution in Nicaragua overthrew the repressive Somoza regime. The Sandinistas, who assumed power, launched social reform through a national literacy campaign, construction of health clinics, and the organization of agricultural cooperatives. They created space for political pluralism. They brought great hope to those who had suffered so grievously for so long.

With its economic interests threatened, the Reagan administration determined to undo the Sandinista revolution. It was no secret that one of President Reagan's top foreign policy objectives was to destroy the Sandinista government—using U.S. political, economic, and military power to attack a country with three million citizens—equal to the population of the city of Philadelphia.

The CIA began covertly training and funding former members of Somoza's barbaric National Guard. Dropping military supplies from planes onto mountaintops in Honduras and Costa Rica, our government turned this defeated and scattered band into a fighting force known as the Contras. Their grisly attacks on Nicaraguans included rape, decapitations, kidnappings, and massacres.

I was inspired by the Sandinistas' vision of a just society organized for the benefit of the poor. What a rare blessing it was to be among people experiencing a sense of dignity and hope they had never before known. I wept to see the Nicaraguan people being attacked daily by my own country.

Walking for an hour in mud sometimes up to our knees, our delegation visited a small agricultural cooperative called El Juste, where the most sophisticated equipment with which to work the land was a hoe. Eight families lived there in shacks. They had been attacked repeatedly by the Contras. Ten of their family members had been murdered.

One woman had been killed by a bullet to her abdomen, which had also shattered the leg of the baby she held in her arms, which had to be amputated. Another woman's husband had been killed, and when she remarried, her second husband was also murdered by the Contras. After our group had walked back through the mud to our bus, she came riding up to us on her pony, with a beautiful smile and a pan of very small ears of corn she had cooked to share with us. Her name was Socorro—"Aid."

We visited a hospital and met a woman who had stepped on a land mine, the blood oozing through the bandages that wrapped what was left of her legs. We visited another community called Jacinto Baca, where the Contras had murdered fifty people in this agricultural cooperative of eighty families, leaving many orphans. The community had two hundred children and no school, since the teacher was among those who had been killed. The Contras had also burned the cooperative's one tractor and only community truck.

I stayed in the home of a family in which the father had been killed in a Contra ambush, leaving behind his wife and five children. They gave me a hammock for sleeping. I found a couple of trees on which to tie it, not realizing it was over a camouflaged trench in the ground. The woman of the house said, "You can hang that there, but we'll have to go under you to hide if the Contras come."

The eldest child, Navidad—which means "Christmas" in Spanish—was fifteen years old. He worked in the agricultural cooperative seven hours a day and then tended the family's plot of beans, corn, squash, and bananas to support and feed his loved ones. He made toy trucks for his younger siblings out of discarded scraps of wood and metal. When I looked into his beautiful brown eyes, tears welled up in my own. He carried so much weight on his young shoulders.

On my return trip three years later, once again as part of a U.S. peace delegation sponsored by Witness for Peace and the Fellowship of Reconciliation, I was traveling with my daughter, Heidi, and my niece, Andrea. We rode in a van to a remote village nestled in the hills east of Nicaragua's capital city of Managua, where we planned to stay with a family. On our way, the van's radiator burst, which our Nicaraguan comrades informed us was a frequent occurrence.

That moment was very frightening for us all. Contra death squads were constantly on the prowl in that area, and before leaving on our journey, we had been warned that it was important in Nicaragua to always arrive where you were going well before nightfall. Questions scurried through my mind: Will we be stuck here all night? Will we be attacked? Will we be shot at or taken prisoner? Will this be our last night alive? I was particularly concerned about Heidi and Andrea.

We were completely in the hands of our Nicaraguan driver. Fortunately, someone on our delegation had brought along some chewing gum. The driver used it to plug the hole in the radiator, then filled it with water from a nearby stream, and we continued on our way. I breathed a sigh of relief when we made it safely to the family's home before dark.

I still remember the toy the children there had. Their nicest plaything consisted of a piece of string tied to a coffee can, with wheels made out of bottle caps. That simple toy drove home to me what life was like for this family, impoverished and constantly vulnerable to violence. I was astounded that the simple lives of these beautiful people were perceived as a threat by my government.

In Managua, I talked with the U.S. editor of a business newsletter that was read throughout Central America. He told me that the United States had "blown it" in Nicaragua. After the triumph of the Sandinista revolution, we had the opportunity to help nurture a new kind of society—pluralistic, nonaligned, democratic, and committed to meeting the needs of its people. But the Reagan administration chose to name Nicaragua its enemy, making every effort to dominate and undermine the newly hopeful nation militarily, politically, and economically. Once again, we were on the wrong side of the world revolution for justice.

Nicaragua's southern neighbor, Costa Rica, has been politically neutral and without an army since 1948. I was dismayed while I was there to discover an intense hate campaign directed against Nicaragua in the news media, which was controlled by extreme right-wing elements.

The U.S. government was involved in many efforts to draw Costa Rica into the war with Nicaragua: encouragement to remilitarize, overtures to train Costa Rican military in counterinsurgency warfare, offers to build roads and airport runways in the north, and the opening of a just-completed, highly amplified Voice of America radio station in northern Costa Rica, constantly beaming the U.S. version of "truth" to the Nicaraguan people.

In the face of overwhelming pressure, members of the Costa Rican peace movement were attempting to keep their country truly neutral and nonmilitarized. They were promoting nonviolent civilian based defense as a means to defend Costa Rica against attack. While I was there, they were planning presentations, strategy games, and study groups across the country to help strengthen people's understanding of nonviolent civilian defense and to try to stave off the drive to militarize the country. I worked with several people in Costa Rica's Peace Center, to help them gain the skills and confidence to lead nonviolence training workshops and to support their explorations of developing a nonviolent peacekeeping force along the Nicaragua–Costa Rica border.

I also visited the community of Monte Verde high in the mountains. It was founded by U.S. Quakers, who had been conscientious objectors during World War II and had left the United States to escape the militarism in our country and establish a new life in this peaceful one. Apparently they couldn't escape forever. Thirty-five years later, the members of this peace-loving community, and all of Costa Rica, were being threatened again by U.S. military power.

While I was in Central America, I was plagued with questions about my country's role there. Why do we prop up dictatorial governments in El Salvador and Guatemala? Why do we try to overthrow a democratically elected government in Nicaragua that is sincerely attempting to meet the needs of the poor majority? Why do we attempt to embroil Costa Rica in a regional war?

One of the Mothers of the Disappeared in El Salvador, who had lost thirteen members of her family, asked me to convey this question and plea to the people of the United States: "Why does your government support our government, which kills those who struggle against injustice? Tell your government to stop the military intervention in El Salvador. We believe that if the American people knew about the tens of thousands of people you are assassinating, you would stop the madness immediately. Don't send more military supplies, airplanes, and bombs. It is better to send clothes, medicines, professors, and nurses. We don't want more war and death."

During my stay in El Salvador, I asked many people how long they felt their government could last without U.S. military and economic support. The range of answers I received was from one day to three months, but almost all felt that without U.S. backing, the Salvadoran government would have been forced to negotiate a political settlement and end the civil war.

The Catholic Church in El Salvador had initiated a national dialogue as an effort toward peace. Monsignor Urioste told us that it was not likely to end the war, because the military, wealthy Salvadorans, and the U.S. government collaborated in believing that the way to a solution was through more war. This meant that many more poor people were going to die.

I believe that if we in the United States had possessed faith and courage equal to what I witnessed in most Central Americans, we could have stopped the wars and ended U.S. intervention. I was so moved by the dedication of Christians there to follow what they understood to be God's will for them: to meet the needs of the poor, the hungry, and the homeless, even when these acts were viewed by their governments as subversive and punishable by death.

I could not help feeling the challenge to us as U.S. Christians and people of conscience to live our faith and beliefs, even when risks are involved. I felt it even more strongly when I pondered the truth that it was our country that was supplying the planes, helicopters, bombs, munitions, and military training whose devastation I saw everywhere. It was my country that was crucifying these people.

One Salvadoran pleaded with us, "The people of the United States need to come to understand the reality of the people of El Salvador— what your tax dollars are doing and paying for." He reminded us that our government was pumping in more than two million dollars *each day* to support the government and the war in El Salvador. "The only thing that can stop the war here," he said, "is the American people."

Some of us in the United States took those words seriously. I was part of several efforts aimed at stopping U.S. intervention in Central America. One was Witness for Peace. This nonviolent, faith-based effort was launched in 1983 after a church delegation from North Carolina discovered that their presence in Jalapa, near Nicaragua's border with Honduras, was enough to stop Contra attacks there. On their return to the United States, they called together a national meeting of peace activists, who decided to organize a permanent presence of North American citizens in Nicaragua's war zones, to provide peaceful, prayerful protection for vulnerable Nicaraguans.

I co-led a nonviolence training for a long-term Witness for Peace team—a very courageous group of sixteen people who had committed to live among and work with the Nicaraguan people for at least six months. They lived in areas under Contra attack, to say as strongly as possible to the U.S. government and to the Contras: "If you continue to attack and kill the people of Nicaragua, you will have to risk killing us as well."

One of their critical roles was to host short-term teams—three groups of twenty people each month from across North America. These teams spent two weeks in Nicaragua, gathering eyewitness testimony, documenting Contra atrocities, holding vigils, and offering prayers. They then returned home to share their experiences and tell the truth about the Contras, which the Reagan administration's propaganda consistently referred to as "freedom fighters" and compared to our "founding fathers."

I spent a couple of weeks in the northern border area with Witness for Peace volunteers. I trained some of the long-term team members to become trainers themselves, so that they could offer nonviolence training to other North Americans and Nicaraguans in the religious community who wanted to participate in Witness for Peace actions. And I helped to develop a library on nonviolence at the Witness for Peace office in Managua.

One of the great blessings on one of my trips was a long visit with Miguel d'Escoto Brockmann, Nicaragua's foreign minister, who was a Maryknoll priest who would later serve as president of the United Nations General Assembly. D'Escoto has been a strong and persistent proponent of nonviolence. He explained, "Creative, active nonviolence is not to be confused with quietism or resignation in the face of evil. Rather it is active, persistent opposition to violence in all its forms. This is the core of the message Jesus brings to us."

For too long, he said, the church had been a pillar of support for the old, established order. Too many church leaders in Nicaragua, according to d'Escoto, were "lackeys of imperialist interests." And too many in the United States were silent in the face of the conflagration being perpetrated against Central America. The church, he told us, should be taking the lead in transforming societies toward brotherhood and sisterhood. It "needs to provide leaven in the loaf, to provide vision."

D'Escoto understood well the risk of renouncing injustice, exploitation, and violence. "What happened to Jesus is what happens when one order is being challenged by another," he said. "The cross is the inevitable consequence of following the teachings of Jesus. To fulfill our responsibilities as Christians, we need to risk our lives." That requires grace and courage, according to d'Escoto, who advised, "Start by reflecting on the message of Christ and then pray for the strength to live it."

D'Escoto declared, "There comes a time when you must put conscience above all. To preserve my life is not as important as following my Father's will." The reprisals that came down on him included being suspended from the priesthood by the Vatican. I was surprised to hear the weight of this burden for him. "Death would be easier than being suspended from the priesthood," he said.

"Nonviolence requires more than ordinary power," he continued. "But we can get it. To be truly Christian is to be dedicated to this kind of social transformation." The Sandinistas, he added, "have shown that religion and gospel values can be very helpful in creating a new society."

D'Escoto and other Nicaraguan government leaders were convinced that only dialogue and negotiation could bring true peace, aware that their best guarantee of a stable future was to develop diplomatic and trade relationships with many countries. The Sandinistas had made repeated overtures toward ending the Contra attacks and normalizing relations with the United States. But the Reagan administration had recently broken off bilateral talks with Nicaragua and tried to block the Contadora process, a diplomatic effort by the foreign ministers of Mexico, Venezuela, Colombia, and Panama to stabilize Central America by preventing confrontation between neighboring nations and ending direct military intervention by the United States. Our government continued to escalate its intervention, pushing Nicaragua to build up its military defenses "to protect itself from the most powerful nation in the world," according to d'Escoto. "If Reagan wants to end military development in Nicaragua," he asserted, "he can do that by immediately stopping the war against Nicaragua."

He added, "The only thing standing in the way of a U.S. invasion of Nicaragua is the will of the American people. The United States is likely to continue along this road of attrition. Its options are to blast everything out of existence, or to slowly bleed the country to death. Inflicting violence and death and suffering on the Nicaraguan people is not what America should be about."

Those of us with Witness for Peace who were his guests agreed. We were battling to overcome our love of comfort and our fear of persecution. We wanted to offer ourselves freely to stand with our Central American sisters and brothers, whatever the consequences.

The thousands of North Americans who went to Nicaragua, El Salvador, and Guatemala in those years felt very intensely the pain and suffering the wars were inflicting on the people there. We returned wondering what more we could do at home to stop the madness. In the wake of the U.S. invasion of Grenada of 1983, we were particularly concerned about the possibility of an invasion of Nicaragua.

In the East, Sojourners Community and the people gathered around *Sojourners* magazine were talking about launching a Pledge of Resistance. Out West, we were having discussions about an Emergency Response Network. Ken Butigan represented our West Coast group at an East Coast meeting where we joined forces.

About fifty thousand people all over the United States signed the pledge to publicly and nonviolently resist if our government invaded Nicaragua or further escalated the war there or in El Salvador. For several years we mobilized people to do nonviolent actions at local military bases, federal buildings, and other sites of U.S. militarism. We used the Pledge of Resistance handbook to train many people, who in turn trained thousands of others in nonviolent resistance.

I helped to organize hundreds of people to surround the federal building in San Francisco and shut it down for a while. People felt empowered throughout that event. Individuals approached the microphone we had set up and explained why they felt called to participate.

Our numbers and our resolve were strengthened by the fact that so many of us had visited Nicaragua with Witness for Peace, the Fellowship of Reconciliation, and other groups—as well as by the presence of many Central American refugees who had fled the persecution and violence in their homelands and were being offered safe haven in our communities as part of the Sanctuary Movement. After that event, through various contacts, we received word that a few folks in the Reagan administration had quietly said, "We could fight these wars if the Christians were not in the way."

Rarely do we receive so clear a word about making a difference. I was enormously grateful that so many of us had figured out how to get in the way. We were about to escalate our efforts, the tragic results of which would shock us all.

CHAPTER 10

Assault on the Tracks: Facing Violence with Love and Courage

September 1, 1987, was a bright, sunny day, with a strong breeze blowing off the Suisan Bay. Having earlier faced the bay's rough water and high waves in small boats, we had decided to shift the focus of our campaign to block shipments of weapons from the Concord Naval Weapons Station to land rather than water. About fifty of us gathered at ten o'clock that morning for an interfaith worship service on the train tracks that led to Port Chicago, where weapons from trains were loaded onto ships.

For eighty-three days, we had held peace vigils on these tracks. I had no idea that morning how different this day would be. How could I have known that two hours later I would be cradling one of my dearest friends as he clung tenuously to life, mangled by a 125-ton train carrying bombs and munitions, whose operators had been ordered to deliberately run him over?

Like many visitors to Central America, I had returned from my trips with renewed determination to try to end U.S. military intervention and the wars there. So had Brian Willson, a Vietnam War veteran whose job with the Air Force had included going into villages after U.S. bombing and strafing missions to assess the damage. One particularly unforgettable mission put him on the path from patriotic warrior to peace activist.

An hour after U.S. bombs fell on a small Vietnamese village, Brian was in a sea of crying and moaning humanity. Almost all of the victims, who had been attending to their farming and domestic chores that day, were women and children. Sobbing and gagging from the horror he was witnessing, Brian stumbled upon the body of a young woman, still clutching her three small, shrapnel-riddled children. Napalm had blackened their bodies and partially melted the woman's face, but her vacant eyes stared right at Brian.

Almost two decades later, Brian witnessed a small caravan of horse-drawn wagons on its way to a cemetery in Nicaragua, carrying the bodies of five women and a child who had been killed by U.S.-supported Contras the day before in an attack on a coffee cooperative. The simple caskets were open, and Brian could see the faces of the dead. He had a flashback to his time in Vietnam, and he knew that he needed to do all that he could to stop the U.S.-sponsored terror in Nicaragua.

In the fall of 1986, four Vietnam veterans fasted for forty-seven days on the steps of the Capitol in Washington, DC, in an appeal to Congress and the people of the United States to stop supporting the killing in Central America. Brian Willson was one of those veterans, and Charlie Liteky, who lived in San Francisco, was another. I was impressed with their witness and began doing nonviolence training with war veterans in the Bay Area.

I was profoundly moved that these veterans—who admitted to collectively killing hundreds of people in combat and on bombing runs— were willing to risk their lives for peace. After a weeklong training, some of them went to Nicaragua and walked more than seventy miles throughout that country's war zones—through ambushes, past bombed vehicles, and over mined roads—in a witness to peace and reconciliation. Brian was part of that team, and when he returned, we spent a long night talking about the agony he felt over what he had seen.

In Nicaragua, Brian had met with Eugene Hasenfus, a U.S. arms transporter who had parachuted to safety when his plane was shot down over southern Nicaragua. Hasenfus and his crew had been secretly dropping weapons to the Contras. The CIA and the Reagan administration denied any connection to him. But the downed plane and Hasenfus's confession blew the lid on the secret activity and exposed what would come to be known as the Iran-Contra Scandal: a doubly illegal covert U.S. operation that involved selling arms to Iran in exchange for their help in securing the release of U.S. hostages in Lebanon, and using the cash from Iran to buy weapons for the Contras—all in violation of congressional prohibitions.

I was pretty sure I knew the point from which those weapons had been deployed. In early 1987, I took Brian out to the Concord Naval Weapons Station (CNWS). We found a hillside honeycombed with literally hundreds of bunkers, each one filled with munitions. Bullets, mines, and bombs were being transported from the storage bunkers in trains and trucks across a public highway, then out to the Port Chicago pier, where the deadly cargo was loaded onto ships that carried it into the San Francisco Bay, beneath the Golden Gate Bridge, and then to other parts of the globe.

Months of research uncovered the horrific reality that millions had died as a result of weapons that had been shipped along the tracks at Concord and then been dropped on, or shot at, people in Vietnam, Korea, Chile, the Philippines, the Middle East, and Central America. We were able to document that arms were going from CNWS to El Salvador for use there, and for trans-shipment to Nicaragua and Guatemala.

A Freedom of Information request from the San Francisco Pledge of Resistance revealed that weapons shipped from Concord to El Salvador's port of Acajutla included more than six thousand high-explosive rockets and almost three thousand demolition and fragmentation bombs for the quick destruction of homes; thousands of white phosphorous rockets with the incendiary capacity to burn flesh to bone; several million cartridges for General Electric machine guns mounted on helicopter gunships that could fire a hundred bullets per second; and almost 1,800 fuse extenders used to increase a bomb's impact and the intensity of damage from shrapnel. The U.S. government was literally sending bombs from our backyard to the front yards of brothers and sisters we had met in Central America.

Brian and I and several others agreed that we needed to escalate our efforts for peace. We decided to launch a sustained, nonviolent vigil at the road and the tracks, supporting people who were led by conscience to block the trucks and trains carrying weapons. We were prepared to put our bodies between the bombs and the people of Central America.

Our goal was to try to stop the arms shipments, but also to speak to the hearts and consciences of the American people about the insanity of our nation's policies of fighting and killing the people of Central America. Many of us wondered why more German people had not protested and acted to stop the shipment of millions of Jews to their deaths in concentration camps during the Third Reich. Were they afraid that if they acted to stop the genocide they too might end up in concentration camps? How did German Christians reconcile their faith with allowing this horrible mass slaughter to go on?

At Concord our government was not sending people on trains off to death camps, but instead was sending death itself along the tracks.

Every train that passed through the base's main gate meant that more people would die in another corner of the globe. As people of faith committed to creating a peaceful world, we were confronted with a question that echoed what we had asked about Hitler-era Germans: What is our responsibility to speak out and act to stop this crime against humanity?

I wrote these words at the time:

> For those of us who call ourselves Christians and people of faith, there is a clear moral choice. We can pretend we don't know these bombs are being shipped from our neighborhood and, as a result, people are dying. We can argue that we have written our Congress people and encouraged them to act to stop this war. We can say the issue is so complex, we are not well enough informed about the issue to act.
>
> We can also argue that literally putting our bodies in the way of these trains could mean death for us if the trains run over us, or, more likely, the possibility of long jail terms for interfering with the war effort. We can ask ourselves: "What good would it do? Who is going to care if a few people get out on the tracks to pray and try to stop a death train?"
>
> Or, we can say: "We have a moral responsibility to act in the strongest nonviolent way we can to stop the killing of innocent men, women, and children in Central America and other parts of the world." If we see ourselves as a human family, we have a responsibility to our brothers and sisters whom our government has decided to declare our "enemies" and kill.

I wrote that, as Christians and Jews, we felt a moral obligation to uphold God's laws "Thou shalt not kill" and "Love one another." And we also felt a legal responsibility to uphold international law, particularly the Nuremberg Principles.

After the Second World War, Nazi leaders were put on trial at Nuremberg. A frequent response to questions about their participation in the atrocities of the Third Reich was "I was just following orders." The Nuremberg Principles that arose from that tribunal declared that soldiers are morally obligated to refuse orders that violate conscience; and, furthermore, that it is the responsibility of citizens to try to stop the war crimes, crimes against humanity, and crimes against peace being committed by their governments.

These crimes include the wanton killing of civilian populations— which we had witnessed throughout Central America being carried out

With Dorothy Granada, blocking the first truck with munitions headed for El Salvador as part of Nuremberg Actions at Concord Naval Weapons Station, CA (June 1987).

by military personnel and death squads armed, funded and trained by our government. The United States, which had called Nazi leaders to account for their crimes in the Hitler era, was acting without any accountability in direct violation of the principles it had instituted four decades before.

Complicity in crimes against humanity, through silence or passive approval by inaction, was itself defined as a crime at the Nuremberg tribunal. So we decided to call our nonviolent witness at the Concord Naval Weapons Station "Nuremberg Actions." We did not see ourselves as breaking the law, but rather as participating in "civil obedience," or "holy obedience," attempting to uphold both international law and God's law. We did not view our actions as "disturbing the peace," as others would charge, but "disturbing the war."

We launched our witness on June 10, 1987. I was among the initial four who blocked trucks that day. Every truck and train that carried munitions was marked with a large red or orange placard reading "EXPLOSIVES," so it was easy to identify what to block.

We were kneeling on the cement roadway—a public space about 150 feet wide that was bordered on both sides with a heavy yellow line demarcating Navy property. We claimed that public strip as "people's land." On that sweltering afternoon, we were reading the Nuremberg Principles aloud as a munitions truck approached and stopped.

For about forty-five minutes, we were on our knees in front of the truck. The authorities didn't know quite what to do. I finally handed an extra copy of the Nuremberg Principles to a friend to carry to the truck driver, so he would know why we were there.

A Marine, who was among the 350 assigned to CNWS to keep the base secure, stopped my friend and said, "You can't cross this yellow line." When my friend explained what he was trying to do, the Marine said, "I'll give it to him." So I watched as a Marine handed a copy of the Nuremberg Principles to the driver of a truck loaded with bombs headed for Central America!

We refused to move when ordered to do so. Eventually the county sheriff and his deputies arrested us. We and the groups that followed us successfully blocked three trucks that day, all of which turned back with their cargo. The driver of a security truck stopped and rolled down his window as we were being taken off to jail and said, "Real good job there, you fellows." I was always moved to find people on the "inside" who supported us.

We spent three days in jail and returned to the tracks. Despite temperatures that sometimes rose to 120 degrees, we maintained an ongoing vigil throughout that summer. After that first encounter, the deputies arrested us quickly whenever we blocked trains or trucks.

In August, Brian Willson declared at the tracks, "One truth seems clear: if the munitions train moves past our blockade, other human beings will be killed and maimed. *We are not worth more. They are not worth less.* Let us commit to ourselves and the world that we will claim our dignity, self-respect, and honor by resisting with our lives and dollars, no matter what it takes."

In an August 21 open letter to Captain Lonnie Cagle, the commander of CNWS, Brian wrote that the authorities had the choice of "suspending movements of munitions, removing our bodies, or running over us." He requested a meeting with Cagle. The base commander neither answered the letter nor responded to two follow-up phone calls from Brian.

Brian echoed the words of the letter when he addressed the base authorities at a press conference at the tracks on the morning of September 1, as he prepared to block a train and begin a forty-day fast. Referring to those who were being killed by our weapons in Central America, he asked, "Am I more valuable than those people? If I say no, then I have to say, you can't move these munitions without moving my body, or destroying my body."

About an hour later, at 11:40 a.m., Brian, along with veterans Duncan Murphy and David Duncombe, took their positions in front of our blue "Nuremberg Actions" banner on the tracks. Brian and I had been strategizing, and we had planned to block the first train together. But at the press conference after the worship service, I had asked if anyone who had not yet received nonviolence training wanted to join the ongoing blockade. Many people came forward, and I was the only one there at the time that could do the training, so I agreed to do that instead of blocking the first train. I planned to block the next train with others later that day.

I remember that the mood at the base felt more uneasy and sinister that day than it had before. About ten minutes before Brian, Duncan, and David moved onto the tracks, two truckloads of Marines wearing flak jackets drove close to our vigil, got out, pointed their M-16 rifles at us, and then sped off. A few minutes later, a carload of Marines drove by us, and one of them shouted, "We hear there's going to be violence today." But still I didn't imagine what was about to happen.

I was standing in front of Brian, Duncan, and David, at the edge of the tracks. The munitions train had been sitting for about half an hour with its headlights blazing about five hundred feet away. We sent a couple of people over to deliver a copy of Brian's letter and tell the person in charge of security that we were beginning the blockade of the train. A guard in the security office picked up a handheld radio and told someone—presumably the engineer of the train—that people were on the tracks. The two members of our vigil heard the voice on the radio respond, "I think you're crazy. We have our job to do."

As they were walking back toward us, the train began moving. As it got closer and closer to us, it kept picking up speed. On the cowcatcher platform at the front of the locomotive stood two spotters, whose job it was to make sure the tracks were clear.

I was waving my arms frantically over the tracks and looking those guys in the eyes, shouting, "There are people on the tracks! Stop the train!" They just looked straight ahead and kept coming. We learned later that the train was going about seventeen mph when it reached us—more than three times the five mph speed limit.

The train hit my arm and knocked me to the ground. From that vantage point, I could see underneath the wheels, and I was appalled by what I saw. David had leapt off the tracks, and Duncan had managed to jump up ten feet to grab the railing of the cowcatcher. But Brian

We come to the aid of Brian Willson, who was run over by a train with two boxcars of munitions at Concord, CA (September 1, 1987). [Photo: John Skerce]

had been run over and was being dragged by the locomotive, getting smashed from side to side as the train continued another four hundred feet before stopping. As I got up and ran toward Brian, I first came to one of his legs, which had been severed by the impact.

Witnessing Brian's mutilation was the most horrible experience of my life. He had a gaping hole the size of a lemon in his skull. I knelt over him, trying to protect his exposed and bleeding brain. He reached up and felt the wound and said, "Oh my God, I'm gonna die." Friends surrounded him, telling him they loved him, encouraging him to hold on. I think everybody there believed he was going to die, and several people made a point of assuring him that the witness at the tracks would go on.

Blessedly, Holley Rauen, a midwife whom Brian had married just ten days before, had studied emergency medical care in preparation for peace walks on mined roads in Nicaragua's war zones. She and others used pressure to control the blood gushing from the stump of Brian's leg and other injuries. Duncan's training and experience as an ambulance driver during World War II was also invaluable at that moment. Though in excruciating pain, Brian's chief concern was for his thirteen-year-old stepson, Gabriel, who had witnessed the whole grisly spectacle.

A Navy ambulance arrived. I looked at the sea of Brian's spilled blood and begged the crew, "Please, take this man to the hospital! He's dying!" One of them said to me, "We are not allowed to." They left, having provided no medical assistance or transportation, explaining that Brian's body was lying in public space and not on Navy property. Seventeen more precious minutes elapsed before the county ambulance arrived.

Holley remained amazingly composed, tending to Brian and also trying to calm Gabriel, who screamed out his rage and grief. Incredibly, Brian stayed conscious and kept talking. I invited Holley to switch places with me. I thought she should be the one to hold him and try to communicate with him in his final minutes and hear what I assumed would be his last words.

Three or four times, Brian said, "Take the stuff out of my pockets." So I went through his pockets and pulled out his keys and some change, thinking that this was a crazy use of my time at that moment. But Brian explained later that he thought he was going to jail, and he didn't want the jailers to lose his ID or keys.

The wars came home in a powerful way that day. What our government had long been willing to do to poor people and people of color in other parts of the world, it was also willing to do to peaceful protesters in the United States who tried to impede the war effort.

That Brian survived was nothing short of a miracle. He suffered a total of nineteen injuries, including a skull fracture, a damaged kidney, and broken ribs, wrist, and shoulder. He spent eight hours in surgery that day. One leg had been severed in the collision, and the other was so badly twisted and mangled that it needed to be surgically amputated below the knee. One ear had to be reattached. Brain surgery was necessary to clean Brian's brain of grease, dirt, and debris, and to extract a piece of skull that had lodged in his frontal lobe.

I felt a heavy responsibility, because I had helped to organize the blockade. I feared first of all that this beautiful man and dear friend was going to lose his life—and, secondly, that if he survived, he would be horribly physically maimed and mentally debilitated. So three days later, when a few of us were allowed into his hospital room, seeing Brian alert and talking was one of the most joyful moments of my life. Although his body was badly battered, and literally every part of it was bandaged, his spirit was still very much alive and free.

Brian asked about Gabriel and wanted to know what was going on at the tracks. I shared with him that we were going to hold a huge rally there the next day, and I asked if there was anything he wanted to communicate to those who would gather. From beneath that massive bandage covering his whole body came a voice with an unwavering commitment to nonviolence, love for the people who would be killed if the trains got their weapons to their destination, and determination to continue the struggle. It was obvious that, rather than being destroyed by the train assault, Brian's conviction about nonviolence had deepened.

Brian had a tube in his throat, which made it difficult for him to talk, and he was in overwhelming pain. But he dictated this message, which I wrote down and typed up, then read over the loudspeaker at the rally the next day:

> I want to thank all of you for coming to Concord today out of concern for the violence which the death train inflicted on me last Tuesday. But please remember that the same horror—and much worse—is happening every day to the people in Central America.
>
> I am grateful you are here today to demonstrate your concern for peace in Central America. I hope you will come back day after day after day after day to nonviolently block the trains and trucks carrying bombs and munitions to ships bound for Central America and other parts of the world. Tomorrow, the next day, and the next day and the next—come a day, a week, a month—for as long as you can.
>
> As soon as I am able, I will be back on the tracks. Hopefully, we can get enough people to stop the arms shipments from Concord, and then the blockades will spread throughout the rest of the country.
>
> Despite your anger and outrage at what has happened, I ask you to express your opposition to this violence here on the tracks, and in Central America, *nonviolently*. We must confront violence with nonviolence.
>
> We all have to put our lives on the line for peace and justice. It does not have to be in front of a train. If we want peace, we can have it, but we are going to have to pay for it.
>
> Is there anything of higher value than peace and justice? A boat? A VCR? What is standing in the way of your journey to liberation with the people of the earth? We of the First World need to learn the lessons of the Third World—that justice is the foundation for peace.
>
> This is the time to call for the creation of a peace force, where people will work full-time to stop the arms race, consistent with President Eisenhower's statement: "I think that people want

peace so much that one of these days governments had better get out of the way and let them have it."

Every time those munitions trains go past us, some people are going to be killed or maimed. When we come to sincerely feel that the lives of those people are worth no less than our own lives, we become fully liberated.

We're talking about nonviolent revolution—of our lifestyle and attitudes and values—so we can join the Third World revolution for justice and stop the madness, greed, and war which come out of the First World. Our government can only continue its wars with the cooperation of our people, and that cooperation is with our taxes and with our bodies.

Our actions and expressions are what are needed, not our whispers and our quiet dinner conversation. Martin Luther King Jr. said, "Injustice anywhere is a threat to justice everywhere." When someone is hurting in El Salvador or Nicaragua, we are hurting, too.

I never thought I would lose my legs here in the U.S.—maybe while walking for peace in Nicaragua, but not here. I hope everyone will search their hearts about what they can do to stop this madness. We each need to take responsibility. I want to call on everyone to speak out and act as strongly and powerfully and honestly and nonviolently as possible. Together we can stop these death trains and the horrible wars in Central America.

Four days after the train assault on Brian, ten thousand people heard these words at the tracks. They had come in response to the tragedy, to express their commitment to stopping the continued export of violence to Central America. Among them were Daniel Ellsberg, singer Joan Baez, and presidential candidate Rev. Jesse Jackson, who declared from the stage, "If more people had sat on the tracks in front of trains taking people to death camps forty-five years ago, six million people might not have died."

Jackson named other activists who, like Brian, had made great sacrifices for peace and justice during the civil rights era and at other critical times in our nation's history. And he compared "the first Concord," where the Boston Tea Party took place, to "California's Concord, where people are again trying to bring this country to its senses." After the rally, I took him to the place where Brian had been hit, where his blood was still visible, and Jackson knelt and offered a prayer.

We were particularly moved that Rosario Murillo, wife of President Daniel Ortega, came from Nicaragua with their four children. President Ortega sent a letter addressed to Brian, which said in part, "Your body, mutilated by those who make war, is part of our sadness, but it is also part of our hope for a better future." Murillo, too, wanted to see the place where Brian had been hit, and I took her there early Saturday morning before the rally. When she saw his blood, she said, "I think that this was a very Christian act, what he did, in terms of expressing his love and being willing to risk his life out of love for other people."

Brian had declared just minutes before he was run over that he hoped that our action was the beginning of a new era of sustained resistance—equivalent in moral power and in nonviolent spirit to the Salt March that liberated India from British control, or the Montgomery bus boycott and Birmingham campaign during the civil rights movement in our own country. He saw our witness as a declaration that "We the people are the ones who are going to make peace." His prophetic vision began to take shape at the tracks.

After September 1, we had people at or on the tracks twenty-four hours a day seven days a week, maintaining a permanent encampment so that trains and trucks could not sneak by in the middle of the night and building a growing community of commitment. Almost fifty churches, synagogues, Buddhist communities, Friends meetings, and peace groups committed to being present one day each month. Thousands of people kept vigil, prayed, fasted, leafleted the base's workers, and sat on the tracks. Over the next couple years, more than two thousand arrests were made as we blocked the trains and trucks loaded with munitions.

Detractors passing by in their cars showered us with "gifts"—often insults and obscenities and blaring horns. A few threw trash our way, and one person hurled a dead skunk at us. There was an incident with a shot fired toward the tracks, but fortunately no one was hurt.

In a very different spirit, supporters showed up regularly with food. Occasionally someone would hand us a twenty-dollar bill and say, "I'm glad you're here." And a passing busload of school kids flashing us the peace sign would make it all feel worthwhile.

Instead of barreling through our demonstrations, after September 1 the trains crept at about one-half mile per hour. Still, the base authorities tried all kinds of intimidation to get us to give up our nonviolent protest. Drivers of the munitions trucks threatened to run us over. A phalanx of Marines and sheriff's deputies appeared every day, intent on forcibly removing us from the tracks. They threatened us with police dogs and stun guns.

On November 10, I was kneeling in prayer with a few others on the tracks, facing the munitions train as it approached. A deputy ordered us to leave, and I responded, "We will get off the tracks when you stop shipping bombs to kill our brothers and sisters in Central America."

The deputy grabbed my arm and twisted it until I could no longer stand the pain. I got up and walked off the tracks, with him still restraining me. We walked another fifteen feet, and then the deputy—warning, "This is to make sure you leave the tracks next time"—twisted my arm with such force that it broke in two places. I blacked out from the pain. Two other demonstrators also had their arms broken that day.

Such experiences were indeed painful, but we kept reminding ourselves that our suffering was miniscule compared to the immense violence being inflicted on the people of Central America every day by American guns and munitions. After the train passed that day, I went back to the tracks, sat down, and wept.

The tears were partly a result of the pain of my broken arm; partly my awareness of the pain of the people of Nicaragua and El Salvador who would die as a result of the trainload of munitions that had just passed by; and partly a response to the beauty and power of our sustained nonviolent action there on the tracks, our saying "No" to the death trains. I thought to myself as I spilled my tears on the tracks, "They can injure and break our bones, but they cannot kill our spirit and our determination to live as one human family."

I went to the hospital instead of jail that day, to get my arm set. It was a Tuesday, and I was usually at the tracks on Tuesdays and Thursdays. When Thursday came, Rev. David Wylie, who had also had his arm broken, and I showed up with our casts. We were asking ourselves and each other whether we were going to block another train. We acknowledged that there was still a lot we could do with one broken arm. But with two . . . well, that was another story.

We joked uneasily about the things we wouldn't be able to do with two broken arms—bathroom activities being high on the list. But after we consulted our consciences, we both decided to block the train that day.

The beautiful thing was that the more violent the authorities became, the deeper became our understanding of, and commitment to, nonviolence. We did not express anger or violence to the deputies who injured us, or to the Marines who hurled epithets at us. We felt concern for them and saw them as part of our human family as well.

With my parents, Ray and Ruth Hartsough, before being arrested blocking a weapons train at Concord, CA (1988).

Apparently the Navy thought that running over protesters would end our witness. Instead, for more than two years—875 days, to be exact—we blocked every train and truck that carried arms at Concord Naval Weapons Station. Sometimes two buses were needed to carry off all the arrested demonstrators. Some people ended up spending as much as three months in the county jail.

One of the high points of my life was having my parents join the vigil. Mom and Dad came with a group of Quakers and war-tax resisters from Sonoma County each month to vigil at the tracks. Though my mom had been arrested with me at Livermore, my dad had never been arrested.

Dad was seventy-eight and severely crippled from Parkinson's disease. It was a cold day, and he was wearing several layers of warm clothing and a brightly colored knit hat that I had brought him from the highlands of Guatemala, an area where many civilians had been killed with U.S. weapons. Though he could barely walk or talk, he wanted to come out to Concord to join his voice with others in saying "No" to the killing in Central America.

He and I were sitting and holding crosses on the tracks that day—his emblazoned with the radical idea "Love one another," and mine bearing the name of Valentina Castellon, who had been killed by Contras with U.S. weapons in Nicaragua in February 1986. As a munitions train with several boxcars loaded with bombs came into sight, I asked dad if he would like to block the train with me. Struggling, he managed to say, "Y-e-s . . . l-e-t's . . . **b-l-o-c-k**."

I helped him up. Lieutenant Doug Sizemore from the Sheriff's Department approached us. I gave him a handshake and said, "I'd like you to meet my dad, Ray Hartsough." A pained look overtook the sheriff's face, and he blurted out, "He's not going to get arrested, is he?"

I beamed him a smile and said, "Lieutenant Sizemore, that is up to you. I'm not going to arrest him."

Dad and I were placed under arrest, handcuffed, and taken to the side of the tracks as the train laden with its deadly cargo rumbled through. When I looked at Dad, whose Parkinson's had robbed him of most of his capacity for facial expression, his face lit up with a brilliant smile, and he crowed triumphantly, "They arrested me!"

For a second time, I didn't go to jail. I think the authorities thought my dad was too old or infirm to go, so they released us both.

My mom got arrested about a month later trying to block a truck. A tiny woman, she was still able to fit into her wedding dress on her fiftieth anniversary. As the police officer put her into the police van, I pleaded with him, "Be gentle, you have some precious cargo."

Mom was taken, as we all usually were, to the county jailhouse. The women were in one room and the men in another. The men had to go past where the women were being held to use the water fountain. My friend Russ Jorgensen, who also got arrested that day, told me that one of the male inmates saw this "little old lady with silver hair in a blue coat" sitting among the mostly young women who had been picked up for prostitution. He asked Russ, "What was she arrested for?"

Russ answered, "She was arrested for blocking an eighteen-wheeler!" Suddenly all the men felt a need for a drink of water—just so they could get a glimpse of this tiny old woman who had stopped a semi trailer loaded with bombs!

We had themes for many of our days of vigil: Women's Day, Human Rights Day, World Hunger Day. On February 14, we decided to make valentines, acknowledging that what we were really about in this movement was love. My mom was there, and she and others made valentines for the new commander of the base, Richard Owens, who was much more open in his approach than Captain Cagle had been. We invited him to come out and receive them, which he did.

My mother read her valentine message aloud: "We're here because we love the whole human family, and we don't appreciate the Navy sending all these bombs to kill the people we love. We invite you to join us in loving these people, and stop the shipment of bombs." The commander very graciously accepted the valentines, and I believe he was moved by the gesture. I think we touched his humanity that day and throughout the entire time we kept vigil at the tracks. I believe he appreciated that we didn't treat him as an enemy, even though we were totally opposed to what the Navy was doing at Concord.

I was grateful that we maintained a spirit of nonviolence throughout those many months, and for the instances of genuine mutual respect and caring between us and the authorities. Our nonviolence covenant was very clear that we considered all base workers, security personnel, and police as our brothers and sisters, and that we would treat them as such.

On the day of the big rally after the assault on Brian, about fifty people who had nothing to do with Nuremberg Actions came prepared to tear up the train tracks. Holley and I and several others pleaded with them to maintain the spirit of nonviolence, which for us included a covenant not to destroy property. But they refused to listen. They had large hammers and crowbars and massive bolt cutters, and they succeeded in removing a couple of lengths of track.

But then I gathered a few people to sit on the tracks with me, and soon others who saw what was happening joined us, so that we had about a hundred people. The sparks were flying—literally, off the hammers—within six inches of us. About seventy-five police cars were there for the rally, and I went with a couple of others to tell the police captain what was going on. He thanked us and told us he'd let us deal with it.

I stayed at the tracks that night until about eight thirty, after the sun had set and the crowd had left. The captain of Marine Security came by, and he told me he was impressed that we weren't just talking about nonviolence, but that we were willing even to sit on the tracks to block their destruction. He also assured me that he had given every truck driver and train engineer instructions to stop until people are removed from the tracks. And he said, "If for whatever reason they don't, I personally will get out in front of them and make sure they do."

An amazing, inspiring community grew up around the Concord tracks. There was a gathering every morning to share stories about what had happened during the night. People from many walks of life appeared, from teenagers to retirees, developing a deep appreciation and affection for one another. A few ex-CIA agents and many war veterans joined us. Our sense of community eventually grew to include members of the Contra Costa Sheriff's Department who, though still continuing to carry out orders, showed increasing respect toward us.

David Duncombe, a former weapons designer, served as a chaplain at the University of California San Francisco Medical Center. He and his wife had been riding along the bike path in Sausalito one day when I happened to see them. I said, "Well, Dave, we are going to start blocking trains and trucks carrying bombs to Central America on June tenth, and I thought you might be interested."

He not only blocked the train with Brian on September 1, he ended up taking off two days each week from his work for three years to be present at the tracks. He was our unofficial chaplain, providing a lot of Spirit and sustenance for the group. David was arrested more than a hundred times, received several long jail terms, and fasted three times, each for more than forty days in prison and on the tracks.

Diane Poole, who had a high-paying computer job in Silicon Valley, quit it to live at the tracks. During one arrest after blocking a train, she was handcuffed and sitting in the jail bus. She saw another train coming down the tracks. A guard blocked the bus's front door. A sign over the back door read "For Emergency Use Only." Declaring, "Well, this is an emergency," Diane walked back the aisle and, with her hands still cuffed behind her, opened the back door.

Diane got back on the tracks to block the next train. The Navy was especially upset with her and tried to charge her with attempting to escape from prison, but she hadn't been booked yet. So instead they settled for charging her with stealing government property: the handcuffs!

Abraham Zwickel, who was in his nineties and lived near the base, came virtually every day to the tracks with his Buddhist drum. Whenever he got arrested, the authorities always tried to expedite his processing and get him out of jail as quickly as possible. I think they were worried he was going to die on their watch.

When I went to El Salvador in 1988, I was in a village where there were no radios, no electricity, and no newspapers. But people there had heard about Brian Willson—and about the many people who were blockading the trains and trucks that were carrying the bombs that were killing their family members.

It was amazing that everywhere I went—even in the most remote villages and refugee camps in El Salvador and Nicaragua—people had heard about our witness. One peasant man in El Salvador said, "It fills us with hope and joy that there are North Americans who are willing to risk their lives to try to stop the horrible violence and killing being inflicted on our people." I heard similar sentiments over and over, all across Central America.

I remain grateful for the many outcomes of the Nuremberg Actions. It is no longer a secret that arms are shipped from Concord Naval Weapons Station. Thousands of people felt personally touched by the wars and confronted the question: what am I willing to do to stop the killing? We learned of two munitions truck drivers who quit their jobs because they felt they couldn't in conscience continue their work, and a few Marines who refused orders to keep us off the tracks. They joined the thousands of others who were declaring with our bodies "The war stops here."

Our witness gave great encouragement to people in Central America and around the world. We learned that in Palestine and Pakistan, in Iraq and Afghanistan, from Korea to Cuba and Colombia, people at "the other end of the tracks" were moved by what we had done.

We built a sustained, nonviolent resistance community and played a part in inspiring others to develop similar nonviolent campaigns and communities at military facilities around the United States. In the spring of 1988, in a coordinated effort organized by the Pledge of Resistance, nonviolent actions took place at forty-five military facilities supporting the war in Central America.

Over time, the broken places in Brian's body healed, and he gradually recovered his strength. Before long, he was taking his first steps on prosthetic legs. I felt like I was witnessing life after death: resurrection!

Unbelievably, in February 1988 the train crew sued Brian, claiming he had caused them to suffer mental anguish and posttraumatic stress because he had sat on the tracks and got run over by them. Because no criminal charges had ever been brought against the crew or their Navy superiors, Brian's lawyer convinced him to countersue. Thus began a three-year legal morass.

The engineer, conductor, and supervisor of the train that ran over Brian all admitted to investigators that they had been under orders from their superiors not to stop the train. One of the two spotters standing on the front of the locomotive said in a report that he "felt the protester who had been hit was beyond help, so he did not tell the engineer to stop." The lawsuit against Brian was eventually dropped, and the U.S. government offered him a substantial cash settlement, which he understood to be an acknowledgment that the Navy's actions had been intentional and deliberate.

Brian, Holley, and Gabriel lived with our family for four years after Brian was released from the hospital. They owned no property, and their "bank account" was a coffee can in our basement, hidden behind the freezer. Brian had been a war tax refuser for many years, and he knew that a considerable amount of the settlement money was vulnerable to seizure for back taxes.

He directed his lawyer to establish the Brian Willson Trust, over which Brian had no control. When the government check arrived in the mail, he deposited it immediately into the trust account. Within two hours, IRS agents showed up at the house to seize the unpaid taxes, and Brian answered honestly, "I don't have the money." It has paid for Brian's considerable medical expenses and supported many good causes, including his travel to war zones around the world.

In 2011, Brian published his memoir. As part of a speaking tour to promote it, I organized several events for him in the Bay Area. One of them was a book party at the Mount Diablo Peace and Justice Center in Walnut Creek, not far from the Concord Naval Weapons Station. On our way there, we stopped at the base.

We stood at the place where Brian had been run over and snapped a few pictures. Within minutes, sirens blared from all directions. Security vehicles surrounded us, and an officer in a black uniform ordered us to put our hands behind our heads. "It is illegal to take pictures here!" he barked at us. Then he asked what we were doing there.

"I am on a speaking tour, with my book," answered Brian.

"What's the book about?"

"It's called *Blood on the Tracks*—and it is my blood, on those tracks."

The man in charge became more cordial then. He told Brian, "You know, I was just a kid when that train incident happened." He had fought in the wars in Iraq and Afghanistan in the meantime. "You were a legend," he continued, "and everybody in this town knew about you. I am glad to meet you!" We invited him to the book party, and he promised to buy Brian's book. Before we left, he said, "Oh, by the way, you are not under arrest."

I continue to be moved by Brian's spirit and determination. And by his profound insight that our lives are not worth more, and the lives of other people around the world are not worth less. Taking seriously this notion—so radical and unpopular in this age of "American exceptionalism"—has great implications for how we view others and how we live in the world.

I think that for Brian, seeing the agony in Central America was like a parent discovering their child is in a burning house. No parent would question whether to run into a burning house to save their child. That's how Brian felt about the children he had met in Nicaragua and El Salvador—all the ones who were traumatized or orphaned or missing legs because of land mines.

Brian and I had conspired together to do the action that ended up with him losing his legs and almost getting killed. I know that he doesn't regret it, and he doesn't blame me. In fact, our sharing in that tragic event forged a special lifelong friendship and partnership in our work for peace and justice.

But it has not been easy for Brian to do what he has had to do all these years. Like him, I don't regret that we organized the Nuremberg Actions. But when I think about the suffering and hardship of my friend living the rest of his life without his legs, I feel very sad. He paid a very high price for putting into action his love for his sisters and brothers living in war zones.

As part of his book speaking tour, Brian rode more than seven hundred miles from Portland to San Francisco, pedaling his hand-powered tricycle and peddling his book. I rode my bike the last seventy miles with him. As we approached the last big hill rising from Sausalito to the Golden Gate Bridge, Brian was assessing how long and steep it was and pondering if he could make it.

I followed behind him, encouraging him, as he rode more and more slowly, trying to get up that long hill. Eventually I got off my bike, and with one hand on it, and one on his back, I pushed him the last couple hundred yards. He probably would have made it without my help. But that moment seemed symbolic of all the little ways I've tried to be supportive and loving to him over all these years. He is such a gift to the world.

CHAPTER 11

The World Is Watching: Facing Down Death Squads

J ust as the war in Vietnam finally ended, so did the worst of the violent conflicts that devastated Central America a decade and a half later. But the U.S. war machine has a perpetual mission, and other targets were being sought for its firepower and domination.

In February 1986, the surprising "People Power" Revolution in the Philippines nonviolently overthrew the ruthless U.S.-supported regime of Ferdinand Marcos—known as "the Hitler of Southeast Asia." It brought high hopes for fundamental change in that suffering country. But the anticipated end to corruption and greed, and the advent of agrarian reform, never materialized. Massive structural injustice persisted, and so did a guerilla insurgency committed to political change.

In April 1989, a large-scale government military campaign named Operation Thunderbolt took aim at the southern portion of the Philippine island of Negros. In the name of "wiping out the Communists," thirty-five thousand people were driven out of their homes under the bombs of helicopter gunships and F-5 fighter jets supplied by the United States. General Raymundo Jarque, commanding officer of the army's 301st Brigade in Negros, is reported to have said, "I am willing to kill a million people if need be to flush out the insurgents and save democracy."

Three months later, at the invitation of the Philippine Council of Churches, I joined a delegation from the Northern California Ecumenical Council, with a desire to understand the challenges and struggles that the Filipino people faced. We spent most of our time in Manila, and we also visited the U.S. Naval Base at Subic Bay. We heard a great deal of criticism and resentment of the U.S. military presence.

One angry Filipino told us bitterly, "The U.S. bases do not represent peace on earth but war on earth. The U.S. military bases here are a pact with the devil."

Toward the end of our trip, I went with a few others to the small, stricken island of Negros. It was eerily reminiscent of the tragedies I had witnessed elsewhere. Almost the entire island was covered with sugar plantations. The sight of them brought back memories of Cuba, though the poverty there made Cuba look almost rich. Most of the people lived in extremely substandard housing, with virtually no clothes and very little to eat.

I visited one family whose little home was built on stilts. They had one small wooden bed in which the whole family slept. The man worked twelve hours a day in the sugar cane fields—the only job available—receiving a dollar and a half for a day's work. Like thousands of others, he was exploited so that we Americans could eat and drink plenty of sugar at cheap prices.

Our delegation met with Deputy Chief of Staff Fidel Ramos, who was one of two generals who had defected from the Marcos government during the revolution. Ramos made very clear to us that the military was still running the show in terms of "security." The prevailing mindset required herding people into "strategic hamlets"—our failed strategy in Vietnam. As in that neighboring Asian country, this plan was backed up with bombing runs against the civilian population.

The bombing target was an area about the size of the state of Rhode Island. Most of the people living there had fled the lush and tropical rolling green hills of their ancestral lands, leaving behind livelihoods and livestock, carrying only their children, the sick, and the elderly. Some trekked for weeks to escape the bombs, and hundreds—mostly children—died from exhaustion and hunger.

Many took refuge in church buildings and the grounds around them, mostly Catholic. In Bacolod, the capital of Negros, we visited the social hall of the Sacred Heart Seminary. Six hundred refugees were huddled in groups all over the floor, sitting on small piles of bedding, with the cries of the young and coughs of the old filling the air. We heard stories of unconscionable brutality.

Sixty-year-old Dionisia Grande told us that her son Freddie had gone to the river near their home to bathe and wash clothes. Armed vigilantes accused him of being part of the New People's Army guerilla movement. They stabbed him, cut off his head, and took the head to the military commander, who rewarded them with a bag of rice.

A family who fled bombing and sought shelter in a church hall with six hundred other refugees in Bacolod, Negros, Philippines (1989). [Photo: David Hartsough]

Joni González was a very small fourteen-year-old. Soldiers entered his home and brutally killed his father in front of his entire family. Joni, his mother, and his four younger brothers fled into the forest, where they subsisted for two months on roots, bananas, and wild fruits and suffered oppressive heat and cold. Weakened by hunger and exposure, Joni's mother and one of his brothers contracted malaria and died. Joni was left with the responsibility of caring for his surviving three brothers.

Soldiers had fired into the home of the Alohado family, shooting infant Boyet Alohado in her mother's arms. Her young parents walked three hours to the nearest town, carrying their wounded baby. She died soon after their arrival, for lack of medicine at the clinic there.

In one corner of the hall, an elderly man lay still on a blanket, his family all in tears, sobbing as the reality sunk in that they had lost not only their home and their village, they had also lost their father. No words were spoken as this family was overwhelmed with grief.

Not long after I sat with them, I heard that in another corner of the room a baby had been born. Rejoicing drifted through the hall at the good news that he had been born alive, even healthy, under such tragic circumstances. But it didn't take long for people to wonder sadly what kind of life this child would have.

The infant Jerilyn Briones died while we were visiting the refugees. Her beautiful little body was placed in a tiny homemade wooden coffin and taken to the front of the chapel. I knelt with her family and wept with every pore of my body, feeling as if I had lost my own daughter.

Pawns in the war games of others, the people had fled to this church hall to save their lives. They were hoping against hope that they could someday return home. In trembling voices, they told us that not long before our arrival, death squads had visited the hall and threatened to kill them all if they didn't leave within three days and "surrender to the governor." The threat was broadcast on several radio stations.

This was the refugees' punishment for walking to the governor's office to request compensation for their destroyed homes, livestock, and crops. They had also asked that the military disband paramilitary vigilante groups known as CAFGUS (Civilian Armed Forces Geographical Units) in their area, so that they could return home and live safely. A representative of the governor told them they could return home only under the conditions that they submit to military control and that all their men join the CAFGUS.

Unwilling to inflict on others the torture and violence that they had suffered, the people refused these terms. The military responded by sending eight truckloads of soldiers, who surrounded the refugees and drove them at gunpoint back to the seminary. Soon after, the death squads arrived, spewing their terrible threat.

Bishop Antonio Fortich lived at the seminary, in a home that had been both burned and bombed because of his courageous calls for land reform. He said of his persecutors, "I have forgiven all of them." In stunning and characteristic good humor, the bishop appealed to the military: "Please do not bomb my house; it is hard to rebuild. And please do not bomb my residence; it is hard to sleep."

As in Central America, religious leaders working for justice were specifically targeted for repression. Thirty-seven Catholic priests in Negros were on the death squads' hit list, and eleven pastors of United Church of Christ congregations had been murdered. Many religious leaders had received death threats with the message "Your days are numbered," signed "KKK CAFGUS."

Bishop Fortich was nominated that year for the Nobel Peace Prize by the American Friends Service Committee. I was the first Quaker he met after the nomination, and I was on the receiving end of a great deal of love and appreciation from him. He felt deeply the pain of the people in the church hall and wept as we related what we had seen and heard. They had already suffered so much. Where could they go? What could they do?

I shared some of the experiences of Witness for Peace and Peace Brigades International in Central America, and his eyes lit up. I watched the despair that had been written on the bishop's face melt into hope. He said, "That's what we will do. We will invite international religious people to come and be present with these refugees until the threat is over."

We had very little time. The death squads' deadline was looming. It was about six thirty in the morning, and our delegation was scheduled to catch a plane back to Manila at seven thirty. So the bishop hastily dictated a letter inviting international religious people to come to the church hall in Bacolod. Our group flew to Manila, typed up his invitation, and faxed it out to every international we knew who was connected to any kind of religious institution. Many, including several Catholic Maryknoll missioners, were already in the Philippines.

Within thirty hours we had twenty-five international religious people—from the Philippines, the United States, Australia, France, and Switzerland—present in that church hall in Bacolod. Surrounded by the vulnerable refugees, we held a press conference. Addressing the members of the death squads, we said, "We are appealing to you to treat all of these people as your brothers and sisters, and as children of God, and not to carry through on your threats to kill them. We want you to know that we are going to be here with them, and whatever you do to them you will have to do to us. We also want you to know that the eyes of the world are watching what happens here."

I canceled my flight home and stayed with the others in the hall for a few days, until it was clear that the death squads had backed down. I spent a few more days with a family that lived nearby, trying to spread the word about the witness in Bacolod. This was in the early days of computers and e-mail, and the five-year-old and his family helped me figure out how to use it to tell my family I was okay.

In the weeks that followed, the refugees slowly filtered home. They established "zones of peace," as proposed by Bishop Fortich. Some of the international religious witnesses agreed to help organize long-term protection for the victims of the civil war and remained in the area.

I witnessed once again the power of nonviolent presence and solidarity, the profound truth of our common humanity, and the transforming role that Christians and other religious and concerned people can play—usually at fairly low cost to ourselves—to help protect people who are struggling for justice or are caught in war zones. If ever

I doubted, I knew then that we are one human family, we really do have a responsibility to stand up for one another, and we can actually make the world safer for all of us when we act on that belief.

That trip to the Philippines gave me the inspiration for the next years of my journey. I wanted to explore even more deeply nonviolent witness in conflict zones around the world. I decided to start by returning to places that had opened my eyes and changed my life when I was a young man.

Russia

On August 19, 1991, citizens of Moscow woke up to find thousands of tanks on their city streets. Some disgruntled members of the Soviet government were staging a coup to oust President Mikhail Gorbachev. They were hardline Communists opposed to Gorbachev's reforms—particularly *perestroika* (economic, political, and social restructuring) and *glasnost* (openness and détente with the West). I visited right after the coup attempt and heard the extraordinary story.

The coup leaders had instituted a curfew and ordered the military to attack and bomb the "White House," the Russian parliament building. Boris Yeltsin, president of the Russian republic, arrived at the White House and called for a general strike and resistance to the coup. Thousands of ordinary citizens all over Moscow gathered up their courage and risked their lives in this effort to save their society and support its movement away from the dictatorship of the past and toward democracy.

They surrounded the tanks and greeted the soldiers with cakes, cigarettes, and roses. Some knocked on the tanks and shouted questions: "Why are you here?" "Who gave you orders?" "Who are you going to shoot?" Women and girls showered the soldiers with kisses and hugs and pleaded with them not to kill the people.

For three days and nights, between ten thousand and forty thousand people surrounded the White House, much of the time in driving rain. They linked arms, forming a "Living Ring" to nonviolently protect their elected government, erecting a human barrier between the building and the tens of thousands of soldiers and their tanks.

The protesters built barricades out of trolley cars, buses, pieces of metal, and box springs. They weren't naïve enough to believe that these would stop the tanks, but the barricades bought time, enabling them to enter into dialogue with the attacking soldiers about what they were doing and to try to convince them to turn around.

Ten thousand Soviet citizens form a "Living Ring" around the Russian White House (Russian Parliament building) in Moscow to protect elected President Boris Yeltsin from the armed forces under command of the leaders of the coup d'état.

I will never forget my friend Valya, who had a daughter and young grandson. She and her daughter felt that this was a critical moment in history, and this was a cause for which they were willing to die. They took turns at the barricades, so that if one was killed, the other could raise the young boy.

The Russian women kept reminding other protesters not to hurt the soldiers: "They're our sons and brothers." Ruzanna Ilukhina, chair of the Russian Peace Society, said, "We women must be the first to meet the soldiers with words of kindness. We are standing not for struggle, but for peace. Our goal is nonviolence, our 'arms' are words and kindness." She added, "We shouldn't be frightened of anything. Our people are around us. We are defending justice, legality, and freedom."

Many of the soldiers were won over. Troops under the direction of the KGB, the Soviet Secret Police, refused orders to enter Moscow and attack the White House when they learned that they would have to kill hundreds, or even thousands, of civilians to fulfill their mission. Some courageous media people refused to censor their reports, and a few employees of banned newspapers published an underground paper, mimeographed and photocopied for dissemination and posted at bus and subway stops.

Mayor Sobchak of Leningrad (now St. Petersburg) went on TV and encouraged people to gather at the Palace Square the next day. Word spread, and four hundred thousand people showed up. The Russian people had overcome their fear.

The coup leaders had at their disposal almost four million soldiers, thousands of tanks, and sophisticated aircraft and nuclear weapons. The world's second most powerful military machine was overcome by a people armed with courage and conviction, who were no longer willing to cooperate with illegitimate authority or be scared into submission by threats of death or imprisonment. Without the cooperation of the Soviet people—including many in the armed forces, police, and media, as well as ordinary citizens—the coup leaders were powerless. After three days, the attempted coup was defeated.

During my visit that August, members of the Living Ring invited some of us from the United States who were knowledgeable about nonviolence to train them in civilian-based defense. They wanted to be even better prepared to defend their society nonviolently against future coup attempts. Under the sponsorship of Nonviolence International, we returned in mid-November.

Four hundred Russians participated in the workshops we organized. We honored our hosts' request to lead trainings in nonviolent defense, but we felt we had a great deal to learn from them as well. Many positive developments followed.

The group Golubka—"Peace Dove"—organized an international conference on nonviolence on the first anniversary of the coup attempt. Some Russians began working to get conscientious objector legislation passed. Others were cooperating with the Mujahideen—their former enemies in Afghanistan—to find ways to end that senseless war, which was killing a hundred people every day.

The coup attempt and the people's Living Ring were a major contributing factor to the destabilization and eventual dissolution of the Soviet Union on Christmas Day, 1991. The Berlin Wall had already come down in November 1989, and reforms and liberalization were transforming the nations of the formerly pro-Soviet Eastern Bloc.

That moment provided an unprecedented opportunity to drastically cut back the Soviet and U.S. military establishments and convert both nations into peacetime societies committed to meeting the needs of their citizens. Both were in economic distress, struggling under the stranglehold of massive, resource-draining military machines. Conditions were particularly grim in Russia.

In the three weeks that I was there in November and December 1991, I hardly met a Russian who had eaten what Americans would consider a full meal. Long lines created waits of up to eleven hours for staples such as bread, eggs, meat, fish, and milk. Shelves in the grocery stores I visited were 95 percent empty. The official word was that Moscow had only a three-day supply of food.

Hundreds of thousands of people were losing their jobs in the crumbling Soviet society. Fuel shortages were expected that winter—in a country where temperatures could reach forty degrees below zero Fahrenheit. High inflation had reduced the value of a typical Russian salary to the equivalent of $2.50 to $7.50 per month.

I was involved in efforts to send financial support for food and medicine to Russia, and I encouraged "sister city" and "sister church" partnerships between the United States and Russia. I also asked people in the United States to put pressure on their legislators to follow Russia's example and halt further nuclear weapons development, and to call for massive cuts in the U.S. military budget.

Big changes on the world's political scene were mirrored in my personal desire to shift my vocational energy. After eighteen good years working with the American Friends Service Committee, budget cuts and my hope to channel more energy toward international peacemaking spurred a change.

In 1993, I became the executive director of Peaceworkers, a community of activists, primarily in the San Francisco Bay Area, whose mission is to strengthen and promote nonviolent movements for peace and justice in the United States and around the world. Supported entirely by donations, I wrote articles, spoke at conferences, and led workshops to build momentum for Peaceworkers.

Unfortunately, my hope that the United States and Russia would view the end of the Cold War as a perfect moment to convert both our societies to peacetime economies was quickly dashed. Our nation chose instead to show its muscle as the only remaining superpower and escalate its obscenely massive investments in war-making. And, tragically, the commitment to military dominance was matched by an equally fervent pursuit of political and economic domination around the globe.

On January 1, 1994, the North American Free Trade Agreement (NAFTA) between the United States, Canada, and Mexico went into effect. Supporters, including many of the world's largest corporations, claimed it would create jobs and raise standards of living. Opponents, which included many labor, religious, and environmental groups, saw

NAFTA as a vehicle for outsourcing U.S. jobs, undermining democratic control of domestic policy making, raising corporate profits, and
threatening health, environmental, and food safety standards. As we
now know, this disastrous experiment has wreaked havoc on millions
of lives here and in Mexico and Canada.

Mexico

The same day that NAFTA took effect, the Zapatistas launched their
uprising in Chiapas, Mexico. Viewing NAFTA as the start of major
globalization and the beginning of the end of their indigenous way
of life, they demanded a better life for peasants, self-determination,
and fair elections. This revolutionary group was in a standoff with the
Mexican military when Samuel Ruiz, the Catholic bishop in Chiapas
and the primary mediator between the government and the Zapatistas,
appealed to internationals to come and be a peaceful and protective
presence.

Inspired by Ruiz's call, Medea Benjamin of Global Exchange, Phil
McManus of the Fellowship of Reconciliation, and I organized a delegation of leaders from religious communities around the United States.
We spent ten days in Chiapas. The poverty and violence that I had witnessed a decade before had only intensified.

Our delegation went to Chiapas to observe and report the truth,
encourage dialogue between the factions, support a negotiated settlement, discourage human rights abuses on all sides, and accompany those working for a peace process. Observing how entrenched
the challenges were, we launched a new organization called SIPAZ
(International Service for Peace), which has maintained an international nonviolent presence in Chiapas ever since.

I returned again to Chiapas with another delegation in February
1995. We were in the town of San Cristóbal de las Casas when word came
that Mexican President Ernesto Zedillo was sending the military into
the surrounding Lacandon jungle to capture five Zapatista leaders. We
watched, horrified, as thousands of soldiers and hundreds of machine
gun-mounted armored personnel carriers rolled into villages all across
Chiapas to set up staging areas for their attacks.

Fear was rampant in Chiapas, and so was suspicion that the U.S.
government was putting pressure on Mexico to resolve the Zapatista
problem quickly. U.S. military attachés had been sighted, and Chase
Manhattan Bank had reportedly circulated a memo calling for more
aggressive military actions by the Mexican government to "eliminate

the Zapatistas." As a sign of support, the United States extended a $51 billion line of credit to the Mexican government.

Some of our group went to the office of CONPAZ, the nongovernmental coordinating committee for humanitarian aid in Chiapas, where they escorted the staff out past special police armed with machine guns and plainclothes police with pistols, who had arrived in unmarked cars. Others went to the Catholic chancery in San Cristóbal, which housed the diocesan human rights office. And still others went to the home of Amado Avendaño Figueroa, head of the transitional government in rebellion and recently installed as governor of Chiapas by the Zapatistas, who claimed that the PRI (Institutional Revolutionary Party) had stolen the gubernatorial election.

A Catholic priest, Padre Joel from Simojovel, a village two hours away, wanted to return to be present with his people during the escalating military occupation. Marlene Bertke, a Benedictine sister from Erie, Pennsylvania, and I volunteered to accompany him.

Marlene had been with the group that went to the chancery, and while there she had handed Bishop Ruiz a brochure about the upcoming national assembly of Pax Christi, the Catholic peace organization. When she asked the bishop if he was still planning to be the keynote speaker, he replied, "If I am alive and can leave the country, I will be there."

Those words were on both our minds when Marlene and I met the priest. He was a beautiful, dedicated man with a deep love for his people. He lived in Simojovel but circulated among many other small communities, visiting each once every three months or so. He had recently been detained for fifty days by police because of his work for justice. He knew that it could happen again at any time.

The military had occupied his village two months before, arriving just before Christmas as he and his congregation's children were walking out of the church. They were keeping the annual ritual of *La Posada*, a pilgrimage from house to house seeking a place for the Christ child to be born. The soldiers stepped back as the procession of singing children passed.

Padre Joel told us he felt fear about returning to his village. But he wanted to be with his people as the tanks and soldiers were converging again. We agreed to leave at six o'clock the next morning.

That evening, Marlene and I talked about which one of us would sit next to the priest in the front seat of the pickup truck, recognizing that whoever sat there was the more likely to get shot. We agreed that

I would take that seat, and I brought along a couple of extra T-shirts to use to help stop blood flow if needed. We left contact information and instructions for one of our group to get in touch with family members if we got killed.

We were nervous as we started out early the next morning. It did nothing to reassure us when the priest said, "My life is life only if I am willing to hand it over." I hoped to be able to claim that kind of courage and faith.

As we approached the first military checkpoint, my heart was pounding and I took a deep breath as Marlene dangled her rosary out the window, believing that the soldiers were likely Catholic and would honor it. We had contingency plans in place: if Marlene and I were stopped, the priest would return with us to San Cristóbal; if he was arrested, we would demand to be taken with him to jail.

Thankfully, we were waved through without any trouble. The trip turned out to be an uneventful four-hour drive, a long Spanish lesson for Marlene and me—once Padre Joel turned off the radio—with a wonderfully devoted man of faith and compassion. Marlene and I rode a bus back to San Cristóbal later that day.

The next evening, when our group went to our usual restaurant for dinner, the owner handed us a flyer. He told us that copies had been distributed widely in the city and warned us to be careful. The message of the flyer was essentially, "Get rid of the foreigners. Get rid of those collaborating with them." It was a little hard to enjoy our meal that night.

A few positive signs appeared while we were there. On February 14, President Zedillo called for the Mexican army to halt all offensive military operations in Chiapas. Chiapas's Governor Robledo offered to resign. For the moment, at least, a few steps had been taken back from the brink.

I spent another month with SIPAZ in Chiapas in 1996, and then an additional week on the edge of an indigenous settlement that sympathized with the Zapatistas. Its members were working to build a self-reliant community beyond the grasp of NAFTA. A Mexican human rights organization was setting up "peace houses," where international teams lived in the threatened communities in an effort to discourage military attacks on the villages.

Other organizations committed to a peaceful resolution in Chiapas joined Peaceworkers in sustaining the work of SIPAZ. Eventually we expanded the project to include other parts of Mexico, including Oaxaca and Guerrero.

A campaign of peaceful civil resistance was launched in the neighboring state of Tabasco, also with support from Peaceworkers. As in Chiapas, the PRI had stolen the 1994 election for governor—from Andrés Manuel López Obrador, the progressive candidate. Thousands of people marched more than six hundred miles to Mexico City to protest.

A truck loaded with fourteen boxes of original documents appeared in the square. They were evidence that the PRI had spent $70 million on the election. An amount more than Bill Clinton had spent that year in the entire United States on his presidential campaign, this came to $250 per vote in a state with two million inhabitants—illegal under the Mexican constitution and more than likely financed from illegal drug sales.

The other part of the Tabasco resistance campaign included protests at Pemex Oil installations. These had contaminated the lands, lakes, and lagoons—and destroyed the lives and livelihoods—of thousands of farmers and fishermen throughout the region. As I visited former fishing areas totally contaminated with oil, and homes and farms of *campesinos* with oil pipelines through their front yards and across their fields—often leaking and sometimes even exploding—my heart wept.

Peaceworkers helped get the word out in the United States about the plight of the Mexican people who were victims of our oil addiction. We supported Rafael Landerreche, a Mexican with Servicio Paz y Justicia (Service for Peace and Justice), who helped to organize the nonviolent campaign in Tabasco. Demanding that Pemex stop drilling oil wells until the company compensated those who had suffered losses, hundreds of people blockaded the oil installations in twelve-hour shifts around the clock. Their strategies included a march of thirty thousand people, hunger strikes, and filling the jails to expose the destruction of their communities.

I was heartened that Peaceworkers was able to support such courageous campaigns in many corners of the globe. That year, I knew I needed to return to one more place that held many warm and profound memories for me. Sadly, it was now known as "the former Yugoslavia."

CHAPTER 12

A Force for Peace: Creating a Nonviolent Army

In the 1990s, terrible violence broke out among many Serbs, Croats, and Muslims in Yugoslavia fueled by the nationalist leaders of Serbia, Croatia and Bosnia. The news of this tragedy overtaking what used to be known as the nation of Yugoslavia was heartbreaking to me. I couldn't fathom how people who had lived in harmony for so long, who had welcomed me so warmly into their hearts and homes, could be reduced to such barbarity and suffering.

After the death of Yugoslavia's President Tito in 1980, and the dissolution of the Soviet Union and the Eastern Bloc a few years later, the United States no longer thought it necessary or important to support Yugoslavia as a bulwark against Russian Communism. With U.S. pressure, the World Bank demanded payback of loans. The Yugoslav government was forced to discontinue its broad economic and social benefits, which had created shared prosperity and security for the people of Yugoslavia.

People began fighting over the crumbs. The era of scarcity created fertile ground for nationalist leaders to emerge in the various republics that were part of Yugoslavia, whipping up enmity and fanning the flames of ethnic strife. I agonized about the conflict and began strategizing with Kathy Kelly of Voices in the Wilderness, who was organizing an international nonviolent presence in Bosnia.

During the summer of 1996, I spent two months in Bosnia-Herzegovina, Serbia, and Croatia with a Fellowship of Reconciliation peace delegation. We arrived just after the Serb militia's shelling of Sarajevo had ended, in the aftermath of the civil war that had devastated the region. We lived with families, getting to know the people and the situations they were enduring.

The change from my visit as a college student was shocking. Still carrying with gratitude my warm memories of that unforgettable summer, I was stunned to witness the unspeakable horror that had overtaken this place that had elicited such deep affection in me. Bosnia felt like one massive cemetery, with thousands of fresh graves everywhere. More than a quarter million people had been killed in the ethnic strife that had overwhelmed this once peaceful land.

The horrific strategy of the Serb forces had included massive rape, torture, plunder, expulsion, and murder. In Srebrenica alone, they had massacred more than 8,300 Muslims and expelled another twenty-five to thirty thousand the year before. Throughout the region, four million people had fled their homes getting away from the violence which was being committed by all sides and thousands of these homes had been destroyed. The economies of these now separate nations were in ruins, with few jobs available and travel very limited.

The terror and tension of such a violent period will likely take generations to heal. I was heartened to see a few glimmers of hope amid the deep despair. A few brave souls were crossing the lines drawn between nations and hearts, opening themselves and their communities to the possibility of reconciliation and peace.

The Gornji Vakuf Reconstruction Project, supported by the UN Development Program, the Austrian government, and several Quaker and other private groups, was bringing international volunteers from all over the world to rebuild this town on the front lines, which had been 80 percent destroyed during the war. The project had opened a women's center and a youth center, where people from both sides of the conflict were able to meet one another and share their experiences. Sixteen men—eight from each side—were learning carpentry and construction skills and were together rebuilding destroyed homes, as they also rebuilt trust.

In Mostar, which also had been terribly devastated during the conflict, I attended a powerful play put on by youth from both sides, a silent performance that portrayed the horror of their experiences during the war. In this city where a historic five-hundred-year-old bridge, or *most*, had been destroyed, young people from across Europe had developed a youth center called Mladi Most, or "Young Bridge," where youth from both sides could gather, do photography, play sports, and rebuild a sense of community.

In Sarajevo, I encountered a very courageous Serbian man named Bozidar (Gayo) Sekulic. He was developing a Citizens Alternative

Parliament, to represent the people of all parts of Bosnia who were committed to creating a democratic, nonnationalistic, and peaceful future, rather than allowing their fate to be determined by the ruling nationalistic political parties. In Belgrade I met the Women in Black, who had been bravely demonstrating every week for more than four years against the militarism and nationalism of the Serbian government.

I spent time with very talented journalists who worked with WIN (Weekly Independent News). They were trying to start an independent television station in Serbia, to counter the lies, propaganda, and nationalism of President Slobodan Milosevic's brutal regime. The cost of setting up the station and funding it for a year of operation was $3 million—a daunting sum, but less than the cost of one military tank, of which there were many hundreds in Serbia and Bosnia.

I was grateful to meet and hear the inspiring stories of some of the more than one hundred thousand courageous young men who had left Serbia and gone underground rather than fight what they considered an unjust imperialistic war. And I was equally moved by the volunteers with Balkan Peace Teams. They were accompanying local peace and human rights activists throughout the former Yugoslavia, supporting their initiatives for democratic and multiethnic communities.

When the peace delegation headed back home, I decided to stay and go on to Kosovo. I had heard that there was a strong nonviolent resistance movement there. Kosovo was a particularly painful place, but what I witnessed there was amazing and inspiring.

Although 90 percent of Kosovo's population was Albanian by nationality, all political power and most economic power was held by the less than 10 percent who were Serbs. Many Albanians in Kosovo, known as Kosovars, described their society as "worse than apartheid." They expressed their fear that Kosovo was a time bomb waiting to go off.

The Albanian language had been outlawed in Kosovo. Eighty percent of Kosovars who had worked in government, business, the media, and human services were fired in 1990 and remained unemployed. Schools, universities, and hospitals were closed to Kosovars, who were regular targets of gross human rights violations by the Serbs, including beatings, torture, and killings. But, again, I had the privilege of seeing extraordinary signs of hope.

The nonviolent movement in Kosovo had begun in 1989 with thousands of miners marching from the lead mines to Pristina, the capital, to protest their working conditions and exploitation. Hundreds went on a hunger strike for more than a week, almost a mile underground, in temperatures that reached 120 degrees Fahrenheit. The Association of Independent Trade Unions called on Kosovars to participate in a general strike for half an hour every day, demanding a return to autonomy and respect for their rights as citizens.

People lit candles in their windows at night as a symbol of their determination to be free and jangled keys at demonstrations, chanting, "We hold the keys to unlock our prison." After a particularly violent response by Serb police, hundreds of thousands of Kosovars participated in a creative "Funeral for Violence," in which they carried a coffin labeled "Violence" to a cemetery and ritually buried it.

While I was there, I got to know Adem Demaci, considered the "Nelson Mandela of Kosovo." He had spent twenty-eight years in prison for speaking out against the unjust treatment of the Albanian majority. An ardent proponent of nonviolent struggle for freedom and justice for the two million Kosovars, he served as president of the Council for the Defense of Human Rights in Kosovo.

The Kosovar Albanians were establishing a complete alternative society. They formed a parallel government to represent their needs and a tax system to fund a university and alternative schools that operated out of private homes. Claiming the name of a famously compassionate native daughter, they set up a network of "Mother Theresa medical centers," where doctors and nurses donated their services. The Kosovars established farmers' markets and launched several alternative periodicals to spread news and build their movement.

The Serb crackdown was swift and brutal. Serb police officers raided the alternative clinics, seizing medicine, and arrested schoolteachers. Some Serb citizens and police stole food from the markets. Still, most Kosovars persisted in their nonviolent resistance and their support of one another through their alternative network.

The Post Pessimists were an energetic group of Albanian and Serbian youth who were meeting together to work toward a peaceful, just, and democratic future. The Kosovo Peace Group had a similar aim, creating dialogue between individuals from the two ethnic groups. But increasing pressure was being put on Serbs in both groups to end their association with Albanian Kosovars.

From 1996 to 1998, I focused a lot of my energy on trying to bring the nonviolent movement in Kosovo to the attention of the world and drum up support for it. Kosovars from all sectors pleaded for international people to come and be present to make it safer for them to escalate their nonviolent struggle. They asked for pressure to be put on

Twenty thousand Kosovar students march nonviolently toward their former university Pristina, Kosovo, demanding the right to study there (September 1997). [Photo: Ilaz Bylykbashi]

the Serbian government to stop its repression of the majority population, just as international sanctions had successfully pressured the apartheid regime in South Africa. "If there is not change soon," many told me, "this situation will explode."

Recognizing the extreme urgency, I traveled around Europe speaking and writing articles, and then did the same in the United States. I shared my experiences of Kosovo, the urgency and volatility of the situation, and the Kosovars' impassioned call for an international nonviolent presence. A lot of people looked perplexed and responded with, "Where is Kosovo?"

It was an unfamiliar name, and people were busy and preoccupied with other concerns. Kosovo simply wasn't a priority. I believe that the world passed up an extraordinary opportunity to support a bold and creative nonviolent movement and a peaceful resolution of that conflict.

I was in Kosovo again in 1997. Seventy percent of Kosovars were under thirty years old. On September 1, twenty thousand students—who had to attend classes in living rooms, kitchens, garages, and mosques—staged a march to the university that had once been open to everyone. They invited me to accompany them.

All the students wore white shirts, with flowers in their lapels. They marched quietly and peacefully toward the university they were banned from attending. About a mile down the road, and still a great distance from their destination, they came to a line of Serbian police who were blocking their way. The marchers stopped and stood in total silence, facing the armed police. It was the most disciplined large nonviolent action I have ever witnessed.

After a tension-filled ten minutes, the police burst into action, firing teargas to disperse the marchers and riding their horses roughly into the crowd. The students ran in all directions, coughing, choking, trying to escape. Some were hurt, and many were in shock from the effects of the teargas and the violence of the police. Spirits were very heavy in the aftermath.

I spent the following month strategizing with the students, who were deeply committed to continuing their nonviolent struggle despite the assaults. I shared with them the history of nonviolent movements. I gave them books on nonviolence, including Gene Sharp's *From Dictatorship to Democracy* and the encyclopedia of nonviolent action, *Protest, Power and Change.* I led nonviolence trainings, emphasizing the need to maintain a nonviolent discipline even in the face of police repression.

Every month the students tried again to march to their former university—only to face police roadblocks and brutality each time. After I left Kosovo, we kept in communication by e-mail and continued our discussions about strategy. They invited me back in the spring of 1998. I recruited four young American students to go with me to support the courageous Kosovars in their nonviolent resistance struggle.

The Serbian regime's reign of terror in Kosovo had escalated. In early March, Serbian police had killed eighty villagers in the Drenica region. We watched as more than one hundred thousand Kosovars—students, young families with babies, and older, feebler folks, some of whom were on crutches—marched in protest through the streets of Pristina. They were armed with nothing more than flowers, candles, and pictures of Mother Theresa—against Serbian machine guns and riot gear. They ended their march at the Catholic church with an interfaith memorial service for the victims.

The next day we accompanied twenty thousand women who attempted to march the thirty miles from Pristina to Drenica, carrying loaves of bread to villagers who had fled their homes when the massacre took place. Serbian police turned them back and refused to allow any food or medicine to get through. Even personnel from the International Red Cross received death threats for trying to help the refugees.

The American students and I led a nonviolence training with a group of about eight hundred people crowded into a large auditorium. The day after the training, all five of us were arrested, under orders of President Milosevic. We were sentenced to ten days in jail.

The jail time was not a pleasant experience. The food was terrible, and the cramped cells reeked of cigarette smoke. The weather outside was frigid and snowy, and the prison had no heat, so we wore all the clothes we had just to keep from freezing. The prison authorities had shaved our heads. We had one hat between the four of us men, which we passed back and forth every hour or so, trying to share the warmth. The one woman in our group was in a different jail and fortunately got to keep her hair.

We were extremely uncomfortable, but the Kosovars faced far worse punishment for their protests against the Serb repression. One of our group witnessed a man getting his hands smashed because he had asked permission to use the telephone. We saw evidence that our fellow inmates were being physically abused by our captors.

A hundred thousand Kosovars demonstrating for justice every day for many weeks never made the international news, but five Americans in jail hit the front pages all around the world! We didn't realize when we were sitting behind bars how much attention we were getting, but apparently the Serbian authorities were uncomfortable with the publicity and decided to expel us from their country. They released us after three days and dumped us at the Macedonian border, stamping our passports with a warning that we were banned from returning for ten years.

After our release, we did what we could to try to put the real story into the press, alerting the world about the apartheid system in Kosovo. The intergovernmental Kosovo Verification Mission eventually established a presence and began monitoring the situation and helping to limit the violence. But the nonviolent movement continued to be largely ignored by the world.

In contrast, once some frustrated Kosovars decided that nonviolence wasn't getting them anywhere and formed the guerilla Kosovo Liberation Front, the CIA and the U.S. military stepped in to support their armed struggle. When the situation exploded as many of us had predicted, President Clinton went on national television, declaring that ethnic cleansing was taking place in Kosovo. He said essentially that the United States had two alternatives—to look the other way and do nothing, or to go in and start bombing. The Kosovo Verification

Mission was withdrawn, and the bombs began dropping on March 24, 1999. This was dubbed "humanitarian intervention" which those of us who had worked with the nonviolent movement in Kosovo totally rejected. Bombing, from our perspective, can never be considered humanitarian.

Those of us who had been in Kosovo knew that there was a third alternative: to support the nonviolent movement there with our bodies and our resources. At the time of Clinton's statement and the launching of the NATO (North American Treaty Organization) bombing campaigns, I was in The Hague, in the Netherlands, with nine thousand other peace activists from all over the world. A century after the first Hague Appeal for Peace, we had come together from 130 different nations to explore how we could put an end to war.

I was leading a five-hour workshop every day on the situation in Kosovo. One afternoon, during a panel discussion, I laid out my vision for an "international nonviolent peace army." Standing against the back wall of the packed room, listening in stunned amazement, was Mel Duncan, an organizer from St. Paul, Minnesota. Mel had arrived at the conference hoping to drum up support for the same idea, which had come to him during a retreat at Plum Village, the meditation center founded in southern France by Vietnamese Buddhist monk and peace activist Thich Nhat Hanh.

Mel was feeling rather overwhelmed by the crowd at the conference—twice what had been expected. Every venue was jammed. He had called his wife, Georgia, the day before and told her, "I can't organize here. I could stand on a chair and, even if I shouted, I'd get lost in the background noise." She very wisely counseled, "Well then, be quiet and listen."

Mel followed her advice and showed up at the panel discussion the next day. When it was over, he pushed his way through the crowd toward me. He told me that if I was serious about what I had said, he was ready to sign up and collaborate to formulate a plan. Thus was hatched the Nonviolent Peaceforce.

It was not a new idea. Before Mahatma Gandhi's assassination in 1948, he was building a *shanti sena*, or "peace army." We were also inspired by the work of Christian Peacemaker Teams, Voices in the Wilderness, Balkan Peace Teams, and other groups that had been involved for years in similar work. My experiences with Peace Brigades International in Guatemala, Witness for Peace in Nicaragua, the ecumenical delegation to the Philippines and elsewhere, had convinced

With Mel Duncan, as cofounders of the Nonviolent Peaceforce (2001).

me of the protective power of peaceful presence. We hoped through the Nonviolent Peaceforce to send peacekeepers into conflict situations by the hundreds instead of by the handfuls and hopefully help the world learn that there is a better alternative than violence and armed intervention.

The struggle in Kosovo had given birth to this vision that I had been pondering for quite some time. That dire situation provided strong motivation to get the Nonviolent Peaceforce off the ground. I remain convinced that, had the international community rallied around the nonviolent movement there, a peaceful resolution could have been reached and a costly military conflict averted—costly in the loss of lives, in the billions of dollars expended, and in the escalated ethnic hatred and mistrust that will be the legacy of Kosovo for years to come.

The NATO bombing of Kosovo and Serbia continued for three months, with many civilian casualties, causing Serbs to rally more fervently around their dictator. Serb security forces eventually withdrew from Kosovo, but Milosevic remained in power. Although the International Court of Justice in The Hague indicted him for genocide and crimes against humanity, his stranglehold grip on what was left of the former Yugoslavia held for many months.

What NATO firepower couldn't accomplish, a determined group of twelve nonviolent student activists eventually did. They launched the youth movement Otpor! (Resistance). Organizing marches aimed at overthrowing Milosevic, they grew a movement that eventually included more than seventy thousand supporters. Almost two thousand were arrested in a massive crackdown, many of them beaten in police custody.

The symbol of their movement, a clenched fist, appeared all over the former Yugoslavia, stenciled by the intrepid and persistent students. Otpor! was credited with playing a key role in the overthrow of Milosevic on October 5, 2000. The fallen dictator ultimately surrendered to security forces on March 31, 2001, after an armed standoff at his fortified villa in Belgrade, and died in a jail cell in The Hague five years later.

But in March 1999, Kosovo was still embroiled in violence and very much on our minds at the Hague peace conference. Mel Duncan and I shared our hope with everyone who would listen, and several attendees committed themselves to working with us toward building a global Nonviolent Peaceforce.

Those of us who were part of its founding wanted to create a trained nonviolent army that would respond to invitations from local peacemakers in areas of violence and war around the globe. This corps of trained civilians would be available to accompany threatened activists and communities, protect human rights, work with local groups to prevent violence, summon the attention of the international community for peaceful intervention, and create space for peaceful resolution of conflicts.

We hoped to have our first group "non-combat-ready" by 2003. We were aiming for an initial contingent of two hundred active participants, four hundred reservists, and five hundred supporters of an emergency response network, committed to receive urgent-action alerts and send e-mails, make phone calls, and urge the press to turn the spotlight on specific conflicts.

We wanted to be international eyes, ears, and conscience. Our mission was to help save the lives of people being targeted because of their work for justice and peace, and to protect civilian communities that so often bear the brunt of violence in war zones. We hoped that never again would the world ignore those who are struggling for justice nonviolently.

I spent the next couple years searching out individuals and organizations that resonated with the idea of a Nonviolent Peaceforce. I met with peacemakers and human rights workers around the United States and in various parts of Asia (India, Japan, Indonesia, the Philippines, Thailand, Cambodia, and South Korea); Europe (Germany, Sweden,

Great Britain, the Netherlands, Italy, Belgium, and Switzerland); and Latin America (Brazil, Argentina, Venezuela, Ecuador, Mexico, Guatemala, El Salvador, and Costa Rica). Fortunately, Servicio Paz y Justicia was convening an international gathering in Uruguay, so Phil McManus, who accompanied me, and I got to meet activists from all over Latin America in Montevideo, Uruguay. A colleague, David Grant, traveled throughout Africa and the Middle East.

We built on groundwork that had been laid in May 1995, when a couple dozen of these peace practitioners had converged for a meeting in Sweden. Their aim was to develop a framework for communication and support. This was a critical step toward making concrete the global peace force, an idea that had surfaced many times through the years.

We learned a great deal during our exploratory visits. First, we learned that creative and courageous peacemakers and human rights defenders are working in the most violent places in the world—and more often than not, this work is being led by women. Second, we learned that no one can make peace for someone else; peacemaking is the job of local people. But specially trained internationals can support these efforts and provide much-needed nonviolent protection, undermining isolation and bringing the world's attention to such local efforts.

As we traveled, we asked two questions: 1) If there was a global Nonviolent Peaceforce, would this be helpful to your part of the world and to your work? and 2) Would you like to work with others to help create the Nonviolent Peaceforce? The answers were overwhelmingly "Yes, yes!" We secured more than three hundred individual endorsements, including from eight Nobel Peace laureates.

We researched more deeply many of these efforts and produced a three-hundred-page feasibility study covering what had worked, what hadn't worked, and what hadn't yet been tried. We wanted to build on previous successes and expand the effort to a scale that we hoped would get the attention of governments, the United Nations, and people around the world interested in an alternative to armed intervention and in helping to end war.

By this time we had received informal invitations from ten conflict areas: Sri Lanka, Palestine/Israel, Burma, Tibet, Korea, the Philippines, Guatemala, Colombia, Zimbabwe, and Nigeria. An interim steering committee analyzed each invitation based on criteria developed from the feasibility study and narrowed the applicants to three. We then sent exploratory teams to each of those areas: Guatemala, Palestine/Israel, and Sri Lanka.

In December 2002, we brought together 130 activists from forty-seven countries and seventy peacemaking organizations for our founding conference outside Delhi, India. There we officially launched the Nonviolent Peaceforce and created an international steering committee as the governing body. The exploratory teams brought their reports to the convening event in India, where delegates discussed, debated, and then chose Sri Lanka as the site of our pilot project.

The Nonviolent Peaceforce (NP) was launched in April 2003 with an eleven-member team in Sri Lanka, a small, lush island southeast of India, thick with tea plantations and violence. The civil war between the Sri Lankan military and the Tamil Tigers, who were fighting for an independent state for the Tamil minority, had claimed sixty-five thousand lives. Assassinations and disappearances of those working for change were common.

In the 1990s, Baddegama Samitha, a Buddhist monk and member of Sri Lanka's parliament, had received death threats because he had hidden young Tamil men being pursued by the government. Members of Peace Brigades International accompanied him whenever he had to travel to the capital city of Colombo. They "really safeguarded my life during that dark period of our history," Samitha said. "They saved my life, I would say . . . I warmly welcome the Nonviolent Peaceforce because we need international peace activists to help defuse our situation."

Though we had been warned by people from the UN and other international agencies to stay out of the area because it was too dangerous, we went to Vakery, a small town where armed confrontation seemed inevitable. Together with local community leaders, we negotiated so that civilians could take shelter in the town's school and church if fighting broke out. On Good Friday the armed conflict erupted, and thousands of people had to flee their homes. They found sanctuary in that school and church.

Our second deployment was to the Philippines in 2007. Before the arrival of the NP, the Philippine government sometimes responded to threats, or rumors of threats, from the Muslim community in Mindanao with violence. People in Mindanao had been found decapitated and local communities had been bombed. The tension threatened to escalate into all-out war, and one hundred thousand people were preparing to flee their homes.

The NP was invited in by both sides of the conflict. I met with the vice president of the Philippine government and the vice chair of the guerilla Moro Islamic Liberation Front (MILF). Both of them wanted

During the war in Sri Lanka, both Tamil and Sinhalese engage in nonviolent protest accompanied by the Nonviolent Peaceforce (2005). [Nonviolent Peaceforce photo archive]

to keep the violence from escalating out of control and work toward a negotiated political settlement of their longstanding differences.

The NP team in Mindanao, which continues its work, has been able to check rumors, get accurate information to both sides, and deter violence. Its presence has enabled civilians caught in the middle to remain in their homes. Serving as a liaison between communities, government officials, and humanitarian service providers, the NP works with local partners to provide safety and security for noncombatants and to strengthen human rights monitoring.

In partnership with UNICEF, Nonviolent Peaceforce launched a program in the Philippines regarding the rights and safety of children. In December 2009, both the Philippine government and the MILF invited NP to serve on the UN's International Monitoring Team for a ceasefire brokered by the Malaysians, specifically to monitor civilian protection. NP continues in this role, with nine teams deployed around the country, making daily reports to the major parties to the conflict and helping to hold the peace.

NP was invited to southern Sudan in 2009 to help prevent violence, protect civilians, and promote stability in the period leading up to the referendum for independence in January 2011. NP unarmed civilian peacekeeping teams have continued in the new nation of South Sudan, helping to stabilize that very fragile new country. They've offered protection in local conflicts—for example, responding to tribal violence through relationship building, regular travel between communities, and providing protective accompaniment.

NP's work in the Yida refugee camp involves communicating and cooperating with international humanitarian agencies such as UNHCR, and nonstate armed actors to protect the civilian population, prevent gender-based violence, increase safety and security, and develop protection trainings.

Currently NP lives and works in several internally displaced people (IDP) camps, identifying and mitigating protection concerns for the IDPs, working closely and delicately with women and children, young men and chiefs, civilians and potential combatants. Women's Security Teams have been formed in several locations, allowing IDP women's voices and concerns to be heard and acted upon for the first time.

We now have NP support groups in forty countries. We estimated that it would cost $1.7 million to sustain the Nonviolent Peaceforce for the first year. That seemed staggeringly daunting when we began, but we reminded ourselves that that amount is less than the U.S. military spends every two minutes.

We've received donations from several religious organizations and grants from a few foundations. Individual contributions have ranged from a pledge of six cents to a check for $40,000 from a teacher who cashed in his entire retirement fund to support us. The Hartsough-Duncan Founders Circle, created by friends to honor Mel and me, has raised several million dollars.

Our commitment is to pay our workers rather than expect them to be volunteers. That enables people of all classes, and from economically marginal parts of the world, to participate. The policy of paying peacekeepers has been particularly critical for team members from Africa and Asia, where an NP worker remains a breadwinner with a reliable source of income and can continue to support a family.

While "in-country," NP workers live as the people around them do: very simply. They can choose to send their pay back to their families, have it deposited in a bank account, or receive it at the end of their two-year term of service. One worker from Kenya was able to build a home for his family when he returned with his earnings.

A paid income enables NP peacekeepers to remain for multiple years, with some now serving for more than six years and other veterans returning after a respite. Most NP workers stay in the same place for an entire two-year term, but some move around. A Pakistani who served in Sri Lanka now leads the work in Mindanao, and three of NP's local staff from Sri Lanka offer leadership in South Sudan.

The criteria and training are rigorous. We require participants to have exhibited a clear commitment to nonviolence. We expect them to have had some cross-cultural experience, so that they will not be scared off by dire poverty or extreme violence. We conduct a four-week training in how to be an effective peace team member, and in addition we provide language training if needed.

Early on in the effort, we had talked with some people at the United Nations about the peace force. Many of them told us they thought it was a great idea. One added this qualifier: "Show us it can work for eight to ten years, and we'll get behind it and take it on."

Increasingly, UN agencies are paying attention and supporting our work.

Rolf Carriere, a Dutchman with whom we connected in South Africa at the Parliament of World Religions, is a retired country director with UNICEF who served in many Asian nations. He has been opening many doors for the Nonviolent Peaceforce. Through his influence, UNICEF has been very supportive of our work, especially in protecting children.

Nonviolent Peaceforce currently has eight contracts with five UN agencies. NP's participation in the international monitoring effort for the ceasefire in the Philippines led, very significantly, to our conducting a nonviolence training at the academy where the United Nations trains its diplomats. In 2012, high-level briefings on unarmed civilian peacekeeping were held at the UN in New York and Geneva.

Even some friendly governments are paying attention now. Nonviolent Peaceforce recently received a grant of five million euros from the European Union to expand our work in the Philippines, and an additional million euros from the Belgian government to extend NP's work into additional communities in South Sudan. The Netherlands, Sweden, Norway, Spain, the United Kingdom, Canada, Australia, and France have also contributed generously. NP has a policy of accepting no more than 10 percent of its budget from the U.S. government. No problem there—NP has only received minimal funding from the U.S. Institute of Peace for the feasibility study at the beginning.

The work has expanded so that NP's annual costs are now about $8 million. This figure is even more daunting than the one with which we began. But it is still less than what the world's nations collectively spend on war and military endeavors every four minutes.

I consider the people I've met around the world who have had key roles in launching and sustaining the Nonviolent Peaceforce part of my community and my family. We are bound together in an exciting project. From the beginning, we've been committed to having both our governing board and our peace teams composed of members that are half from the global South and half from the North.

We did not want this effort to be U.S.-dominated or -controlled, and Mel Duncan and I set out early on to work ourselves out of our jobs. I do best launching new efforts, and I don't enjoy or excel at administration. So I was happy to step back after a few years and focus my time and energy again on Peaceworkers, which we consider the midwife of the Nonviolent Peaceforce.

The work of NP continues. As I write this, NP has been invited to send peace teams to Burma and has found the funding to support them. I'm heartened by the words of anthropologist and UN Messenger of Peace Jane Goodall about our effort: "I carry a photo of the [Nonviolent Peaceforce] team of brave men and women in my briefcase to remind myself that, however terrible things seem, there is a powerful source for good in a world gone mad. . . . In the end, the indomitable human spirit will prevail."

CHAPTER 13

Taking the Long View: Active Nonviolence in Palestine and Averting War with Iran

An "apartheid wall" surrounds and separates the West Bank, Gaza, and East Jerusalem from their Israeli neighbors. Electrified chain-link fencing, concertina wire, steel and concrete barricades stand as grim reminders to Palestinians of their place. In some spots, the wall dissects their villages, separating Palestinians from one another.

In 2009, I crossed this barrier and led an interfaith delegation to Palestine and Israel. One of our memorable visits was to Bil'in, an agricultural village with about 1,800 residents, located in the West Bank just west of Ramallah. More than half of the villagers' farmland was unreachable because of the separation fence constructed by the Israelis.

The Israeli Supreme Court had, surprisingly, ruled in favor of the Palestinians and ordered that the barrier be moved so that the villagers could get to their fields. But for two and a half years, members of the Israeli military refused to comply with the ruling, claiming that they could not afford to move the fence.

Our delegation joined the weekly demonstration with about two hundred local people, accompanied by Israelis and other internationals, marching from the center of Bil'in up a hill to the fence to demand compliance.

As we approached the barricade, Israeli soldiers launched dozens of canisters of tear gas. The gas burned our eyes, seared our lungs and exposed skin, and caused widespread nausea. The attack was much more potent than anything I had ever before experienced.

With the frightening explosions of concussion bombs all around us, our delegation turned around abruptly and stumbled blindly over the rocks and back down the hill. The villagers, exposed to this toxic gas every week, continued the nonviolent protest quite close to the fence. Some wore face masks or held plastic bags up to their faces to deter the noxious fumes. A man in a wheelchair stayed the longest, able to leave but unwilling to surrender his place on the line.

Perhaps no other conflict on the globe has seemed so intractable, or required such courageous perseverance on the part of peacemakers, as the crisis in the Middle East. When I arrived there in 2009, sixty-one years had passed since my dad had worked in Gaza and Israel distributing tents, food, and medicines to the Palestinian refugees of the 1948 Arab-Israeli War. I found it particularly painful to discover that not only many of those same refugees, but now also their children and grandchildren, are still living in refugee camps in the prison called Gaza.

The people of Gaza are all but completely cut off from the rest of the world. They cannot travel or visit relatives living beyond the barricade, and family members and friends living outside it cannot visit them. Only very limited food and medicines get through the barrier, and building supplies and many other necessities of life are severely restricted.

In December 2008, for more than three weeks, the Israeli military had subjected the people of Gaza to horrific violence during Operation Cast Lead. Israeli air strikes killed more than 1,400 Palestinians. (Thirteen Israelis were killed by rockets shot from Gaza). Five thousand Palestinians were injured, and more than fifty thousand were left homeless. Thousands of homes and dozens of schools, seven hundred factories and businesses, thirty-four clinics and hospitals, twenty-four mosques, and ten water and sewage lines were utterly destroyed.

On the first anniversary of the siege, 1,340 people from more than forty countries gathered in Cairo, Egypt, for the Gaza Freedom March. We joined them after our time in Israel/Palestine and planned to cross the Rafah border into Gaza. Unfortunately, under extreme pressure from Israel and the United States, the Egyptian government denied most of the internationals entry into Gaza. Only ninety of us very fortunate souls were able to get in.

The joy of the Gazans upon seeing those of us who made it, and their awareness that many other supporters were in Egypt in solidarity, was deeply moving. On December 31, 2009, the day of the Freedom March, I walked with two schoolteachers. They were greatly touched that people from all over the world cared enough about their fate that we were willing to take on the expense and overcome all the obstacles to get into Gaza to join them.

Our international group of ninety joined about a thousand people from Gaza in a march to the northern Israeli border checkpoint called Erez Crossing, to demand that the Israeli government end its occupation and siege of Gaza and let the Palestinians live in freedom and peace. We marched through mile after mile of bombed-out homes, factories, and shops. People were everywhere gathering up rubble, recycling rebar, and grinding up smashed blocks to make cement to rebuild their homes and other destroyed buildings.

Dressed in long black coats, with their *payot* curling below broad-brimmed hats, four Hasidic Jewish rabbis from Naturei Karta International, also known as Orthodox Jews United Against Zionism, marched with us. They carried a banner emblazoned with a Palestinian flag and the message "Judaism Demands Freedom for Gaza and All Palestine," and wore buttons proclaiming "A Jew is not a Zionist." The Gazans showed deep gratitude for these Jews, who are committed to honoring the humanity of the Palestinian people and had come to march with them.

After the march, a few of our group went out with some Gazan fishermen in their small boats. The Israeli authorities forbid them from going beyond 2.5 kilometers from the shore, which means few fish are available to them. Israeli soldiers have shot at those who have strayed beyond the imposed limit. Farmers have similarly been targets of Israeli bullets. Gaza's most fertile land is near the border, and if farmers cultivate too close to the wall that separates Gaza from Israel, Israeli soldiers fire on them.

In a refugee camp, our interfaith delegation met a mother racked by grief. On a wall of her small home were pictures of twenty-eight members of her extended family—all killed in the Operation Cast Lead attacks. The cement blocks in the upper part of her home, which had suffered severe damage in the bombings, had been relaid with mud, because cement is not allowed into Gaza. Holes in the roof let in the rain.

The woman's children, who had nothing to play with, were the delighted recipients of a few of the fifty teddy bears a war veteran, Will Covert, from New Mexico had carried to Palestine.

Classes for schoolchildren have to be convened in two shifts each day, to accommodate them all in the few schools that were left standing after the siege. Books and other educational supplies are at a bare minimum. Orphanages are overflowing. Children suffered greatly during the attacks, and the legacy of severe trauma remains.

A Palestinian woman in Gaza pointing out the twenty-eight members of her family killed in Operation Cast Lead in December 2008. [Photo: David Hartsough]

One of the great joys of that trip for me was meeting Dr. Mustafa El-Hawi from Gaza. His father had worked with my dad in a refugee camp in Rafah in 1949. Following in his father's footsteps, Mustafa works for an NGO (nongovernmental organization) called Community Bridge Initiative, providing both humanitarian relief and training in conflict resolution, peacemaking, and active nonviolence.

The NGOs in Gaza feel pressure not only from the Israelis, but also from Hamas, the party of the elected Palestinian government.

Members of a women's NGO told us that because of their affiliation with Fatah, the other main political party, they are often harassed and sometimes arrested. Other groups reported being closely watched.

In the Middle East, the fact that people who have been oppressed often end up being oppressors is abundantly evident. This is the cycle of suffering in which that embattled land has been locked for more than six decades. Israelis who experienced the horrors of the Holocaust are now oppressing Palestinians, cashing an essentially blank check from the United States to purchase their bullets and bombs. And members of Hamas, who have suffered decades of injustice from Israelis, are turning their anger against their own people. The Palestinians are caught in a vise of violence, pressing them from both sides.

Endless checkpoints, twenty-six-foot-high walls, and great fear and mistrust between most Israelis and Palestinians are grimly persistent features of life in Palestine. But I discovered there that violence is not the whole story. An alternative to the cycles of destruction is also being forged on both sides. A larger story is unfolding beyond the script of retaliatory violence—a story of a growing nonviolent movement that both Palestinians and Israelis are building.

Weekly nonviolent demonstrations, like the one in Bil'in, have been held in many Palestinian villages for years. Israelis (including Combatants for Peace and Anarchists Against the Wall) and internationals (including Christian Peacemaker Teams, Ecumenical Accompaniment Program, and Michigan Peace Teams) actively participate in these weekly actions. Occasionally, protestors can claim success. In February 2010, after five years of nonviolent actions in Bil'in, Israeli bulldozers finally began to move the barrier.

But such changes have come at a great cost. On July 28, 2008, ten-year-old Ahmed Moussa was fatally shot by Israeli soldiers during an anti-barrier demonstration in Nil'in, four miles west of Bil'in. On March 13, 2009, U.S. citizen Tristan Anderson of Oakland, California, was critically injured when he was struck in the head by a gas canister, fired by an Israeli soldier after the weekly protest had already ended. Tristan's only "weapon" was the camera he was using to take photographs of the demonstration. When we visited nine months later, he was still in an Israeli hospital near Tel Aviv, just beginning to talk again and get around in a wheelchair.

Other peaceful activists have been killed in these protests, and more than eleven thousand Palestinians have been imprisoned for nonviolent resistance. But the deeply inspiring commitment of Palestinians throughout the region to continue the struggle nonviolently—even when Israeli soldiers shoot powerful tear-gas canisters and grenades, concussion bombs, rubber-coated steel bullets, and sometimes live ammunition at unarmed villagers—is unwavering. They are deeply committed to *al-Samoud*, which in Arabic means "perseverance" or "steadfastness."

Palestinians practice *al-Samoud* daily by refusing to leave, even in the face of heavy intimidation by Israeli military and armed settlers who are trying to confiscate their lands and remove them from their homes. *Al-Samoud* motivates them to replant their olive trees when they are uprooted, to rebuild their homes when they are bulldozed, and to keep walking to school even when Israeli settlers taunt and throw stones at them. The Palestinians are steadfast even when they can't reach their fields, when their homes are raided in the middle of the night, and when members of their families are arrested.

In al-Ma'sara, south of Bethlehem, seventy-five well-armed Israeli soldiers and six military tanks met our peaceful demonstration of approximately two hundred villagers, sympathetic Israelis, and inter-national supporters. At the barricade, a former Israeli bomber pilot who had joined the peaceful demonstration spoke passionately against the apartheid wall. A local woman, accompanied by her two young chil-dren, held up a picture of her older son, who had been arrested with her husband and was being held indefinitely with him in an Israeli prison. Her home had been bulldozed by Israeli soldiers. Her anguish was acute, her determination unwavering.

After the rally ended, people slowly began walking back down the road to al-Ma'sara. The soldiers crossed the barbed wire and began aggressively pushing the crowd back toward their village. A couple of young boys threw small stones at them, and they immediately rushed at the boys and shot off sound grenades, with blasts that were both deafening and frightening.

Backed up by the six tanks, which were roaring their engines, jerking forward, and threatening to run down any demonstrators who did not retreat quickly enough, the soldiers attempted to arrest the boys.

Sami Awad, executive director of the nonviolent, grassroots Holy Land Trust—whose aim is peaceful coexistence between Israelis and Palestinians in Bethlehem—intervened. He told the military com-mander that security and goodwill would not be served by the arrest of the boys or the army's invasion of the village. Once they concluded their show of force, the troops and tanks retreated from al-Ma'sara and people returned to their homes.

Some of our delegation stayed on in the village to offer a protective presence in the event of a return by members of the Israeli military. They didn't come back that night. But a few nights later, soldiers came and arrested one of the leaders of the nonviolent movement. He still sits in an Israeli prison.

In the community of Tent of Nations, outside Bethlehem, I met Daoud Nasser and his family. Daoud's father bought land in 1924 when the area was under Turkish rule. Now, all the hilltops surrounding the farm are overrun with new settlements—homes to some of the half million Jewish settlers who have moved into the West Bank.

Armed Israeli soldiers broke into Daoud's home a few months before our visit and told him that he and his family had to leave, but Daoud refused to go. He has the deed to his home and believes he has a right to stay on the land that has belonged to his family for more than eighty-five years. Settlers raided his farm and uprooted four hundred olive trees, which were the source of most of his family's income. Committed to a nonviolent response, Daoud and his family planted five hundred more trees, but these will take many years to mature and produce olives.

Israeli authorities refused Daoud's family building permits for their house, the greenhouse where they start new seedlings, and the cistern where they collect rainwater. At any time, the soldiers could come and bulldoze their home, forcing them to leave. Daoud and his family are a remarkable example of *al-Samoud*.

Daoud questions, "Why can't all the children of Abraham [Jews, Muslims, and Christians] understand that the basis of all our religions and religious teachings is the same?—that we love one another, that we treat others as we would like them to treat us, and that we are all children of God." I did not observe in him even an ounce of hatred toward the Israeli settlers or soldiers who continually threaten his family with eviction from their ancestral land. Their faith that justice will prevail, and that nonviolence is a more powerful weapon than the gun, sustains them.

Daoud and his family organize camps for young people of all religions, from many countries around the world, to come and live for a while on their land. The camps provide a wonderful opportunity for these young civilian diplomats to discover how much we human beings all have in common. When the young people return to their home countries, they take the message that building understanding and friendship are important parts of nonviolent social change. They have learned that there are better ways to challenge injustice, oppression, and violence than responding with more violence.

While I traveled throughout Palestine, hearing the stories of people who had been uprooted, many families showed me the keys to their original homes in what is now Israel. They are hanging on to them in the hope that someday they will be able to return to their homes. This may seem a dim and distant possibility, but many people and organizations are at work trying to make it a reality.

MEND (Middle East Nonviolence and Democracy) offers nonviolence training to hundreds of young Palestinians throughout the West Bank and East Jerusalem, helping to educate and nurture a new generation with a deep understanding of nonviolent action. The Wi'am Center promotes human rights and helps people to address injustices rather than avenge them.

The Israeli peace movement is also alive and well. More than four thousand "refusers" have disobeyed orders to serve in the illegally occupied territories of the West Bank and Gaza, including seventy-three pilots who refused to participate in bombing missions. Hundreds of high school students are defying Israel's compulsory military service (eighteen months for women, and up to three years for men). Many of these brave people have served time in prison for their stands. Other groups of Israelis working for peace and justice include New Profile, Rabbis for Human Rights, and the Israeli Committee Against House Demolitions. Women in Black have been demonstrating in Israel for peace and justice for Palestinians every week for more than twenty-three years.

I was particularly moved by the Israelis and Palestinians who have joined together in groups such as, Parents Circle Family Forum, whose members have lost loved ones in the conflict. Recognizing that their shared pain unites them, they are speaking together in schools and to community groups. "We refuse to let our grief harden into hatred and actions of retaliation," one of them told me. "Instead, we are turning, in compassion and reconciliation, to each other—Palestinians and Israelis—with the hearts of parents who want to join our voices and hands so that there will be no more bloodshed and no more lives of children wasted."

These people, along with a growing number of others, understand that the security of the Palestinians and the Israelis is inextricably linked. Such significant interdependence exists between these two

Die-in protest on Market Street in San Francisco on the anniversary of U.S. military attack of Iraq (March 2008). [Photo: Meg Whittaker Greene]

peoples in that ancient and holy land that they must work together to find a peaceful resolution to the conflict. As John F. Kennedy once said, "Those who make peaceful change impossible make violent change inevitable."

U.S. support of nonviolent movements in the Middle East would help to make peaceful change possible. Training Palestinian young people in conflict resolution and nonviolence would be a much greater contribution to peace in the region than sending weapons and building walls separating these beautiful people. If we all—Israelis, Palestinians, and Americans—embraced a different way that affirms the rights of all people to live in peace with justice, the whole world would be more secure.

Treating all people as children of God, and with respect as sisters and brothers, is a place to start. That has to include respecting their choices. We in the United States must get clear about whether we really support democracy—or if we support it only when people elect the governments we prefer and pursue the policies that further our self-interest.

Former President Jimmy Carter, who headed up the monitoring mission during the 2006 Palestinian elections, declared them honest, fair, and safe. Should the United States and Israel force the Palestinian people to suffer untold misery through our actions because we do not like their elected government? And is the Hamas government really more terrorist than our own, which has been raining bombs and death on the people of Iraq, Afghanistan, and Pakistan?

For fifteen months during the wars in Iraq and Afghanistan, our peace community in San Francisco held weekly "die-ins" in front of the Federal Building to protest the bombings and the use of torture. As we had done during the Vietnam War, we read the names of the war dead. Then everyone who felt called to do so lay down on the sidewalk with a white sheet covering them, as the dead are covered up in Iraq. Our hope was that hundreds of communities across the country would organize similar activities to resist the wars. We also organized "die-ins" on March 19 each year, the anniversary of the U.S. military's invasion of Iraq.

Iran

Unfortunately, our nation seems to have no shortage of "enemies." At the time of this writing, the target of our disdain is Iran—designated the latest threat to world security and "enemy number one." In 2009 and 2010, I also led delegations to that country.

After all my decades of international travel, I'm still amazed at the similarities in how governments foment mistrust and hatred through relentless propaganda—not much different from our government's campaign against the Russians when I first visited their country half a century ago. And I'm equally amazed to discover many ordinary citizens in these places who are open and kind and willing to go to extraordinary lengths to make me feel welcome.

The Iranian government was mistrustful of our visits—understandable, given the history of U.S.-Iran relations. In 1953, the CIA and British intelligence engineered the overthrow of Iran's democratically elected Prime Minister Mohammad Mosadegh who had nationalized Iran's oil production, enabling the profits to go to programs that benefitted the Iranian people. The United States also installed a military general, and paved the way for the dictatorial reign of Shah Mohammad Reza Pahlavi.

In 1979, a popular revolution deposed the shah, and later that year militants supporting the revolution took over the U.S. Embassy in Teheran and held fifty-two Americans hostage for 444 days. In the 1980s, the United States supported Iraq's Saddam Hussein in his invasion of Iran and a war that cost at least two million lives. And when U.S. Navy missiles shot down Iran Air Flight 655 in its own airspace in July 1988, killing all 290 people on board, instead of apologizing, the U.S. government awarded a medal to the captain of the ship that fired the missiles.

U.S. warnings about Iran are mind-bogglingly hypocritical. Iran has not attacked another country in more than two hundred years—which unfortunately cannot be said of the United States. I find it particularly stunning that the only country on earth that has ever used nuclear bombs against a civilian population would denounce Iran's nuclear program and declare as a threat a nation surrounded on all sides by U.S. Army bases in Afghanistan and Iraq and U.S. Navy ships in the Persian Gulf.

The George W. Bush administration declared Iran part of the "axis of evil." Members of our current government have continued to relate to Iran, a nation whose history reaches back 2,500 years, as if it were a naughty child. The U.S. Congress has voted to spend hundreds of millions of dollars and the CIA has been put to work in an effort to destabilize/overthrow Iran's government. And the United States, along with many other governments in the international community that have followed suit, has imposed very harsh sanctions that are crippling the Iranian economy and making the lives of ordinary Iranians almost unlivable. Israel and some in the U.S. government continue to threaten to bomb Iran.

While our delegation was visiting, the Iranian government kept a close watch on all our movements and refused to allow us to set up many meetings. However, we were able to spend a lot of our time meeting ordinary people in parks and on the streets. And we discovered what I've always discovered in other countries: people refusing to buy into the government propaganda that we are one another's enemies and working to change their governments' policies to be more tolerant and understanding of other nations. In Iran, the professors and poets, the mosques and museums, often reflect a profound reverence for life.

One member of the delegation that traveled to Iran in late February 2009 was Fr. Louie Vitale. A seventy-seven-year-old Franciscan brother who had recently spent two years in jail as a result of his protests against U.S. war-making and torture, Louie shared with Muslim leaders that he has kept the Ramadan fast every year since 2001, which moved them deeply. Their conversation harkened back to St. Francis himself who, centuries before during the Christian Crusades in the Holy Land, offered friendship to the feared and much-maligned sultan, and spoke peace to Muslim brothers and sisters.

In a park in Esfahan, a man approached me, smiling and pointing at my T-shirt, which bore the phrase "Peace with Iran" written in both English and Farsi. He said to me, "Thank you for your message.

Young Iranian women we met in Yazd, Iran, on our citizen diplomacy trip in 2010.
[Photo: David Hartsough]

We are all children of God under one sky on the same earth. We need to see ourselves as brothers and sisters and friends, not as Iranians or Americans or Muslims or Christians or enemies."

The man's name was Hamid, and he was a firefighter at the Shiraz airport, on vacation with his family. His young children drifted toward us from a playground, curious about the American visitor. Hamid continued to talk animatedly, encouraging me to read the Sufi poet Hafez, and gratefully receiving my suggestion that he read Gandhi. He declared at the end of our conversation, "All religions teach us to love one another."

As I made my way through a busy bazaar, a man emerged from a shop and asked where I was from. When I told him, he smiled broadly and cried, "Welcome to Iran. We are very glad to have you here. We would like many more people to come visit us from America. But don't bring your guns!"

Those words still echo in my soul: "Don't bring your guns!" This is the message that I believe most of the world's people want us Americans to hear. But we just keep on developing ever more sophisticated and lethal weapons to use against other people around the globe.

One of the latest horrors is the use of unmanned drones in warfare. At Creech Air Force Base, outside Las Vegas, soldiers sit in trailers at video consoles, tracking people in Afghanistan and Pakistan and then directing drones armed with bombs to kill them. The drones can accurately target a person, but whoever else is in the vicinity also gets killed. It's just one more way we're raising anger across the world and fueling the forces that want to do us in. The military has even announced the prospect of arming drones with nuclear weapons, further escalating the "collateral damage."

In 2008, I was arrested in one of the first protests against drones, along with my wife Jan, Louie Vitale, and several other people, including Gene Stoltzfus, the Mennonite friend from my DC lobbying years who had served with International Voluntary Service in Vietnam. We had requested a meeting with the commander at Creech and were denied. When we stepped onto the base sidewalk, soldiers surrounded us.

While we were waiting to find out what would happen to us, I asked Gene to tell me about his recent trip to Afghanistan—which meant that the young man guarding us also had to hear the story. I imagine that that was the first time this soldier had to listen to the details of the horrific reality on the ground that were the result of the deadly, real-life video game he and his comrades were playing. Sadly, Gene, a stalwart of courage and peacemaking, died shortly after that arrest.

I feel extraordinarily blessed to have stood with so many people in so many places who are committed to ridding the world of its guns and bringing change nonviolently. Although Peaceworkers is a small, low-budget NGO that operates out of my home, we have found ways to leverage resources and play a small part in big changes.

Among the most courageous nonviolent movements of which I'm aware is WOZA (Women of Zimbabwe Arise), which had very little visibility and support when we first learned of them. These intrepid women have persistently challenged the oppressive policies of dictator Robert Mugabe. Despite beatings and arrests—including some of them being jailed with their babies—they continue to sound a clarion call for nonviolent change. Inspired by their courage, men in Zimbabwe have launched an auxiliary effort, MOZA (Men of Zimbabwe Arise).

In 2009, WOZA won the Robert F. Kennedy Human Rights Award, which President Barack Obama presented at the White House to Jenni Williams, the group's leader. She later described how Obama walked in, handed over the award, and left the room. A few minutes later he came back in, explaining that he wasn't quite sure what he was allowed to do. He sat down and listened for more than an hour as the members of WOZA told their moving story.

Peaceworkers has also supported and provided nonviolence training for the Movimento dos Trabalhadores Rurais Sem Terra (MST), the landless workers movement in Brazil, where 4.8 million farmers have no access to land. The largest social movement in Latin America, MST has used nonviolent action to pressure the Brazilian government to give land titles to 150,000 families so far. The organization is supporting another 57,000 families occupying uncultivated land in twenty-three states, shoring up their hopes of receiving parcels to farm.

Diane Emerson, a friend doing relief work in Kashmir, a territory caught for more than sixty years in a violent dispute between India and Pakistan, invited Peaceworkers to get involved in helping to end that tragic conflict. Diane was willing to donate two months of her salary to launch a nonviolent peacemaking project. I got her in touch with Rajiv Vora, who had been Asia Regional Coordinator of the Nonviolent Peaceforce. Rajiv has enlisted the support of many Gandhians in India to become involved in this peacemaking effort, and nonviolent training is now being conducted in Kashmir with young people across religious and political divides.

Peaceworkers has partnered with Mustafa El-Hawi's Community Bridge Initiative in Gaza, offering some financial support. We've also been exploring the possibility of supporting the nonviolent struggle in Burma. I continue to talk with nonviolent activists around the world, helping them strategize and trying to meet expressed needs, such as nonviolence training, funding, accompaniment, and networking.

I'm working with a colleague, Jan Passion, organizing the Rapid Nonviolent Accompaniment and Protection Project (RNAPP), an effort of Peaceworkers that I find especially exciting. The project is designed for individuals who have had significant experience with peace-team work in war zones. RNAPP is developing a roster of people available to go on short notice to volunteer in areas of conflict or extreme repression for up to six months, with the understanding that if a longer-term presence is needed, the Nonviolent Peaceforce or another international peace team could follow. RNAPP is presently sending volunteers to accompany the villagers in the nonviolent movement on Jeju Island off the coast of South Korea who are protesting the building of a new military base on their island by nonviolently blocking bulldozers and cement trucks (Savejujunow.org).

Local residents in Gangjeong Village, Jeju Island, South Korea, block cement
trucks and bulldozers used to construct a huge new naval base to be used by U.S.
warships as part of the "Pacific Pivot" (2013). [Photo: Regis Tremblay]

I've distributed thousands of copies of a documentary DVD called
A Force More Powerful in many languages all over the world. It shares
the stories of people engaged in significant nonviolent movements
that have had success bringing fundamental change. These include
India's independence struggle and South Africa's peaceful transition
from apartheid to democracy, Denmark's nonviolent resistance to
Nazi persecution of the Jews and Poland's Solidarity movement, the
American civil rights movement and Chile's overthrow of the dictatorship of Augusto Pinochet.

I've also spread around copies of *Bringing Down a Dictator*, the
story of the student-led nonviolent movement of massive nonviolent
civil resistance that forced Serbian dictator Slobodan Milosevic out
of power in 2000. And *The Orange Revolution*, which documents the
extraordinary story of massive nonviolent demonstrations in Kiev,
Ukraine, against the fraudulent 2004 election and the poisoning of
opposition candidate Viktor Yushchenko—when twenty thousand
people camped out in front of the capitol building for two weeks in
twenty-below-zero weather until the election was declared null and
void. I'm grateful to the International Center for Nonviolent Conflict,
which has sent, at their own expense, thousands of copies of these
excellent resources all over the world when I request them—a wonderful contribution to increasing global understanding of the power of
nonviolent people's movements.

I feel a bit like a Johnny Appleseed, spreading the seeds of nonviolence—and nurturing those seeds around the world. I'll never
know where they all land, how they might take root, or what fruit they
might produce. I've always appreciated a prayer, often attributed to

Archbishop Oscar Romero of El Salvador, but written by Bishop Ken Untener of Saginaw, Michigan, in honor of the archbishop's martyrdom. It reads in part:

It helps, now and then, to step back and take a long view . . .
We accomplish in our lifetime only a tiny fraction
of the magnificent enterprise that is God's work . . .
We plant the seeds that one day will grow.
We water seeds already planted,
knowing that they hold future promise . . .
We cannot do everything,
and there is a sense of liberation in realizing that.
This enables us to do something, and to do it very well.
It may be incomplete, but it is a beginning,
a step along the way,
an opportunity for the Lord's grace to enter and do the rest . . .

CHAPTER 14

Transforming Our Society from One Addicted to Violence and War to One Based on Justice and Peace with the World

Things undreamt of are daily being seen, the impossible is ever becoming possible. We are constantly being astonished these days at the amazing discoveries in the field of violence. But I maintain that far more undreamt-of and seemingly impossible discoveries will be made in the field of nonviolence. —Gandhi

In early 1959, Fort Detrick in Frederick, Maryland, underwent a massive expansion, making it the largest bioweapons facility in the world. Among its projects was the development of "Q Fever." A small amount of this lethal bacterium with horrific side effects could wipe out whole populations, and it is now on the official government list of Weapons of Mass Destruction. I knew that the Nazis had worked on developing germ warfare during the Second World War, but I never expected it here at home—and just forty-five miles from Washington, DC.

Longtime Quaker peacemaker Larry Scott put out a call for people to join a vigil in protest at Fort Detrick. My mother, who was a first-grade teacher then, was particularly disturbed by the developments at the base. She spent most of her summer vacation in 1959 standing at its entrance, holding a sign and keeping silent vigil with many others, largely Quakers from the East Coast.

After I hitchhiked back from Cuba, where I had spent that summer, I joined my mom and the others for a few days. I admired their courage and persistence. The summer outside the base had been sizzling hot, and the winter was icy and cold. And on the face of it, the witness

Vigil at germ warfare plant at Fort Detrick, MD, 1959. My mother, Ruth, is third from the right.

seemed to be totally ineffective, as if these faithful souls were holding a candle in the dark against the death machine and nobody cared.

The response of the base members was largely to ignore us. The authorities decided not to make arrests, and they told the workers to refuse our leaflets and not look at us. As they drove through the entrance, almost all of the base personnel kept their eyes straight ahead. Despite the snubs, for three years in a row my mom spent her summer vacations there—a wonderful contribution from our family to try to stop the madness of war.

In the late 1960s, my parents were living in Salem, Oregon. My mom was perusing the shelves in a bookstore one day. A stranger approached her and asked, "Were you in that vigil at Fort Detrick about ten years ago?"

Flabbergasted, she said yes.

He told her, "I just want you to know that I was working at Fort Detrick at that time, and because of you folks, I resigned my job."

A decade later, and 2,500 miles away, a man who had been instructed not to look or pay attention to the people on the vigil line recognized and remembered my mother's face. And he wanted her to know she had made a difference. That story helps me remember that we don't always see the results of our actions immediately. When a small pebble is thrown into the water, the ripples go out, and one can never know quite where they are going to spread, or what impact they may have.

One of the plagues of our day is that it's easy to feel overwhelmed and powerless in the face of massive violence, poverty, and injustice around the globe. More than 180 million people died in wars in the twentieth century, the deadliest in human history, and warfare has only become more sophisticated and lethal in the first years of the twenty-first. One of the greatest needs in this country is for us to have some hope, and to feel empowered that as ordinary people we can make a difference.

The world is shifting. Johan Galtung, a Norwegian sociologist and a principal founder of the discipline of Peace and Conflict Studies around the globe, predicts that the American Empire will be over by 2020. He believes that many people around the world are no longer willing to put up with U.S. military, political, and economic domination of their countries and our treatment of them as pawns, cheap laborers, and second-class citizens.

Militarily, we in the United States are stretched by several wars and the maintenance of more than 760 bases in 130 countries, spending more on the military than all the rest of the world's nations combined. Politically, we're descending into partisan bickering and deadlock, losing both our moral grip and the world's respect. Economically, we're imploding—overwhelmed by the cost of our massive military infrastructure while our schools, parks, hospitals, and highways suffer for lack of funds and care, and more and more of our citizens lose their jobs and their homes.

Whether or not 2020 is the year the American Empire will collapse I don't know. But I believe a transition is inevitable. As Americans, we face a key question: Will we join people around the world to try to make this transition as peaceful as possible, or will we try to hold onto our privileges and our world-dominating way of life?

Consumerism is an addiction in this country. We're devouring the world to maintain a lifestyle that deprives other people around the world of their livelihoods—and, for many, of life itself. When I was in high school, I learned that we in the United States made up about 6 percent of the world's population and were consuming about 40 percent of its resources. This terrible disparity has continued—we are now 4.5 percent consuming more than 25 percent. That's almost six times our rightful share of the world's resources.

We each need to ask ourselves these questions: Who is my family? Who is my neighbor? If there's not enough room in the house for all the kids, would a parent put some of them outside in the cold and give them only scraps to eat? In reality, this is what we are doing to billions of the world's most vulnerable citizens.

Countries that were once able to feed their people are now suffering massive starvation, as more and more land gets devoted to cash crops such as sugar and coffee for export to the United States. NAFTA and other free trade agreements are not only throwing many Americans out of work, they're undermining economies in Latin America and Africa. If we wonder why so many Mexicans are streaming into our country "illegally," we need only look at our own policies: U.S. manufacturing companies that pay Mexican workers pennies a day, and massive influxes of cheap and subsidized U.S. corn that has undermined Mexican agriculture, making it impossible for families to support themselves.

We've structured the world to feed our greed. And that means, according to the policy makers, that we have to protect what we have and control or kill the people who get in our way or demand a fair share of the world's resources. We're now spending trillions of dollars on military "security"—bases, bombers, battleships, drones, nuclear weapons, personnel, intelligence—much of it under the cloak of government secrecy. But these have not bought us security.

The most powerful and militarized country in the world could not prevent the terrible destruction and loss of life on September 11, 2001. Two days after the horrendous attacks on the Pentagon and the World Trade Center, I wrote a letter that was published in the *Washington Post*. It said in part:

> I believe that the only way we can build real security for the American people is for the United States to become a real friend of the world's people. Instead of spending hundreds of billions of dollars for weapons of destruction, we should allocate hundreds

of billions for feeding the world's hungry, housing the homeless, healing the sick, and helping heal the wounds of war and hatred around the world. This would do more to win friends and real security than all the weapons in the world combined. It is time to understand the unity and interconnectedness of all people around the world and build our security system based upon that understanding. May we use this horrible nightmare as a spring-board for a new beginning.

Unfortunately, that vulnerable moment in our nation's history was not a spark for changing direction. Instead, we squandered the sympathetic good will of the world and launched wars of revenge. We proclaimed the nations of Iraq and Afghanistan our latest enemies.

And that declaration became self-fulfilling: our arrogance and destruction had the effect of fomenting anger, mistrust, and hatred, thereby enlisting more enemies in the fight against our domination. Our government's response to 9/11 has created hundreds of thousands more casualties in the world, dug us trillions of dollars deeper into debt, and made us all less secure. It is time to declare the "war on terror" an utter failure.

Many years ago, on my eighteenth birthday, my parents gave me a copy of Gandhi's *All Men Are Brothers*. I would expand its language to be inclusive of women and sisters while the heart of its truth remains. That book transformed my life profoundly and continues to affect how I view the world.

Part of our task as children of God is to celebrate that all people are made in the image of God and refuse to cooperate with the powers-that-be as they try to divide us and pressure us to forget our common humanity. As I've had the opportunity to travel all over the world—especially to countries declared to be "the enemy" or a threat to our nation's security—I have discovered as I've gotten to know people that they are not the menace our government would like us to believe they are. Most of them are searching for the same things we are: safety, a decent life for their children, and an opportunity to live in peace.

As Brian Willson reminded us from his hospital bed after being run over by a munitions train, President Dwight Eisenhower once said, "I think that people want peace so much that one of these days governments had better get out of the way and let them have it." That's the challenge before us. How much do we want peace? How fervently are we willing to work for it?

Building a powerful nonviolent movement in the United States is crucial. People waking up and feeling motivated to act is the first necessary ingredient for a vital movement. The second is realizing that hundreds of thousands—perhaps millions—of others feel the same way. And third is being willing to commit ourselves to long-term nonviolent struggle—even at some cost to ourselves.

I have learned through many years of involvement in nonviolent actions, campaigns, and movements that thinking strategically is critical. Identifying our opponents' weaknesses, searching for potential allies, and reaching out to all who support an alternative vision can help bring success. A powerful movement has the capacity to touch the hearts and consciences of Americans and people all around the world.

One of the great signs of hope to me has been the Occupy movement that sprang up in September 2011. It was inspired in part by the "Arab Spring"—civil uprisings that forced leaders from power in Tunisia and Egypt and led to sustained protests in several other countries including Bahrain. Protesters in the United States first occupied New York's Wall Street, calling for a turn from corporate greed and the vast disparities of wealth in our society.

From that spark, the protest and the hope spread. All across the country, hundreds of thousands of people representing a broad spectrum of classes, races, religious traditions, and ages—especially young people—picked up the cry and said with their bodies, "We're not going to take it anymore." Their refusal to put up with a society skewed toward corporations and the wealthy, and undermined by military overreach, has given me more hope than anything I've experienced since the civil rights and antiwar movements of the 1960s.

My wife, Jan, and I participated in Occupy San Francisco and Occupy Oakland on the West Coast and also the Freedom Plaza Occupation in Washington, DC. The site of our sustained occupation two blocks from the White House was named in honor of the people of Egypt who had occupied Freedom Square in Cairo. Charging dictator Hosni Mubarak with refusing to listen to the Egyptian people and address their needs, these courageous souls had forced his resignation. Jan and I spent ten days in our U.S. Freedom Plaza, joining many others of the "99 percent" to declare that our government is not listening to us, and to demand a return to democracy that serves the people.

A young African American man I met there summed it up well: "This is the most exciting moment of my life. I've been waiting for it my whole life. . . . We need a nonviolent revolution to take back this country

One of thousands of "Occupy" protest signs in hundreds of cities across the United States. Freedom Plaza, Washington, DC (2011). [Photo: David Hartsough]

for the people. We need a government of, by, and for the people, not just the rich and the corporations. I have found a community of people here who care and are ready to commit our lives to changing our society to one where there is justice and we are at peace with the world. . . . We shall overcome!"

During our occupation, we walked each day to a different manifestation of the military-industrial-financial complex to "speak truth to power," voice our concerns, and announce our determination to bring change. We marched to the office of General Atomics, which produces military drones, demanding an end to these long-distance death machines; we were chased out of the building. We were tear-gassed at the Air and Space Museum, which was hosting a drone exhibit.

At the Chamber of Commerce, we shouted "We want jobs!" We called for an end to war profiteering in front of Washington's Convention Center, which was hosting a weaponry fair at which arms manufacturers were displaying and selling to representatives of the U.S. Army their guns and tanks and every conceivable type of military equipment. We filled the atrium of the Hart Senate Office Building with banners from the balconies of all seven floors and chanted "Stop the Wars! Tax the Rich!"

We marched to the White House, where veterans of the Iraq and Afghanistan wars and military families requested a "beer summit" with President Obama, to share their personal experiences and the urgent need to end these wars and military occupations immediately. Twelve of us were arrested occupying the National Security Agency.

Each night we came together in a General Assembly, where all major decisions were made by consensus of the hundreds of people present. We heard inspirational talks by many people, including consumer protection advocate Ralph Nader and clown-physician Patch Adams. Comedian Dick Gregory told the crowd, "We need to be like a turtle—hard on the outside, soft on the inside, and willing to stick our necks out. . . . We have already won. We have given people hope."

I find hope not only in this movement, but also in the many that have persevered for decades. Tri-Valley CARES (Communities Against a Radioactive Environment), the organization born out of our protests at the Livermore nuclear weapons laboratory, is still going strong. The group has remained faithful for more than twenty-five years to its mission to stop nuclear weapons production and divert resources to alternative energy development.

Our reaching out to the humanity of the workers at the lab and to the arresting police officers has garnered support for our actions and led to a few resignations over the years. Recently, Tri-Valley CARES exposed high levels of radioactive tritium in the ground water and soil around Livermore, including at the city's playground for children. And every Good Friday in collaboration with the Ecumenical Peace Institute, we gather for an interdenominational worship service, walking the "Stations of the Cross," kneeling and praying at the gates, and getting arrested—I call it praying for peace without a permit.

I have discovered hope in other corners as well. My children, and their children, give me great hope. Peter and Heidi seem not to have suffered too much from their preschool-age arrests at the White House. In fact, they have embraced the values that are so important to Jan and me.

Peter, who was once so inquisitive about our canoe that was confiscated by the government, now has a PhD in hydrology. He lives in Davis, about an hour and a half away from us, and works in California's Sierra Mountains, researching the impact of climate change on water retention in the soil. He is married to Rachel, and they have two children, Gracie and Ray.

Heidi met her husband, Oliver, in the Peace Corps in Togo, where her work was focused on maternal and child health and nutrition. She is currently a labor-and-delivery nurse at the University of California at San Francisco hospital. She wants to become a midwife and hopes to go back to Africa with her family someday to work again with people there. She and Oliver have two daughters, Sequoia and Masai, and live downstairs from Jan and me in our duplex. Our granddaughters now attend the same nearby public school that Peter and Heidi once did, which is now a Chinese immersion program.

Like Jan and me, both of our children enjoy international travel and are nourished by the beauty of nature. While growing up, they benefited greatly from living in intentional community, surrounded by role models doing good work and trying to change the world. And because sharing in community allowed us to live simply, both Jan and I usually worked only half-time, allowing us more time with our children.

We have had people living with us almost continuously for the past thirty-eight years. We once had three families living in our house— three sets of parents, five young children, and one teenager—all connected through work with the United Farmworkers Union and the American Friends Service Committee. Now, Heidi is grateful to have her children's grandparents upstairs and available babysitters on the scene. Jan and I love having our grandchildren nearby and feel their love and excitement about life, which renews our commitment to helping build a world in which all children can look forward to a future of peace and justice.

We all need community to keep us from going numb, to offer one another mutual support for the hard work of staying faithful to our deepest values, to keep us committed and hopeful. It's the best way I know to overcome the plague of "consumeritis" that affects us all.

Nonviolence is not simply a commitment not to kill people. It means trying to withdraw from the American Way of Life—what Brian Willson calls "going AWOL." It means living in ways that are sustainable for the planet, so that the earth's ecosystem can heal, and our children, grandchildren, and great-grandchildren can inherit a livable planet and the resources necessary to have a future.

Devoting my life to peace and justice work means that I don't often see immediate successes. I think of all the times I tried to blockade or trespass or encourage change and got thwarted in the attempt. But there are always hopeful stories that keep me going. One of my favorites is from the days of our Peace Navy.

Those of us in the American Friends Service Committee were working to strengthen our support of the antiapartheid movement in

Peace Navy join longshoremen in successfully blocking the unloading of South African cargo ship from all ports on the West Coast (San Francisco, 1985). [Photo: Mary Golden]

the 1980s. When we learned that a South African ship was coming into San Francisco Bay to unload cargo, we decided to protest there. The Peace Navy went out in our boats, and one of our group wrote "Stop Apartheid" with spray paint on the side of the ship that was docked there. Not surprisingly, this made the newspapers.

A spokesperson for the longshoremen told us that if we set up a picket line and made a commotion, they would not cross it and would declare to their supervisors that the situation was unsafe for them to do their work. We picketed by land and sea for several days. The ship finally gave up because no workers would unload its cargo.

The ship went north to Portland, Oregon, and protesters there organized a similar picket line. The same thing happened in Seattle. That South African ship was not able to unload its cargo anywhere on the West Coast, and it eventually went back home. Nelson Mandela came to San Francisco after he was elected South Africa's president and thanked all of us for the work we had done. That story reminds me that sometimes we actually do win, and that should inspire us all to keep trying.

South Africa is a stunning example of the power of nonviolence. For decades, observers looked at the ruthless grip of apartheid on that nation and doubted that a peaceful transition to racial equality and majority rule was possible, declaring that change would come only with a horrendous bloodbath. The people of South Africa, under the gracious and generous leadership of Nelson Mandela, Archbishop Desmond Tutu, and others, proved them all wrong.

And South Africa is only one of thousands of success stories for nonviolent resistance. I have seen with my own eyes the power of nonviolence to bring transformation in the Philippines, in Central America, in the Middle East, in Eastern Europe, in the American South. The list of countries where powerful nonviolent movements have brought down dictatorships is stunning: South Africa, India, the Philippines, South Korea, Chile, Bolivia, Poland, East Germany, Czechoslovakia, Serbia, Ukraine, Tunisia, Egypt, Liberia, and too many others to name.

More than half of the world's people live in countries that have had powerful nonviolent movements. Erica Chenoweth and Maria Stephan studied 323 major nonviolent and violent movements for change over the past 110 years. In their book *Why Civil Resistance Works: The Strategic Logic of Nonviolent Conflict*, they concluded that the nonviolent movements were twice as likely to be successful and also far more likely to bring about democratic societies and not revert to civil wars.

Their book provides clear evidence for the argument that active nonviolence is not only the morally right thing to do, it is also the most effective. All over the world, people are increasingly embracing nonviolent action as the most legitimate and effective way of waging struggle against oppression, injustice, and dictatorship. We are all learning from one another's struggles. My hope is that the rest of the world will realize that violence and war are costly, outmoded, ineffective, and morally tragic means of resolving conflict.

I think often of the brave students I met in Serbia. Billions of U.S. dollars, arms, and bombs were not successful in bringing down the dictator Slobodan Milosevic. But twelve students with nonviolent training, good strategic thinking, and courage sparked the movement that did.

I'm convinced that if those students had decided to challenge Milosevic's ironclad rule with guns, they would have suffered a terrible bloodbath, and Serbia likely would still be under his dictatorship. The same is true of the struggle against Marcos in the Philippines, the response to the attempted coup in the Soviet Union, and the Solidarity Movement in Poland. The power structures in all these situations had lots of guns—and they knew how to put down violent insurrections. What they were not prepared to deal with were inspired and courageous nonviolent movements—*A Force More Powerful*, as the moving documentary on nonviolent movements is titled.

And that force keeps moving and growing. Many people in non-violent movements in other parts of the world speak of how they were inspired by Martin Luther King and the courage of the students in the civil rights movement here. During the "Arab Spring," Egyptians had access to a comic book history of the Montgomery bus boycott translated into Arabic. "We Shall Overcome" was sung in Cairo's Freedom Square, just as it had been sung a few decades before in China's Tiananmen Square.

And now, that inspiration has come back to us in the United States, nurturing our Occupy movement and other efforts for justice and peace. Living in the age of electronic media and social networking enables us to observe instantly the courage of the people in Cairo. We can hear the stories of one another across the world in seconds, exchanging the inspiration back and forth, watching the global nonviolent movement swell. And the powers-that-be now know that the world is quite literally watching everything they do.

I have often been inspired by Dr. King's quote "One with God is a majority." He said once in a church basement, "We have the power in this room, if we mobilize it, to change the future course of America." Only thirty-five people were in that room, and perhaps at the time they thought he was delusional. But he acted on that belief and together they woke up the whole nation and helped create fundamental change in our society.

In 1992, I was on a retreat. During guided meditation, the facilitator invited the participants to put ourselves in a very special place. So I was sitting on a park bench perched on the side of a mountain above Grindelwald, Switzerland—a beautiful area I had visited.

The facilitator then instructed us to invite someone to come and interact with us. So out of the silence came Martin Luther King. He put his hands on my shoulders and said, "David, I know that being a part of the struggle for a peaceful and just world can be lonely, and I want you to know that I'll always be with you." That was a very special message that I'll carry as long as I live.

I take comfort in another of King's well-known quotes: "The arc of the universe is long, but it bends toward justice." The work of transformation is a long-haul struggle. We are up against entrenched, systemic structures that are not going to change overnight. And moving them will require extraordinary love and persistence on our part. I love the translation of the word for *nonviolence* in Brazil—"relentless persistence"—which is crucial for effective nonviolent change.

A few years ago, I attended a conference of the September Eleventh Families for Peaceful Tomorrows organization, which was founded by families who had lost loved ones in the 9/11 attacks. It was a gathering near New York City of people from all over the world who have been on the receiving end of horrendous violence: Russians whose children had been killed in a school bombing, Israelis and Palestinians who had lost loved ones in the conflict there, a woman whose brother had been murdered for his political courage in Colombia, a South African who had been maimed by a letter bomb and many others.

Committed to working toward a world in which no one else will ever suffer what they have suffered, all the participants in the conference were seeking loving ways to respond, to break the vicious spirals of violence and counterviolence, hate and counterhate. They founded the International Network for Peace, an organization that stretches all across the globe, enabling people to share their experiences and support one another in their efforts toward forgiveness and reconciliation.

A British woman named Jo Berry was there. Her father, who had been a Member of British Parliament, was killed by an IRA (Irish Republican Army) bomb several years before. When the bomber, Patrick Magee, was released from prison after the Good Friday Peace Accords were signed between Britain and Northern Ireland, Jo contacted him and asked if they could meet. Though it was uncomfortable at first, she shared her story, and then he shared his. They now travel together on speaking tours, talking about the power of overcoming enmity. A film called *Everyman: Facing the Enemy* is the story of their rare friendship.

It is much cheaper to make friends than to fight enemies. The U.S.-funded Marshall Plan that reconstructed Western Europe after the Second World War was one of best investments our country ever made. Maintaining a Nonviolent Peace Force in a country costs literally one-millionth of what a typical military response to a conflict costs. It's also generally more effective, and it doesn't create the terrible death, destruction, and hatred generated by war, which can last for generations.

Imagine how the world would change if we recruited millions of people for the Peace Corps, nonviolent peace teams, and other constructive efforts, rather than for our military forces. Think of how much safer we all would be if the world knew Americans as healers and teachers, builders of clinics and schools, and supporters of land reform, rather than as deadly dominaters.

It is my hope that every individual and faith community will consider being part of such an effort, or sponsoring someone who can be.

We learned through Witness for Peace in Nicaragua the power of thousands of religious people going to a war zone, offering protection and carrying home poignant and compelling stories to their communities. Nothing can really substitute for the experience of going someplace with open eyes and heart, meeting the people and seeing what our government is up to.

If we observe firsthand the wars, poverty, and injustice that are generated by our nation's militarism and consumerism, we will be in a better place to listen to what the Spirit and our consciences are calling on us to do. And we may just be convinced that we have far better alternatives than sending in the Marines, bombing or deploying the drones.

I'm convinced that if our faith communities were bolder in their prophetic witness and more engaged in the world's needs, people would be flocking to them. If observers saw members of religious institutions putting their beliefs into action—including loving one another not only within families and communities, but across borders of race, religion, politics, and nationality—the world would move a long way toward universal brotherhood and sisterhood.

But too many religious leaders are afraid to risk paycheck or reputation. And many Christians simply concede that the Religious Right controls the money, wields the power, and dominates the airwaves. In his book *No Bars to Manhood*, peace activist, prophet, and poet Daniel Berrigan wrote these indicting words:

> We have assumed the name of peacemakers, but we have been, by
> and large, unwilling to pay any significant price. And because we
> want peace with half a heart, and half a life and will, the war, of
> course, continues, because the waging of war, by its very nature,
> is total—but the waging of peace, by our cowardice, is partial. . . .
> Of course, let us have the peace, we cry, but at the same time let us
> have normalcy, let us lose nothing, let our lives stand intact, let us
> know neither prison nor ill repute nor disruption of ties.

Thankfully, some people have been willing to take great risks for peace. I'm grateful for many "spiritual giants," who have given their lives in very powerful, beautiful ways, following their hearts and God's leadings, with deep commitment to transforming our society and world. Many of them have become my friends, and many of their names appear in this book. Some are no longer alive, but their spirits and the memories of their courage give me great strength.

I believed when I was in Nicaragua, Guatemala, and El Salvador that if even a small percentage of people in the United States had determination and courage equivalent to that of the people I met in Central America, we could change U.S. policy and turn our nation around. I have had a similar feeling in many other situations since. We do have the power to create change. We just need to believe it and act on that belief.

We never know where the next Rosa Parks may show up. We never know from what seemingly hopeless corner transformation will be sparked. Once people have overcome their fear and sense of powerlessness, anything is possible. "When people decide they want to be free," declared Archbishop Tutu, "there's no stopping them short of victory."

This is my faith—that we can be co-creators with God in helping to build a world of peace, justice, and human dignity for all people. We have all that we need to bring about transformation, and we are all critical to the struggle. God's only hands are our hands, and God's only feet are our feet.

Many years ago, as a young man, I went to Berlin and had my life changed. I lived just a few blocks from Checkpoint Charlie, the security point between East and West, where U.S. and Soviet tanks were in a face-off, threatening all-out nuclear war and possibly ending all human life on our planet. That spot of earth was a hated symbol of division and domination.

Many years later I returned to Berlin. The dividing wall between East and West had been dismantled. And I was delighted to discover that, where Checkpoint Charlie had once towered menacingly, a massive mural of a smiling Gandhi had been painted.

Transformation of Checkpoint Charlie from a trigger point for nuclear war to a museum housing the exhibition From Gandhi to Walesa: Nonviolent Struggle for Human Rights Worldwide. [Photo: Verlag Haus am Checkpoint Charlie]

I followed the arrow below the mural to the From Gandhi to Walesa exhibition. It portrays in photographs and in many languages the history of nonviolent struggle, from India's campaign for independence under Gandhi's leadership to Poland's Solidarity Movement, led by Lech Walesa. What a beautiful and remarkable symbol of transformation!

What other spots on our earth are waiting for such stunning change? What corner is beckoning to your heart and spirit? Where is God leading you to invest your life on behalf of a world where all God's children share the abundance and live as one family in peace and harmony with the earth?

Deep in my heart, I do believe, that—*together*—**We Shall Overcome!**

Proposal for Ending All War: An Idea Whose Time Has Come

I would like to invite you to become active in a worldwide movement. David Swanson and I wrote a proposal to build a movement to End All War: An Idea Whose Time Has Come. With very positive response, people from around the world are now organizing: **World Beyond War: A Global Movement to End All War and Promote Enduring Peace**.

We hope you will sign the Declaration of Peace and help build this movement.

All individuals and organizations all over the world are invited to sign a Declaration of Peace and help build a World Beyond war, a global movement to end all war. This is the statement:

> I understand that wars and militarism make us less safe rather than protect us, that they kill, injure, and traumatize adults, children, and infants, severely damage the natural environment, erode civil liberties, and drain our economies, siphoning resources from life-affirming activities. I commit to engage in and support nonviolent efforts to end all war and preparations for war and to create a sustainable and just peace.

To sign this, and to get involved in many different ways, visit http://worldbeyondwar.org.

Public opinion is moving against particular wars and the world's spending of $2 trillion every year on war and preparations for war. We plan to announce the launching of a broad movement capable of ending war preparations and transitioning to a peaceful world. We are creating the tools necessary to communicate the facts about war and discard the myths. We are creating ways to assist organizations around the world that are working on partial steps in the direction of a war-free world—including developing peaceful means of achieving security and resolving conflict—and to increase widespread understanding of such steps as progress toward war's complete elimination.

If unnecessary suffering on an enormous scale is to be avoided, we must abolish war. Some 180 million people died in wars in the twentieth century and, while we have not yet repeated a war on the scale of World War II, wars are not going away. Their devastation continues, measured in terms of deaths, injuries, trauma, millions of people having to flee their homes, financial cost, environmental destruction, economic drain, and erosion of civil and political rights.

Unless we want to risk catastrophic loss or even extinction, we must abolish war. Every war brings with it both massive destruction and the risk of uncontrolled escalation. We are facing a world of greater weapons proliferation, resource shortages, environmental pressures, and the largest human population the earth has seen. In such a turbulent world, we must abolish sustained and coordinated militarized combat between groups (primarily governments) known as war, because its continuation puts all life on the planet at risk.

If we abolish war, humanity can not only survive and better address the climate crisis and other dangers, but will be able to create a better life for everyone. The reallocation of resources away from war promises a world whose advantages are beyond easy imagination. Some $2 trillion a year, roughly half from the United States and half from the rest of the world, is devoted to war and war preparation. Those funds could transform global efforts to create sustainable energy, agricultural, economic, health, and education systems. Redirection of war funding could save many times the lives that are taken by spending it on war.

While abolition is a larger demand than partial disarmament, which will be a necessary step along the way, if the case for abolition is made convincingly it has the potential to create support for serious and even total disarmament among people who would otherwise favor the maintenance of a large military for defense—something that we've learned does not work, creates more enemies and generates pressure for offensive warmaking. The first step in such a campaign must be persuading people of the possibility of, and the urgent need for, abolishing war. Awareness of the effectiveness of nonviolent action, nonviolent movements, and peaceful resolution of conflicts is growing rapidly, creating the increased possibility of persuading people that there are effective alternatives to war to resolve conflicts and achieve security.

The reduction and eventual elimination of war and the repurposing of the military-industrial complex could be of great benefit to sectors of the world economy and of public services to which that investment could be transferred. We are creating a broad coalition encompassing civilian industries and advocates for green energy, education, housing, health care, and other fields, including civil liberties, environmental protections, children's rights, and the governments of cities, counties, states, provinces, and nations that have had to make major and painful cuts in social programs for their people. By demonstrating that war is not inevitable and that it is actually possible to eliminate war, this movement will develop the allies needed to make it a reality.

Resistance, including by those profiting financially from wars, will be intense. Such interests are, of course, not invincible. Raytheon's stock was soaring in the summer of 2013 as the White House planned to send missiles into Syria—missiles that were not sent after dramatic public opposition arose. But ending all war will require defeating the propaganda of war promoters and countering the economic interests of war promoters with alternative economic possibilities. A wide variety of support for "humanitarian" and other particular varieties, or imagined varieties, of war will be countered with persuasive arguments and alternatives. We are creating a resource center that will put the best arguments against various types of war support at everyone's fingertips.

By organizing internationally, we will use progress made in one nation to encourage other nations to match or surpass it without fear. By educating people whose governments make war at a distance about the human costs of war (largely one-sided, civilian, and on a scale not widely understood) we will build a broad-based moral demand for an end to war. By presenting the case that militarism and wars make us all less safe and decrease our quality of life, we will strip war of much of its power. By creating awareness of the economic trade-offs, we will revive support for a peace dividend. By explaining the illegality, immorality, and terrible costs of war and the availability of legal, nonviolent, and more effective means of defense and conflict resolution, we will build acceptance for what has only relatively recently been made into a radical proposal and ought to be viewed as a common sense initiative: the abolition of war.

While a global movement is needed, this movement cannot ignore or reverse the reality of where the greatest support for war originates. The United States builds, sells, buys, stockpiles, and uses the most weapons, engages in the most conflicts, stations the most troops in the most countries, and carries out the most deadly and destructive wars. By these and other measures, the U.S. government is the world's leading war-maker, and—in the words of Martin Luther King Jr.—the greatest purveyor of violence in the world. Ending U.S. militarism would eliminate the pressure that is driving many other nations to increase their military spending. It would deprive NATO of its leading advocate for and greatest participant in wars. It would cut off the largest supply of weapons to the Middle East and other regions.

But war is not a U.S. or Western problem alone. This movement will focus on wars and militarism around the globe, helping to create examples of effective alternatives to violence and war, and examples of demilitarization as a path to greater, not lesser, security. Short-term goals may include economic conversion commissions, partial disarmament, elimination of offensive but not defensive weapons, base closures, bans on particular weapons or tactics, promotion of diplomacy and international law, expansion of peace teams and human shields, promotion of nonmilitary foreign aid and crisis prevention, placing restrictions on military recruitment and providing potential soldiers with alternatives, drafting legislation to redirect war taxes into peace work, encouraging cultural exchange, discouraging racism, developing less destructive and exploitative lifestyles, the creation of a peace conversion taskforce to help communities make the transition from war-making to meeting human and environmental needs, and expanding the global nonviolent peaceforce of civilian, trained, international, nonviolent peacekeepers and peacemakers who will be available to protect civilians and local peace and human rights workers endangered by conflicts in all parts of the world and to help build peace where there is or has been violent conflict. To get involved, go to http:// worldbeyondwar.org.

Resources for Further Study and Action: What You Can Do

If you have been moved by the stories in this book, here are some things you can do.

Together we can make peaceful change possible!

PERSONAL DEVELOPMENT

1. Practice nonviolence in all areas of your life—thoughts, conversations, family and work relationships, and with challenging people and situations. Read Gandhi and King to gain a deeper understanding of nonviolence, and how to integrate nonviolence into your life as you work for change. One valuable resource is http://www.godblessthewholeworld.org

2. Explore nonviolent ways of relating and communicating where compassion and active listening guide your interactions with others. Alternatives to Violence Project (http://www.avpusa.org) and Nonviolent Communication trainings (http://www.cnvc.org) are excellent and engaging ways to practice these invaluable skills.

3. Watch or listen to *Democracy Now!*, *Bill Moyers Journal* on PBS, and public news stations which are independently operated, noncommercial, and listener-supported. They provide a more progressive political orientation and counterbalance what is promoted by the mainstream media: http://www.democracynow.org, http://www.pbs.org/moyers/journal/index.html, http://www.pbs.org.

4. Participate in a Global Exchange "Reality Tour." These socially responsible educational tours develop a deeper understanding of the poverty, injustice and violence facing so many around the world. Frequently, long lasting personal relationships are made as you empower local communities and learn how to work for change in American polices, which are often the direct cause for these adverse conditions: http://www.globalexchange.org/tours.

5.   Be the change you want to see in the world. People seeking a caring, compassionate, just, environmentally sustainable and peaceful world can begin by living their own lives by the values they would like to see in the world.

PERSONAL WITNESS—SPEAKING OUT

6.   Write letters to the editor of your local newspaper, and to members of Congress, about issues which concern you. By contacting local, state, and federal elected officials and government agencies, you are "speaking truth to power."

7.   Participate in a short-term international delegation to get to know people living in conflict areas, and to experience their reality. Meet locals who are working for peace and justice, and learn how you can become their ally. Witness for Peace (http://www.witnessforpeace. org); Interfaith PeaceBuilders (http://www.interfaithpeacebuilders. org); Meta Peace Teams (http://www.mptpeaceteams.org), Christian Peacemaker Teams (http://www.cpt.org), Friends Peace Teams (http:// www.friendspeaceteams.org) all offer these valuable opportunities.

8.   Contact the above groups and volunteer to work on a peace team in a conflict area to help support local human rights defenders, protect civilian populations (an estimated 80 percent of the people killed in wars are now civilians), and support local peacekeepers working for nonviolent resolution of conflicts. Ask a local church, religious community, or civic organization to support you in volunteering for three months to a year doing this work.

9.   Counter-recruitment—Educate young people who are considering the military (frequently to get financial assistance for a college education) about the reality of that choice, and the horrors of war. The War Resisters League (http://www.warresisters.org/counterrecruitment) and the American Friends Service Committee (http://www.afsc.org/ resource/counter-recruitment) both offer good educational resources for these efforts.

Assist those who are considering the military with viable, peaceful alternatives and introduce them to veterans who have witnessed war directly such as Veterans for Peace (http://www.vfp.org). Where appropriate, help them to apply for Conscientious Objector status. The GI Rights Hotline offers good information regarding that process (http://

girightshotline.org). Invite a Veterans for Peace speaker to come to your school/college or religious community.

DISCUSSION AND STUDY GROUPS

10. Together with others who have read this book, share insights and stories which touched you, or empowered you to address the problems of war, injustice, racism, and violence in our society. Which accounts motivated you to help create a more just, peaceful, nonviolent, and environmentally sustainable world? What would you like to do differently as a result of reading this book?

11. Watch the DVD *A Force More Powerful* with others in your church, community, school, or university. It documents the history of six powerful nonviolent movements around the world. Discuss each featured episode, which explores some of the twentieth century's major struggles in which nonviolent people-powered movements have overcome oppression, dictatorship, and authoritarian rule. Downloadable study guides, and comprehensive lesson plans for high school students, are available on the website. The DVD is available in more than a dozen languages: http://www.aforcemorepowerful.org.

12. Read articles in *Waging Nonviolence: People Powered News and Analysis* by authors like George Lakey, Ken Butigan, Kathy Kelly, John Dear, and Mary King. These articles are filled with stories of ordinary people facing conflicts, using nonviolent strategies and tactics, even under the most difficult of circumstances, discuss your responses with others, and decide what you would like to do to create nonviolent change: http://www.wagingnonviolence.org.

13. Create a study/discussion group to read or view DVDs and books in the Resources Section of this book. Discuss your feelings, responses, insights on how nonviolent struggle works, and what you might like to do together to put your beliefs into action.

14. To honor Martin Luther King on January 15 (or any other day), organize a showing of one of the excellent films on Dr. King such as *King: From Montgomery to Memphis*, or *KING: Go beyond the Dream to Discover the Man* (by the History Channel). Afterward, talk about what relevance King and the Civil Rights Movement have for your lives, and for our nation today. A Study Guide for this film is available for download: http://www.history.com/images/media/pdf/08-0420_King_Study_Guide.pdf

15. In addition, large public libraries often have good collections of DVDs on MLK and the Civil Rights Movement, like *Eyes on the Prize:*

America's Civil Rights Years 1954–1965. Listen to some of the amazing talks at http://www.godblessthewholeworld.org and discuss them with friends. This free online educational resource features hundreds of videos, audio files, articles and courses on social justice, spiritual activism, counter oppression, environmentalism, plus many other topics on personal and global transformation.

16. Organize a study group using Pace e Bene's workbook titled *Engage: Exploring Nonviolent Living.* This twelve-part study and action program offers participants a wide variety of principles, stories, exercises, and readings for learning, practicing, and experimenting with the power of creative nonviolence for personal and social change: http://www.paceebene.org.

Nonviolent, LOW-, AND NO-RISK ACTIONS

17. Get involved in Pace e Bene's Campaign Nonviolence to build a movement to end war, poverty, and the climate crisis: http://www.campaignnonviolence.org.

18. Identify a problem in your community, the nation or the world, and find others who share your concern. Join together and organize to address that problem, using Martin Luther King's Six Principles of Nonviolence, and his steps in organizing nonviolent campaigns, included at the end of this book. Working together we can create what King called the "Beloved Community."

19. Participate in peaceful demonstrations that focus on your area of concern (antiwar, national priorities, banking reform, immigration, education, health care, Social Security, etc.). They are a good way to expand your contacts and energize your spirit for the longer campaigns.

20. Work at the grass roots level. You don't need to go to Washington to create change. Start where you are, as Martin Luther King did with the bus boycott in Montgomery (1955), and with the voting rights campaign in Selma, Alabama (1965). "Think globally. Act locally."

21. Whatever your spiritual or faith path, live by the values and beliefs you profess. Beliefs don't have much meaning without action. If you are part of a faith-based community, work to help make your church or spiritual community a beacon of justice, peace, and love in the world.

22. All the struggles—justice, peace, environmental sustainability, women's rights, etc.—are interconnected; you don't need to do everything. Pick an issue you feel passionately about and focus your efforts on that. Find ways to support others who are working on different issues, especially at critical times when a major effort is needed.

DIRECT ACTION

23. Participate in nonviolence trainings which create opportunities for participants to learn more about the history and power of nonviolence, share fears and feelings, build solidarity with one another, and form affinity groups. Nonviolence trainings are often used as preparation for actions, and give people a chance to learn specifics about that action, its tone, and legal ramifications; to role play interactions with police, officials, and others in the action; and to practice applying nonviolence in challenging situations. For more information about trainings contact: http://www.trainingforchange.org, http://www.paceebene.org, http://www.ruckus.org, http://www.trainersalliance.org, http://www.organizingforpower.org or http://www.warresisters.org and http://eastpointpeace.org.

24. "Speak truth to power" with others. Develop a nonviolent campaign aimed at a specific injustice or issue, for example: gun violence, the environment, wars and occupations, the use of drones, or redefining our national priorities. Pick an achievable goal, focus on that for some months or even longer. "A campaign is a focused mobilization of energy with a clear objective, over a time period that can realistically be sustained by those who identify with the cause" (George Lakey, "History Is a Weapon: Strategizing for a Living Revolution"). Use King's "Four Basic Steps in Any Nonviolent Campaign" ("Letter from a Birmingham Jail," April 16, 1963) or refer to the Movement Action Plan in Bill Moyer's book *Doing Democracy* (2001), http://www.doingdemocracy.com. One example of a nonviolent campaign is the National Priorities Project: Bringing the Federal Budget Home. They seek to "end the wars and military bases around the world, and bring our tax dollars home—for schools, health care for all, parks, job training, care for the elderly, head start, etc." (nationalprioritiesproject.org).

25. In the spirit of Henry David Thoreau, Mahatma Gandhi, and Martin Luther King, consider engaging in acts of nonviolent civil resistance to challenge unjust laws or policies which you consider immoral, or illegal under international law. These might include the use of drones, the use of torture, or nuclear weapons development. It is highly recommended that you do this with others so you can support one another, and that you go through Nonviolence Training first (see #22 above).

26. Consider refusing to pay some or all of your taxes that pay for war. War Tax Resistance is an important way to withdraw your cooperation from participation in U.S. wars. In order to sustain their war efforts, governments need young men and women willing to fight and kill, and they need the rest of us to pay our taxes to cover the cost of the soldiers, the bombs, the guns, the ammunition, nuclear weapons, the planes and the aircraft carriers that enable them to continue fighting wars. Alexander Haig, President Nixon's chief of staff, as he looked out the White House window and saw over two hundred thousand antiwar demonstrators marching by, said "Let them march all they want to as long as they pay their taxes." Contact the National War Tax Resistance Coordinating Committee (NWTRCC) for assistance and additional information (http://www.nwtrcc.org/contacts_counselors.php).

27. Imagine what might happen if our country put even 10 percent of the money we presently spend on wars and military expenditures into building a world where every person has enough to eat, shelter, an opportunity for education, and access to medical care. We might become the most loved country in the world—and the most secure. See the website for the Global Marshall Plan: http://www.spiritualprogressives.org/gmp.

If you would like to work actively to support nonviolent movements around the world, contact Peaceworkers@igc.org.

Whatever you do, thank you. *Together we shall overcome!*

Ten Lessons Learned From My Life of Activism

1. **Vision.** It is important that we take the time to envision the community, nation, and world we would like to live in, and create for our children and grandchildren. This long-term view, or vision statement, will be a continual source of inspiration. Then we can explore practical ways we can work with others who share our vision to create that kind of world. I personally envision a world without war—where there is justice for all, love for one another, peaceful resolution of conflicts, and environmental sustainability.

2. **The oneness of all life.** We are one human family. We need to understand that deep in our souls, and act on that conviction. I believe that through compassion, love, forgiveness, recognition of our oneness as a global community, and our willingness to struggle for that kind of world, we *will* realize worldwide justice and peace.

3. **Nonviolence, a powerful force.** As Gandhi said, Nonviolence is the most powerful force in the world, and it is "an idea whose time has come." People all over the world are organizing nonviolent movements to bring about change. In *Why Civil Resistance Works*, Erica Chenoweth and Maria Stephan have documented that over the past 110 years nonviolent movements have been twice as likely to succeed as violent movements, and much more likely to help create democratic societies, without reverting to dictatorships or civil war.

4. **Nurture your spirit.** Through nature, music, friends, meditation, reading, and other practices of personal and spiritual development, I have learned the importance of nurturing our spirits and pacing ourselves for the long haul. When we confront violence and injustice it is our spiritual practices that help us discover our inner resources, and

enable us to move forward with the courage of our deepest convictions. "Only from the heart can you touch the sky" (Rumi).

5.   Small, committed groups can create change. Margaret Mead once said, "Never doubt that a small group of thoughtful, committed citizens can change the world. Indeed, it is the only thing that ever has." In times of doubt and discouragement about the current situation, those words, and my own life experiences, have re-inspired me with the certainty that we can make a difference! Even a few committed students can make substantial change, as we did during our lunch counter sit-ins (Arlington, VA, 1960). We had been inspired by four African American freshmen who sat down at Woolworth's "whites only" lunch counter in Greensboro, North Carolina (February 1960). Their action sparked many sit-ins like ours, and led to the desegregation of lunch counters throughout the South. "Ordinary people," can make change. The most successful campaigns I have participated in were with friends who shared concerns, and organized together to make changes in the larger society. Our schools, churches, and community organizations are excellent places to develop such support groups. Although one person can make a difference, it can be very challenging working alone. However, together, we can overcome!

6.   Sustained struggle. Every major movement that I have studied, or been a part of, required sustained struggle over months, and even years, to bring about fundamental changes in our society. Examples include the abolitionist movement, the movement for women's suffrage, the civil rights movement, the anti–Vietnam War movement, the United Farm Workers movement, the sanctuary movement, and many others. All had the common thread of sustained resistance, energy, and vision.

7.   Good Strategy. Yes, holding a sign and putting a bumper sticker on our car is important, but if we want to bring about fundamental change in our society we need to create long-range goals that build toward our vision for the future, and then develop good strategy and sustained campaigns to achieve those goals. (See George Lakey's, *Toward a Living Revolution: A Five-Stage Framework for Creating Radical Social Change*, Peace News Press, London, 2012.).

8.   Overcome our fear. Do everything you can to overcome your fear. Governments and other systems try to instill fear in us to control and immobilize us. Claiming that Iraq had concealed weapons of mass destruction scared people and gave the Bush administration justification to invade Iraq, even though no such weapons were found. We must not fall into the traps of disinformation set by the authorities. Fear is a major impediment to speaking truth to power, to acting to stop wars and injustice, and to whistle-blowing. The more we overcome it, the more powerful and united we become. A supportive community is very important in overcoming our fears.

9.   Truth. As Gandhi said, "Let your lives be 'Experiments with Truth.'" We must experiment with active nonviolence, and keep hope alive. I share Gandhi's conviction that "Things undreamt of are daily being seen; the impossible is ever becoming possible. We are constantly being astonished these days at the amazing discoveries in the field of violence. But I maintain that far more undreamt of and seemingly impossible discoveries will be made in the field of nonviolence."

10.   Telling our stories. Sharing our stories and experiments with truth is critically important. We can empower one another with our stories. There are many inspiring accounts of active nonviolent movements, such as those portrayed in *A Force More Powerful* (Peter Ackerman and Jack DuVall, 2000). Archbishop Desmond Tutu said, "When people decide they want to be free . . . there is nothing that can stop them." I invite you to share your stories of experiments with active nonviolence on the website for this book and help challenge others to join in making a difference.

Hartsough's Sentencing Statement for Nonviolent Protest Opposing Drones at Beale AFB

David was arrested along with eight others blocking two entrances at Beale Air Force Base, where they closed the main entrance for over three hours.

Drones have killed thousands of innocent civilians and are immoral and illegal under U.S. and international law. They also recruit many more people into Al Qaeda.

We are one human family. All people in the world are children of God and are our brothers and sisters. If someone attacks our blood brother or sister, we would do everything in our power to stop them. This is the way we feel about innocent civilians being killed by drones in Afghanistan, Pakistan and Yemen.

One hundred and seventy-eight children and thousands of other civilians have been killed by drones in Pakistan and Yemen. Does this strengthen our national security? Is this making the world a safer place?

Drones are totally immoral and are against everything we have been taught in our religious faiths: love one another, love your enemy and do unto others as you would have them do unto you. This is a question of religious freedom. I am a Quaker and my religious faith requires me to try to stop the killing of innocent people.

How would we feel if Russians or Chinese or Afghanis or Pakistanis were flying drones over the United States and killing American people?

It is illegal under international law to go into another country and drop bombs on people our government doesn't like. The Nuremberg Principles require citizens to attempt to stop crimes against

Along with Shirley Osgood, Janie Kesselman, and Sharon Delgado, my wife Jan and I protested drones and closed the main base entrance for three hours before being arrested at Beale Air Force Base, CA (2012). [Photo: Sherri Maurin]

humanity and killing innocent civilians is a crime against humanity. Doing nothing or remaining silent is complicity in these crimes. In protesting at Beale AFB, I was trying to uphold international law.

The United States is making decisions to kill people without them ever coming before a court or found guilty. The U.S. government is playing Judge, Jury and Executioner. Is this what we call the rule of law?

Using drones and killing many innocent people is creating more and more enemies of the United States. Every person we kill has at least fifty family members and friends who will mourn the loss of their loved ones. Many will seek revenge on the people and nation that has killed their loved ones or friends.

Instead of drones and dropping bombs on people we need to send Peace Corps people to build schools and medical clinics and help people in these countries recover from the wounds of war. We could be the most loved country on earth rather than the most hated.

By our silence we condone this senseless killing. We must speak out and act to stop this madness. By our nonviolent protest at Beale AFB, we were acting to uphold God's law, U.S. law, the Nuremberg Principles and international law.

We call on our fellow Americans, people in churches and synagogues and mosques, students, all people of conscience to join us in stopping drones before they kill more innocent people and recruit more people into Al Qaeda. Unfortunately, our "war on terror" is a recipe for perpetual wars and endless suffering and death for people around the world.

Judge Delaney, at a time when our country is preparing to rain down missiles and bombs on Syria, which could start a much larger war in the Middle East killing thousands or hundreds of thousands of people, perhaps the best place for people of conscience is behind bars.

I am at peace with whatever you sentence me to. I cannot pay a fine or accept probation for a nonviolent action in which I was trying to uphold God's law, U.S. law and international law. Judge, if you so decide, I am ready to do community service or spend time in prison.

Suggested DVDs, Books, and Websites for Further Study and Action

DVDs

A Fierce Green Fire: The Battle for a Living Planet (2012). Spanning fifty years of grassroots and global activism, this documentary brings to light the vital stories of the environmental movement where people fought—and succeeded—against enormous odds.

A Force More Powerful (2000). Documents the power and success of nonviolent movements around the world in the twentieth century; there are six half-hour segments: Gandhi, civil rights movement in United States, nonviolent resistance to Hitler, Solidarity in Poland, peaceful transformation of South Africa, and nonviolent overthrow of dictator Pinochet in Chile.

Beyond Rangoon (1995). Provides a cinematic account of the Burmese nonviolent uprising of the 1980s from the point of view of an American doctor; shows the true story of Aung San Suu Kyi courageously and peacefully confronting and leading a multitude through the line of armed soldiers.

Bringing Down a Dictator (2001). Shows how a nonviolent student-led resistance group built a powerful nonviolent movement which brought down Serbian dictator Slobodan Milosevic.

Budrus (JustVision.org, 2009) Inspiring film about the successful nonviolent resistance of a village in Palestine protesting the separation wall running through their community.

Eyes on the Prize: America's Civil Rights Years (1986). A PBS miniseries that traces the grassroots emergence and progression of the American Civil Rights movement during the King years.

Freedom Riders (2011). A PBS documentary about the courageous and powerful Civil Rights freedom riders, who integrated buses in the South in 1961.

Gandhi (1982). A cinematic portrayal of the life and work of Mohandas Gandhi.

Hearts and Minds (1974). A documentary on the Vietnam War that contrasts the lies of the administrations with the reality of what was happening on the ground in Vietnam. Columbia Pictures refused to distribute the film, and it was only rarely seen publicly until after the end of the war.

King (2008). A documentary that gives viewers a look at the extraordinary life of Martin Luther King Jr., going beyond the legend to portray the man, questions and myths about King; includes interviews with MLK Jr.'s son, his campaigners, Bill Clinton, Condoleezza Rice, and Bono among others.

King: From Montgomery to Memphis (1970). Chronicles the life and work of Dr. Martin Luther King Jr., from the Montgomery Bus Boycott to his assassination in Memphis.

Orange Revolution (2007). Looks at when there were fraudulent elections in Ukraine in 2004 and thousands of people did courageous nonviolent resistance—resulting in the elections being declared null and void. New elections were subsequently held.

Pray the Devil Back to Hell (2008). Details the efforts of the Liberian women whose combined efforts and commitment to active nonviolent resistance forced the government and armed resistance leaders to negotiate an end to the country's civil war.

Sir No Sir (2005). The suppressed story about the powerful GI movement to end the war in Vietnam.

Soundtrack for a Revolution (2010). Highlights the important role that music played during the U.S. Civil Rights movement in the South.

What I've Learned about U.S. Foreign Policy: The War against the Third World (2000). A compilation of videos of key activists by Frank Dorrel that reveals the true nature of U.S. foreign policy (http://www.addictedtowar.com).

You Can't Be Neutral on a Moving Train: A Personal History of Our Times by Howard Zinn (2002). An autobiographical film that provides an eloquent, personal account of the movements for civil rights, against the Vietnam War, and organized labor. It's also very hopeful.

Books

The Power of Nonviolence: Writings by Advocates of Peace (Beacon Press, 2002), 216 pages. A chronological anthology of the most persuasive writings on nonviolence, with an introduction by Howard Zinn.

Peter Ackerman and Jack Duvall, *A Force More Powerful: A Century of Nonviolent Conflict* (Palgrave Macmillan, 2001), 560 pages. The authors share the history of powerful nonviolent movements in the twentieth century which have changed history. This shares in much detail the stories shared in the film, *A Force More Powerful*. We learn how popular nonviolent movements have overthrown dictators and secured human rights and built democratic societies.

Mary-Wynne Ashford with Guy Dauncey, *Enough Blood Shed: 101 Solutions to Violence, Terror and War* (New Society Publishers, 2006), 288 pages. Focuses on the power of ordinary people to make a difference; the author outlines the steps to build a culture of peace.

Peter Blood and Annie Patterson, *Rise Up Singing: The Group Singing Songbook* (Sing Out Publications, 2004), 288 pages. Great collection of songs for peace and justice from around the world.

Andrew Boyd, ed., *Beautiful Trouble: A Toolbox for Revolution* (OR Books, 2012), 460 pages. An excellent compilation of nonviolent tools as proposed by various grassroots organizations working for transformation of our society.

Ken Butigan et al., *Engage: Exploring Nonviolent Living* (Pace e Bene Press, 2005), 320 pages. A study program for churches and other community groups to strengthen their understanding of nonviolence and how to apply it in their everyday lives and how to work for peace, sustainability, and justice in their communities and around the world.

Paul K. Chappell, *Peaceful Revolution: How We Can Create the Future Needed for Humanity's Survival* (Easton Studio Press, 2012), 224 pages. The author shares his journey as a West Point graduate and an Iraq War Veteran to the peace activist he is today, and explains why he believes that nonviolence can end wars.

Paul K. Chappell, *The Art of Waging Peace: A Strategic Approach to Improving Our Lives and the World* (Prospecta Press, 2013), 336 pages. This book shows how we can become active citizens with the skills and strength to defeat injustice and end all wars.

Erica Chenoweth and Maria J. Stephan, *Why Civil Resistance Works: The Strategic Logic of Nonviolent Conflict* (Columbia University Press, 2011), 320 pages. Chenoweth and Stephan study 323 violent and nonviolent movements over the past 110 years and find that nonviolent movements have been at least twice as likely to be successful as armed movements in overthrowing oppressive regimes and creating lasting change; nonviolent movements were also more than twice as likely to end up in democratic societies and not revert to civil wars or dictatorships.

David Cortright, *Gandhi and Beyond: Nonviolence for an Age of Terrorism* (Paradigm Publishers, 2006), 280 pages. The author provides an analysis of nonviolent movements and looks at the philosophy behind nonviolence and how nonviolence can be used effectively in the age of terrorism.

John Dear, *A Persistent Peace: One Man's Struggle for a Nonviolent World* (Loyola Press, 2008), 456 pages. Jesuit priest John Dear's account of his thirty-year journey as an activist. The book focuses on Dear's spiritual journey experimenting with nonviolence.

John Dear, *The Nonviolent Life* (Pace e Bene Press, 2013), 150 pages. John Dear articulates a vision of the power, meaning and impact of the spiritually grounded, nonviolent life and invites us to live a nonviolent life and join the global grassroots movement of nonviolence.

Richard Deats, *Active Nonviolence Across the World* (Create Space Independent Fellowship of Reconciliation, 2012), 102 pages. A booklet giving an overview of active nonviolent movements around the world, in many of which Deats played an active role.

Sharon Delgado, *Shaking the Gates of Hell: Faith-Led Resistance to Corporate Globalization* (Fortress Press, 2007), 176 pages. The author shares how people of faith can challenge corporate greed and globalized institutions.

Louise Diamond, *The Peace Book: 108 Simple Ways to Create a More Peaceful World* (Conari Press, 2001), 191 pages. The author outlines ways to cultivate, promote, and sustain peace.

James Douglass, *JFK and the Unspeakable: Why He Died and Why It Matters* (Touchstone, 2010), 560 pages. An examination of President Kennedy's gradual conversion from cold warrior risking nuclear war with the Soviet Union to working for a policy of lasting peace, and how this contrasted strongly with the Cold War agenda of the military industrial complex, the FBI, and the CIA, and why that conversion got him assassinated.

Lisa Fithian, *Kicking Corporate Booty: A Manual for the People*. A flexible model of strategic organizing to help ordinary people take on corporations and win.

Bruck K. Gagnon, *Come Together Right Now: Organizing Stories from a Fading Empire* (Just Write Books, 2008), 264 pages. Stories about grassroots organizing, international alliance building, the peace and labor movements, the conversion of the U.S. economy from weapons to human needs, the preservation of life on earth and the weaponization of space.

Mohandas Gandhi, *All Men Are Brothers* (Continuum, 1980), 208 pages. A collection of some of Gandhi's most powerful writings on truth, nonviolence, and religion.

Mohandas Gandhi, edited by John Dear, *Mohandas Gandhi: Essential Writings* (Orbis Books, 2002), 192 pages. An excellent collection of Gandhi's writings; gives a deeper understanding of his profound message of nonviolence.

Judith L. Hand, *The Beginning of War, the Ending of War* (Questpath Publishing, 2014), 329 pages. Explores why we have war, why war is not inevitable and a vision and strategy for how we can end war.

Vincent Harding, *Martin Luther King: The Inconvenient Hero* (Orbis Books, 2008), 164 pages. The radical King that the establishment doesn't want us to remember; the King who challenged militarism and economic injustice, as well as racism in our society (an edifice which produces beggars needs restructuring).

Vincent Harding, *Hope and History: Why We Must Share the Story of the Movement* (Orbis Books, 2010), 223 pages. Shares the spirit, history and power of the freedom movement of the 1960s and encourages us all to consider what we can do today to continue that important work.

Chris Hedges, *War Is a Force that Gives Us Meaning* (Anchor, 2003), 224 pages. The author uses his own experiences combined with historical works to illustrate how war can overtake, seduce, and corrupt those who are around it. Hedges believes only massive nonviolent civil disobedience can transform this country into a real democracy at peace with the world; see also Hedges's weekly columns in Truthdig.com

Chris Hedges, *The World as It Is: Dispatches on the Myth of Human Progress* (Nation Books, 2013), 432 pages. A collection of the author's recent articles in which he provides social and political critique on a variety of subjects, including the Middle East and the decay of the American Empire.

Daniel Hunter, *Strategy and Soul: A Campaigner's Tale of Fighting Billionaires, Corrupt Officials, and Philadelphia Casinos* (Hyrax Books, 2013), 340 pages. A great how-to manual for building nonviolent campaigns.

Miki Kashtan, *Reweaving Our Human Fabric: Working together to Create a Nonviolent Future* (Fearless Heart Publications, 2014). An inspiring book that challenges us to live and practice nonviolence in our own lives and in our work for social transformation.

Martin Luther King Jr., *Where Do We Go from Here: Chaos or Community?* (Beacon Press, 1968), 209 pages. King's last book, including his thoughts on the need to build a movement to challenge economic injustice in our society and build a global community based on justice.

Martin Luther King Jr., edited by James M. Washington, *A Testament of Hope: The Essential Writings of Martin Luther King Jr.* (Harper & Row, 1986), 676 pages. A compilation of the most important speeches and writings of Martin Luther King Jr.

George Lakey, *Facilitating Group Learning: Strategies for Success with Adult Learners* (Jossey-Bass, 2010), 304 pages. A great resource for becoming an empowered facilitator/trainer working for social transformation.

George Lakey, *Toward a Living Revolution: A Five-Stage Framework for Creating Radical Social Change* (Peace News Press, London, 2012), 304 pages. A five-stage strategy for transforming our society.

John Lewis, *Walking with the Wind* (Mariner Books; 1999), 496 pages. The personal memoir of John Lewis, SNCC leader and now a member of Congress, details his moving experiences in the civil rights movement.

John Lewis, *March* (Top Shelf Productions, 2013). A graphic novel and vivid firsthand account of John Lewis's lifelong struggle for civil and human rights, meditating on the distance traveled since the days of Jim Crow and segregation.

Staughton and Alice Lynd, *Nonviolence in America: A Documentary History* (Orbis Books, 1995), 535 pages. A comprehensive compilation of documents that detail America's history of nonviolence, from colonial times to present.

Winslow Myers, *Living Beyond War: A Citizens Guide* (Orbis Books, 2009), 180 pages. Wars don't work and there are much better alternatives than war for resolving conflict. We the people have the power to create a world beyond war.

Bill Moyer, *Doing Democracy: The MAP Model for Organizing Social Movements* (New Society Publishers, 2001), 240 pages. Provides a theory and working model for understanding, analyzing and organizing social movements.

Michael N. Nagler, *Is There No Other Way? The Search for a Nonviolent Future* (Inner Ocean Publishing, 2003), 352 pages. The author maps out the historical legacy of nonviolence, from well-known leaders to everyday people, and argues why peaceful action is effective.

David Potorti, *September 11th Families for Peaceful Tomorrows: Turning Tragedy into Hope for a Better World* (RDV Books, 2003), 250 pages. Describes how some families who lost family members on September 11, 2001, rallied to form their own organization dedicated to promoting peace and reconciliation and addressing the root causes of terrorism.

Dennis Rivers, *Prayer Evolving: Five Personal Explorations into the Future of Prayer* (Karuna Books, 2008), 78 pages. Explores the deeper spiritual dimensions of prayer for peace activists: http://www.prayer.evolving.net.

Jonathan Schell, *The Unconquerable World: Power, Nonviolence, and the Will of the People* (Holt Paperbacks, 2004), 448 pages. The author looks at the history of nonviolent movements, both small and grand, and illustrates a way to end modern violent conflicts.

Jonathan Schell, *A Hole in the World: A Story of War, Protest, and the New American Order* (Nation Books, 2004), 208 pages. A look into the current political climate in America, and its focus on war, killing, and death; the author also looks at the future consequences of this emphasis on violence and war as a means of resolving conflict.

Nathan Schneider, *Thank You, Anarchy: Notes from the Occupy Apocalypse* (University of California Press, 2013), 194 pages. An up-close, inside account of Occupy Wall Street's first year in NYC, showing both the spirit and excitement and the challenges of the movement.

Gene Sharp, *Waging Nonviolent Struggle: 20th Century Practice and 21st Century Potential* (Porter Sargent, 2005), 598 pages. The history of powerful nonviolent movements in the twentieth century and budding nonviolent movements in the twenty-first.

Gene Sharp, *From Dictatorship to Democracy: A Conceptual Framework for Liberation* (The New Press, 2012), 160 pages. A guide to overthrowing oppressive regimes; details how to organize movements to withdraw cooperation from and nonviolently overthrow oppressive regimes (available on the web in many languages at http://www.aeinstein.org).

Kent D. Shifferd, *From War to Peace: A Guide to the Next Hundred Years* (McFarland, 2011), 240 pages. Presents a realistic analysis of the extent to which the war system has infiltrated all aspects of Western culture, and how it perpetuates war rather than promotes peace. The values and ideas that have grown out of peace activism offer a very real opportunity to outlaw war in the coming century just as slavery was abolished in the nineteenth century.

Starhawk, *The Fifth Sacred Thing* (Bantam, 1994), 496 pages. An epic tale of freedom and slavery, love and war, and the potential futures of humankind tells of a twenty-first century California clan caught between two clashing worlds, one based on tolerance, the other on repression and how nonviolent defense could work.

Starhawk, *The Empowerment Manual: A Guide for Collaborative Groups* (New Society Publishers, 2011), 304 pages. A comprehensive manual for groups seeking to organize with shared power and bottom-up leadership.

David Swanson, *War Is a Lie* (David Swanson, 2010), 372 pages. Great book sharing the truth that all wars are lies.

David Swanson, *War No More: The Case for Abolition* (2013), 184 pages. This book presents the strongest arguments for the abolition of war, demonstrates that war can be ended, war should be ended, and we the people must end war. A manifesto for the World Beyond War movement.

Michael True, *People Power: Fifty Peacemakers and Their Communities* (Rawat, 2007), 236 pages. Profiles of fifty peace activists from the eighteenth century to the present.

Jim Wallis and Joyce Hollyday, *Cloud of Witnesses* (Orbis Books, 2005), 292 pages. Profiles of inspirational peacemakers and spiritual leaders, from Martin Luther King Jr. to St. Francis of Assisi.

S. Brian Willson, *Blood on the Tracks: The Life and Times of S. Brian Willson* (PM Press, 2011), 472 pages. A chronicle of Vietnam vet turned radical nonviolent activist Brian Willson's battles against social injustice and war, including his involvement in a munitions blockade in which he lost his legs.

Walter Wink, *Peace Is the Way: Writings on Nonviolence from the Fellowship of Reconciliation* (Orbis Books, 2000), 295 pages. An excellent collection of essays by peacemakers that originally ran in *Fellowship* magazine.

Howard Zinn, *A People's History of the United States: 1492–Present* (HarperPerennial, 2005), 768 pages. A detailed and powerful account of the history of the United States as told by the people who are often overlooked by traditional history.

Howard Zinn, *A Power Governments Cannot Suppress* (City Lights Publishers, 2006), 308 pages. The current state of current U.S. policies is critiqued; in addition, the author explains the often-underestimated power of the people.

Howard Zinn, *A Young People's History of the United States: Columbus to the War on Terror* (Seven Stories Press, 2009), 464 pages. Howard

Zinn, with contributions by Rebecca Stefoff, tells the history of America from the viewpoints of workers, slaves, immigrants, Native Americans, women, and others whose stories and impacts are often overlooked by history.

Howard Zinn, *The Historic Unfulfilled Promise* (City Lights Publishers, 2012), 256 pages. Author Howard Zinn questions the political leadership of America, the security of its people, and America's role in the international community.

Howard Zinn, *You Can't Be Neutral on a Moving Train: A Personal History of Our Times* (Beacon Press, 2002), 224 pages. The memoir of Howard Zinn, in which he recalls his life as a teacher, writer, and social activist.

Stephen Zunes, Lester Kurtz, and Sarah Asher, eds., *Nonviolent Social Movements* (Blackwell Publishers, 1999), 330 pages. Shares the stories of major nonviolent movements around the world in the twentieth century.

Websites

Addicted to War: **addictedtowar.com**. Great educational resources for those trying to overcome our country's addiction to war.

Albert Einstein Institution: **aeinstein.org**. The organization founded by Gene Sharp; excellent resources for nonviolent struggle in many languages.

Alliance of Community Trainers: **trainersalliance.org**. Offering knowledge, tools, and skills to individuals, organizations, and communities to empower sustainable transformation.

Alternatives to Violence: **avpusa.org**. A training program helping people learn alternatives to violence in our lives and communities; taught in communities and prisons around the world.

American Friends Service Committee: **afsc.org**. A Quaker organization that promotes peace through justice around the world.

Brian Willson: **brianwillson.com**. Excellent essays and analysis by Brian Willson, author of *Blood on the Tracks*, on the need for radical change in our society and social transformation.

Campaign Nonviolence: **campaignnonviolence.org**. Campaign Nonviolence is building a long-term active nonviolent movement to end war, poverty, and the climate crisis.

Code Pink: **codepink.org**. Code Pink is a women-initiated grassroots peace and justice movement working to end wars and redirect our resources into health care, education, green jobs and other life-affirming activities.

Common Dreams: **commondreams.org**. A nonprofit independent news-center centered on promoting social justice, human rights, equality, and peace.

Democracy Now!: **democracynow.org**. A daily news program on TV, radio, and on the web, which tells the truth about peace and justice and environmental issues around the world. (A necessary ingredient for democracy is for the people to know the truth.)

East Point Peace Academy: **eastpointpeace.org**. The U.S. military trains many of its leaders at West Point. The East Point Peace Academy works to build a nonviolent army investing in peace through nonviolence education.

Fellowship of Reconciliation: **forusa.org**. An interfaith organization committed to replacing violence, war, and economic disparity with nonviolence and justice.

Friends Committee on National Legislation: **fcnl.org**. A Quaker lobby in Washington lobbying for peace and justice, which puts out a good newsletter on issues before Congress and what you can do to influence key legislation.

God Bless the Whole World: **godblessthewholeworld.org**. A fantastic collection of talks by nonviolence, peace, justice, and spiritual leaders. A powerful collection of recordings, speeches, and workshops.

Global Exchange: **globalexchange.org**. A human rights organization dedicated to promoting justice around the world. Check out their Reality Tours to countries around the world.

Global Nonviolent Database: **nvdatabase.swarthmore.edu**. A searchable database of close to a thousand case studies of nonviolent campaigns and case studies, as compiled by students of Swarthmore College.

Institute for Healing of Memories: **healing-memories.org**. Seeks to contribute to the healing of individuals, communities, and nations who are suffering from violent conflict.

International Center for Nonviolent Conflict: **nonviolent-conflict.org**. Great resource for groups around the world; for people to fight for rights, freedom, justice, self-determination, and accountable government through the use of civil resistance—including tactics such as strikes, boycotts, protests, and civil disobedience. ICNC also has a weekly news digest of nonviolent actions and movements around the world.

Liberation Theology: **liberationtheology.org**. Excellent resources on liberation theology from around the world.

National Priorities Project: **nationalpriorities.org**. Offers citizen and community groups tools and resources to shape federal budget and policy priorities which promote social and economic justice—How much money is going from your city and state for wars and militarism, and what could you do alternatively with those resources?

National War Tax Resistance: **nwtrcc.org**. A website dedicated to opposing militarism, war, and social injustices through refusal to pay taxes for war and redirection of those tax dollars for peaceful purposes.

Network of Spiritual Progressives: **spiritualprogressives.org**. Network promoting love and caring for each other and caring for the earth as the new bottom line.

No Nukes: **nonukes.org**. Great website for developments and resources for fighting nuclear weapons and nuclear power around the world.

Nonviolent Action: **nonviolentaction.net**. A collection of some of the best articles on nonviolent action around the world, updated regularly.

Nonviolent Communication: **cnvc.org**. A training program in learning nonviolent ways to communicate.

Nonviolence International: **nonviolenceinternational.net**. Supports nonviolent struggles around the world.

Nonviolent Peaceforce: **nonviolentpeaceforce.org**. The website of Nonviolent Peaceforce, cofounded by David Hartsough and Mel Duncan; includes updates on their projects sending peace teams to areas of conflict around the world and how to get involved.

Pace e Bene: **paceebene.org**. Promotes deeper understanding of nonviolence as a way of life and means of social change. Good resources on nonviolence. They are organizing Campaign Nonviolence, which is building a long-term movement for a nonviolent world to end war, poverty, and the climate crisis.

Parents Circle–Family Forum: **theparentscircle.com**. (PCFF) is a grassroots organization of bereaved Palestinians and Israelis, which promotes reconciliation as an alternative to hatred and revenge.

Peace Action: **peace-action.org**. Peace Action the nation's largest grassroots peace network with local affiliates across the country.

Peaceworkers: **peaceworkersus.org**. An organization dedicated to supporting nonviolent movements, and nurturing peace, justice, reconciliation, and nonviolence around the world and ending all war.

Popular Resistance: **popularresistance.org**. Daily movement news and resources for the Occupy movement and beyond.

Roots Action: **rootsaction.org**. An online initiative dedicated to galvanizing Americans committed to economic fairness, equal rights, civil liberties, environmental protection, and defunding endless wars.

September 11th Families for Peaceful Tomorrows: **peacefultomorrows.org**. Families of September 11th victims working for reconciliation and healing rather than revenge.

Seven Challenges Workbook: **Communications Skills for Life: newconversations.net/sevenchallenges.pdf**. A cooperative communication skills workbook for nonviolent communication and peaceful relationships at home and at work. Includes listening, self-expression, open-ended questions, gratitude, and more. Free to download from website.

Sojourners: **sojo.net**. A faith-based magazine that includes articles promoting peace and social justice.

Training for Change: **trainingforchange.org**. Excellent training resources for nonviolent action and nonviolent movements.

Truth Dig: **truthdig.com**. Includes weekly columns by social change activists including Chris Hedges, who believes that only massive nonviolent civil disobedience can transform our country.

Truth Out: **truth-out.org**. A collection of investigative articles highlighting injustices in the world and the need for change.

United For Peace and Justice: **ufpj.org**. National and international coalition of peace and justice organizations working to end war and oppression, shift resources toward human needs, protect the environment and promote sustainable alternatives.

Waging Nonviolence: **wagingnonviolence.org**. Includes weekly columns by nonviolent practitioners, including George Lakey, Ken Butigan, Mary King, and others.

War Is a Crime: **warisacrime.org**. Exposes the lies that create and sustain wars and occupations and works to hold those responsible accountable. Speakers available.

Western States Legal Foundation: **wslfweb.org**. Working to abolish all nuclear weapons; includes information and analysis on nuclear weapons policies and efforts to work for the elimination of all nukes.

World Beyond War: **www.worldbeyondwar.org**. Building a worldwide movement to end all war and promote enduring peace. They offer resources which challenge the myths about why war in necessary, effective alternatives to war, and suggestions about how all of us can help end/abolish war.

The Six Principles of Kingian Nonviolence

Principle 1: Nonviolence is a way of life for courageous people.
It is a positive force confronting the forces of injustice and utilizes the righteous indignation and spiritual, emotional, and intellectual capabilities of people as the vital force for change and reconciliation.

Principle 2: The Beloved Community is the framework for the future.
The nonviolent concept is an overall effort to achieve a reconciled world by raising the level of relationships among people to a height where justice prevails and persons attain their full human potential.

Principle 3: Attack forces of evil not persons doing evil.
The nonviolent approach helps one analyze the fundamental conditions, policies and practices of the conflict rather than reacting to one's opponents or their personalities.

Principle 4: Accept suffering without retaliation for the sake of the cause to achieve a goal.
Self-chosen suffering is redemptive and helps the movement grow in a spiritual as well as a humanitarian dimension. The moral authority of voluntary suffering for a goal communicates the concern to one's own friends and community as well as to the opponent.

Principle 5: Avoid internal violence of the spirit as well as external physical violence.
The nonviolent attitude permeates all aspects of the campaign. It provides a mirror type reflection of the reality of the condition to one's opponent and the community at large. Specific activities must be designed to maintain a high level of spirit and morale during a nonviolent campaign.

Principle 6: The Universe is on the side of justice.
Truth is universal and human society and each human being is oriented

to the just sense of order of the universe. The fundamental values in all of the world's great religions include the concept that the moral arc of the universe is long but it bends towards justice. For the nonviolent practitioner, nonviolence introduces a new moral context in which nonviolence is both the means and the ends.

The Six Steps of Kingian Nonviolence

Step 1: Information Gathering
The way you determine the facts, the options for change and the timing of pressure for raising the issue is a collective process.

Step 2: Education
The process of developing articulate leaders, who are knowledgeable about the issue.

Step 3: Personal Commitment
Means looking at your internal and external involvement in the non-violent campaign and preparing yourself for long-term as well as short-term action.

Step 4: Negotiation
The art of bringing together your views and those of your opponent to arrive at a just conclusion or clarify the unresolved issues, at which point, the conflict is formalized.

Step 5: Direct Action
Occurs when negotiations have broken down or failed to produce a just response to the contested issues and conditions.

Step 6: Reconciliation
The mandatory closing step of a campaign, when the opponents and proponents celebrate the victory and provide joint leadership to implement the change.

Afterword
by Ken Butigan

The arduous transition to a just and peaceful world will not be accomplished by wishful thinking. It will be achieved by some of us wagering that there is an alternative to two time-honored but dangerous scripts for navigating our lives: violence and passivity.

This will not be easy. Both of these venerable conventions exert powerful gravitational forces that keep them, and us, helplessly in place. There is an alternative, but it requires no less than betting our entire lives that there is a better way—and covering that bet by unleashing the power of the paradoxical qualities of active nonviolence: fierce compassion, contemplative action, global locality, and peaceable rebellion.

Making this shift to a world where everyone matters—where the grip of both violence and passivity is definitively loosened—will require two key ingredients.

First, we must, once and for all, take nonviolent action. The power of nonviolent resistance and public witness for justice and peace has proven itself over the last hundred years. One wave after another of people taking nonviolent action has been key to dramatic change all around the globe. It's now time for all of us to take this up. We must engage. We must experiment. We must join the quiet revolution that has, in spite of all the evidence, been gaining traction and momentum over the past century.

But we also need the second ingredient: *telling the story of the nonviolent action we take.*

We must document, sift, understand. We must remember, retrieve, reclaim, rediscover. We must endlessly share, mull on, and take heart from the stories of love in action.

"Telling the action" is a process of carrying it on in a new way. And, even most critically, it is a way of building a new, more nonviolent world.

A world is made through stories. This has been true for the violent world, but also for all those alternative worlds that have been emerging over the past few hundred years: worlds of emancipation and human rights. These new worlds are rooted in stories that have become increasingly plausible and real, even if they are still unfinished. We help build the nonviolent world by framing it, giving it a home, naming its reality, fleshing out what it looks like and what it means.

Sometimes this is seen in the wishful thinking of a starry vision. Sometimes it is captured in principles, like the Universal Declaration of Human Rights. But sometimes it is found in accounts of specific, concrete actions.

That's what we have in *Waging Peace: Global Adventures of a Lifelong Activist*. Reading this book is breathtaking. Hartsough has lived a life of action for peace and justice from one end of the world to the other. He has participated in many of the nonviolent struggles at the forefront of human liberation over the past half century. He shows us that it is possible to engage, to resist, to "peaceably rebel." He shows us that anyone can do this.

But he has done more than this. This book illuminates how telling the story of nonviolent action is critical. Throughout his life Hartsough has "told the action" in magazine articles, in booklets, in public talks, and—as I first experienced his storytelling—in countless jail cells.

Now we have this book. It is crowded with a dizzying array of accounts of the perils and joys of one person's journey into a terrain beyond violence and passivity, a province of possibilities, options and nonviolent solutions. It is bracing, revealing, and inspiring. It also quietly asks us: *What wager do you want to make?*

David Hartsough has spent his life engaged in nonviolent action. Now he has taken the time to tell the story of this lifelong action and its power—paradoxical and transformative—to invite the rest of us to act and, in turn, to tell.

We all need to read and reread this book—and then get going on own lifelong journey of doing, and telling, nonviolent change.

Ken Butigan is an educator, writer and advocate for nonviolent change. For three decades, he has participated in or organized numerous movements for social transformation. He is the director of Pace e Bene Nonviolence Service and teaches in the Peace, Justice and Conflict Studies

Program at DePaul University in Chicago. He has written or edited a series of books, including Cry of the Environment: Rebuilding the Christian Creation Tradition; From Violence to Wholeness; Engage: Exploring Nonviolent Living; Franciscan Nonviolence; *and* Pilgrimage through a Burning World: Spiritual Practice and Nonviolent Protest at the Nevada Test Site *(State University of New York Press). He also writes a regular online column for* Waging Nonviolence.

About the Authors

David Hartsough is executive director of Peaceworkers, based in San Francisco, and is cofounder of the Nonviolent Peaceforce. He is a Quaker and member of the San Francisco Friends Meeting. He has a BA from Howard University and an MA in international relations from Columbia University. Hartsough has been working actively for nonviolent social change and peaceful resolution of conflicts since he met Dr. Martin Luther King Jr. in 1956.

Over the last fifty years, he has led and been engaged in nonviolent peacemaking in the United States, Kosovo, the former Soviet Union, Mexico, Guatemala, El Salvador, Nicaragua, the Philippines, Sri Lanka, Iran, Palestine, Israel, and many other countries. He was also a peace educator and organized nonviolent movements for peace and justice with the American Friends Service Committee for eighteen years.

Hartsough cofounded the Nonviolent Peaceforce, which now has over two hundred unarmed civilian peacekeepers working in conflict areas around the world.

Hartsough has been arrested more than a hundred times for participating in demonstrations. He has worked in the movements for civil rights, against nuclear weapons, to end the Vietnam War, to end the wars of Iraq and Afghanistan and to prevent an attack on Iran.

Hartsough was arrested at the Creech and Beale Air Force Bases while protesting drones that are killing civilians in Afghanistan, Pakistan, Yemen, and other countries. He has been active in the Occupy movement since its inception, believing that without more equality of income, we cannot have democracy.

Most recently, David is helping organize World Beyond War, a global movement to end all wars.

He has written extensively about his peacemaking work. His articles have been published in *Sojourners*, *Fellowship*, *Peacework*, *Friends Journal*, *Western Friend/Friends Bulletin*, *Waging Nonviolence*, and *National Catholic Reporter*. Hartsough coauthored the book, *Taking Charge: Personal and Political Change Through Simple Living*, published by Bantam Books and republished by Harper & Rowe. Hartsough also wrote and published two small books on his experiences meeting ordinary people in Russia in the early 1960s, *Discovering Another Russia: The Journal of a Camping Trip* and *Backyard Russia: Getting to Know the Russian People*.

He is married and has two children and four wonderful grandchildren.

Joyce Hollyday is a cofounder and copastor of Circle of Mercy in Asheville, North Carolina. She served for fifteen years as the associate editor of *Sojourners* magazine and is the author of several books, including *Clothed with the Sun: Biblical Women, Social Justice, and Us* and *Then Shall Your Light Rise: Spiritual Formation and Social Witness*, and the coeditor of *Cloud of Witnesses*.

ABOUT PM PRESS

PM Press was founded at the end of 2007 by a small collection of folks with decades of publishing, media, and organizing experience. PM Press co-conspirators have published and distributed hundreds of books, pamphlets, CDs, and DVDs. Members of PM have founded enduring book fairs, spearheaded victorious tenant organizing campaigns, and worked closely with bookstores, academic conferences, and even rock bands to deliver political and challenging ideas to all walks of life. We're old enough to know what we're doing and young enough to know what's at stake.

We seek to create radical and stimulating fiction and non-fiction books, pamphlets, T-shirts, visual and audio materials to entertain, educate and inspire you. We aim to distribute these through every available channel with every available technology—whether that means you are seeing anarchist classics at our bookfair stalls; reading our latest vegan cookbook at the café; downloading geeky fiction e-books; or digging new music and timely videos from our website.

PM Press is always on the lookout for talented and skilled volunteers, artists, activists and writers to work with. If you have a great idea for a project or can contribute in some way, please get in touch.

PM Press
PO Box 23912
Oakland, CA 94623
www.pmpress.org

FRIENDS OF PM PRESS

These are indisputably momentous times—the financial system is melting down globally and the Empire is stumbling. Now more than ever there is a vital need for radical ideas.

In the six years since its founding—and on a mere shoestring—PM Press has risen to the formidable challenge of publishing and distributing knowledge and entertainment for the struggles ahead. With over 250 releases to date, we have published an impressive and stimulating array of literature, art, music, politics, and culture. Using every available medium, we've succeeded in connecting those hungry for ideas and information to those putting them into practice.

Friends of PM allows you to directly help impact, amplify, and revitalize the discourse and actions of radical writers, filmmakers, and artists. It provides us with a stable foundation from which we can build upon our early successes and provides a much-needed subsidy for the materials that can't necessarily pay their own way. You can help make that happen—and receive every new title automatically delivered to your door once a month—by joining as a Friend of PM Press. And, we'll throw in a free T-shirt when you sign up.

Here are your options:

- **$30 a month** Get all books and pamphlets plus 50% discount on all webstore purchases

- **$40 a month** Get all PM Press releases (including CDs and DVDs) plus 50% discount on all webstore purchases

- **$100 a month** Superstar—Everything plus PM merchandise, free downloads, and 50% discount on all webstore purchases

For those who can't afford $30 or more a month, we're introducing **Sustainer Rates** at $15, $10 and $5. Sustainers get a free PM Press T-shirt and a 50% discount on all purchases from our website.

Your Visa or Mastercard will be billed once a month, until you tell us to stop. Or until our efforts succeed in bringing the revolution around. Or the financial meltdown of Capital makes plastic redundant. Whichever comes first.

Blood on the Tracks: The Life And Times of S. Brian Willson

S. Brian Willson with an introduction by
Daniel Ellsberg

ISBN: 978-1-60486-421-2
$20.00   536 pages

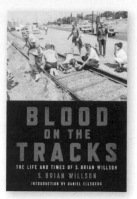

"We are not worth more, they are not worth less." This is
the mantra of S. Brian Willson and the theme that runs
throughout his compelling psycho-historical memoir.
Willson's story begins in small-town, rural America,
where he grew up as a "Commie-hating, baseball-loving Baptist," moves through
life-changing experiences in Viet Nam, Nicaragua and elsewhere, and culminates
with his commitment to a localized, sustainable lifestyle.

In telling his story, Willson provides numerous examples of the types of personal,
risk-taking, nonviolent actions he and others have taken in attempts to educate
and effect political change: tax refusal—which requires simplification of one's
lifestyle; fasting—done publicly in strategic political and/or therapeutic spiritual
contexts; and obstruction tactics—strategically placing one's body in the way of
"business as usual." It was such actions that thrust Brian Willson into the public eye
in the mid-'80s, first as a participant in a high-profile, water-only "Veterans Fast
for Life" against the Contra war being waged by his government in Nicaragua. Then,
on a fateful day in September 1987, the world watched in horror as Willson was run
over by a U.S. government munitions train during a nonviolent blocking action in
which he expected to be removed from the tracks and arrested.

Losing his legs only strengthened Willson's identity with millions of unnamed
victims of U.S. policy around the world. He provides details of his travels to
countries in Latin America and the Middle East and bears witness to the
harm done to poor people as well as to the environment by the steamroller
of U.S. imperialism. These heart-rending accounts are offered side by side
with inspirational stories of nonviolent struggle and the survival of resilient
communities.

*"I was busted with Brian, but I never gave the ultimate as he gave. This book is about a
patriot, the kind of patriot you don't find anymore, the kind of patriot who loves and
believes in his country so much he surrendered his legs in telling his country it's wrong.
Read this book."*
—Edward Asner, actor

*"Brian Willson's courage, compassion, and commitment to fighting for freedom, and
justice, and human rights is an inspiration to the rest of us and a lesson in how to
handle Adjustments in our Plans."*
—Kris Kristofferson, actor, songwriter

We Have Not Been Moved: Resisting Racism and Militarism in 21st Century America

Edited by Elizabeth 'Betita' Martínez, Mandy Carter & Matt Meyer with an Introduction by Cornel West and Afterwords/poems by Alice Walker & Sonia Sanchez

ISBN: 978-1-60486-480-9
$29.95   608 pages

We Have Not Been Moved is a compendium addressing the two leading pillars of U.S. Empire. Inspired by the work of Dr. Martin Luther King Jr., who called for a "true revolution of values" against the racism, militarism, and materialism which he saw as the heart of a society "approaching spiritual death," this book recognizes that—for the most part—the traditional peace movement has not been moved far beyond the half-century-old call for a deepening critique of its own prejudices. While reviewing the major points of intersection between white supremacy and the war machine through both historic and contemporary articles from a diverse range of scholars and activists, the editors emphasize what needs to be done now to move forward for lasting social change. Produced in collaboration with the War Resisters League, the book also examines the strategic possibilities of radical transformation through revolutionary nonviolence.

Among the historic texts included are rarely-seen writings by antiracist icons such as Anne Braden, Barbara Deming, and Audre Lorde, as well as a dialogue between Dr. King, revolutionary nationalist Robert F. Williams, Dave Dellinger, and Dorothy Day. Never-before-published pieces appear from civil rights and gay rights organizer Bayard Rustin and from celebrated U.S. pacifist supporter of Puerto Rican sovereignty Ruth Reynolds. Additional articles making their debut in this collection include new essays by and interviews with Fred Ho, Jose Lopez, Joel Kovel, Francesca Fiorentini and Clare Bayard, David McReynolds, Greg Payton, Gwendolyn Zoharah Simmons, Ellen Barfield, Jon Cohen, Suzanne Ross, Sachio Ko-Yin, Edward Hasbrouck, Dean Johnson, and Dan Berger. Other contributions include work by Andrea Dworkin, Mumia Abu-Jamal, Starhawk, Andrea Smith, John Stoltenberg, Vincent Harding, Liz McAlister, Victor Lewis, Matthew Lyons, Tim Wise, Dorothy Cotton, Ruth Wilson Gilmore, Kenyon Farrow, Frida Berrigan, David Gilbert, Chris Crass, and many others. Peppered throughout the anthology are original and new poems by Chrystos, Dylcia Pagan, Malkia M'Buzi Moore, Sarah Husein, Mary Jane Sullivan, Liz Roberts, and the late Marilyn Buck.

"When we sang out 'We Shall Not Be Moved' in Montgomery and Selma, we were committed to our unshakeable unity against segregation and violence. This important book continues in that struggle—suggesting ways in which we need to do better, and actions we must take against war and continued racism today. If the human race is still here in 2111, the War Resisters League will be one of the reasons why!"
—Pete Seeger, folk singer and activist

Damned Fools In Utopia: And Other Writings on Anarchism and War Resistance

Nicolas Walter
Edited by David Goodway

ISBN: 978-1-60486-222-5
$22.95   304 pages

Nicolas Walter was the son of the neurologist W. Grey Walter, and both his grandfathers had known Peter Kropotkin and Edward Carpenter. However, it was the twin jolts of Suez and the Hungarian Revolution while still a student, followed by participation in the resulting New Left and nuclear disarmament movement, that led him to anarchism himself. His personal history is recounted in two autobiographical pieces in this collection as well as the editor's introduction.

During the 1960s he was a militant in the British nuclear disarmament movement—especially its direct-action wing, the Committee of 100—he was one of the Spies for Peace (who revealed the State's preparations for the governance of Britain after a nuclear war), he was close to the innovative Solidarity Group and was a participant in the homelessness agitation. Concurrently with his impressive activism he was analyzing acutely and lucidly the history, practice and theory of these intertwined movements; and it is such writings—including 'Non-violent Resistance' and 'The Spies for Peace and After'—that form the core of this book. But there are also memorable pieces on various libertarians, including the writers George Orwell, Herbert Read and Alan Sillitoe, the publisher C.W. Daniel and the maverick Guy A. Aldred. 'The Right to be Wrong' is a notable polemic against laws limiting the freedom of expression. Other than anarchism, the passion of Walter's intellectual life was the dual cause of atheism and rationalism; and the selection concludes appropriately with a fine essay on 'Anarchism and Religion' and his moving reflections, 'Facing Death'.

Nicolas Walter scorned the pomp and frequent ignorance of the powerful and detested the obfuscatory prose and intellectual limitations of academia. He himself wrote straightforwardly and always accessibly, almost exclusively for the anarchist and freethought movements. The items collected in this volume display him at his considerable best.

"[Nicolas Walter was] one of the most interesting left intellectuals of the second half of the twentieth century in Britain."
—Professor Richard Taylor, University of Cambridge

Accompanying: Pathways to Social Change

Staughton Lynd

ISBN: 978-1-60486-666-7
$14.95   176 pages

In *Accompanying*, Staughton Lynd distinguishes two strategies of social change. The first, characteristic of the 1960s Movement in the United States, is "organizing." The second, articulated by Archbishop Oscar Romero of El Salvador, is "accompaniment." The critical difference is that in accompanying one another the promoter of social change and his or her oppressed colleague view themselves as two experts, each bringing indispensable experience to a shared project. Together, as equals, they seek to create what the Zapatistas call "another world."

Staughton Lynd applies the distinction between organizing and accompaniment to five social movements in which he has taken part: the labor and civil rights movements, the antiwar movement, prisoner insurgencies, and the movement sparked by Occupy Wall Street. His wife Alice Lynd, a partner in these efforts, contributes her experience as a draft counselor and advocate for prisoners in maximum-security confinement.

"Since our dreams for a more just world came crashing down around us in the late 1980s and early 1990s, those of us involved in social activism have spent much of the time since trying to assess what went wrong and what we might learn from our mistakes. In this highly readable book, Lynd explores the difference between organizing and accompanying. This book is a must-read for anyone who believes a better world is possible."
—Margaret Randall, author of *To Change the World: My Years in Cuba*

"Everything that Staughton Lynd writes is original and provocative. This little book is no exception. Among his greatest contributions on display here is the transformation of the 'organizer' and 'organized' into a collaboration of different people with different skills, each making a decisive contribution."
—Paul Buhle, author of *Robin Hood: People's Outlaw and Forest Hero*

"Accompanying is arguably the most thoughtful examination of Archbishop Oscar Romero's concept of accompaniment insofar as it helps us to understand how liberation theology matured from taking a 'preferential option for the poor' to companionship with the poor as they organize themselves… This legacy flows into the Occupy Movement today when it reclaims foreclosed homes, and occupies banks and spaces collectively and spontaneously. This book would be important at any moment in history, but is indispensable today as we accompany one another in the quest to free ourselves from the shackles of the world the 1 percent has inflicted on us."
—Carl Mirra, Associate Professor of Education, Adelphi University, and author of *The Admirable Radical: Staughton Lynd and Cold War Dissent, 1945–1970*

From Here to There: The Staughton Lynd Reader

Edited with an Introduction
by Andrej Grubačić

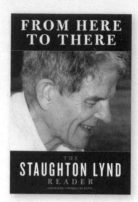

ISBN: 978-1-60486-215-7
$22.00   320 pages

From Here to There collects unpublished talks and
hard-to-find essays from legendary activist historian
Staughton Lynd.

The first section of the Reader collects reminiscences and analyses of the 1960s.
A second section offers a vision of how historians might immerse themselves in
popular movements while maintaining their obligation to tell the truth. In the last
section Lynd explores what nonviolence, resistance to empire as a way of life, and
working class self-activity might mean in the 21st century. Together, they provide a
sweeping overview of the life, and work—to date—of Staughton Lynd.

Both a definitive introduction and further exploration, it is bound to educate,
enlighten, and inspire those new to his work and those who have been following
it for decades. In a wide-ranging Introduction, anarchist scholar Andrej Grubačić
considers how Lynd's persistent concerns relate to traditional anarchism.

*"I met Staughton and Alice Lynd nearly fifty years ago in Atlanta. Staughton's reflective
and restless life has never ceased in its exploring. This book is his great gift to the next
generations."*
—Tom Hayden

*"Staughton Lynd's work is essential reading for anyone dedicated to implementing
social justice. The essays collected in this book provide unique wisdom and insights into
United States history and possibilities for change, summed up in two tenets: leading
from below and solidarity."*
—Roxanne Dunbar-Ortiz

*"This remarkable collection demonstrates the compassion and intelligence of one of
America's greatest public intellectuals. To his explorations of everything from Freedom
Schools to the Battle of Seattle, Staughton Lynd brings lyricism, rigour, a historian's
eye for irony, and an unshakable commitment to social transformation. In this time of
economic crisis, when the air is filled with ideas of 'hope' and 'change,' Lynd guides us
to understanding what, very concretely, those words might mean and how we might
get there. These essays are as vital and relevant now as the day they were written, and
a source of inspiration for activists young and old."*
—Raj Patel

About Face: Military Resisters Turn Against War

Edited by Buff Whitman-Bradley, Sarah Lazare, and Cynthia Whitman-Bradley

ISBN: 978-1-60486-440-3
$20.00   272 pages

How does a young person who volunteers to serve in the U.S. military become a war-resister who risks ostracism, humiliation, and prison rather than fight? Although it is not well publicized, the long tradition of refusing to fight in unjust wars continues today within the American military. In this book, resisters describe in their own words the process they went through, from raw recruits to brave refusers. They speak about the brutality and appalling violence of war; the constant dehumanizing of the enemy—and of our own soldiers—that begins in Basic Training; the demands that they ignore their own consciences and simply follow orders. They describe how their ideas about the justification for the current wars changed and how they came to oppose the policies and practices of the U.S. empire, and even war itself. Some of the refusers in this book served one or more tours of duty in Iraq and Afghanistan, and returned with serious problems resulting from Post-Traumatic Stress Disorder. Others heard such disturbing stories of violence from returning vets that they vowed not to go themselves. Still others were mistreated in one way or another and decided they'd had enough. Every one of them had the courage to say a resounding "NO!" The stories in this book provide an intimate, honest look at the personal transformation of each of these young people and at the same time constitute a powerful argument against militarization and endless war.

Also featured are exclusive interviews with Noam Chomsky and Daniel Ellsberg. Chomsky looks at the U.S.-led wars in Iraq and Afghanistan and the potential of GI resistance to play a role in bringing the troops home. Ellsberg relates his own act of resistance in leaking the Pentagon Papers in 1971 to the current WikiLeaks revelations of U.S. military secrets.

"About Face *gives us important insights into the consciences of women and men who volunteer for the military but find they cannot obey orders to fight in illegal wars. These are brave and loyal Americans who are willing to challenge the U.S. government and perhaps go to jail rather than betray their inner voices that say NO to these wars!*"
—Ann Wright, retired U.S. Army colonel and diplomat who resigned in protest of the invasion of Iraq, author of *DISSENT: Voices of Conscience*

"About Face *pulls down the veil of what honorable service in today's U.S. military really means. When new soldiers swear to support and defend the U.S. Constitution by following lawful orders, what are they to do when they are given unlawful orders?* About Face *provides raw examples of precisely what soldiers are doing who take their oath seriously.*"
—Dahr Jamail, author of *The Will to Resist: Soldiers Who Refuse to Fight in Iraq and Afghanistan*

Towards Collective Liberation: Anti-Racist Organizing, Feminist Praxis, and Movement Building Strategy

Chris Crass, with an Introduction by Chris Dixon and Foreword by Roxanne Dunbar-Ortiz

ISBN: 978-1-60486-654-4
$20.00   320 pages

Towards Collective Liberation: Anti-Racist Organizing, Feminist Praxis, and Movement Building Strategy is for activists engaging with dynamic questions of how to create and support effective movements for visionary systemic change. Chris Crass's collection of essays and interviews presents us with powerful lessons for transformative organizing through offering a firsthand look at the challenges and the opportunities of anti-racist work in white communities, feminist work with men, and bringing women of color feminism into the heart of social movements. Drawing on two decades of personal activist experience and case studies of anti-racist social justice organizations, Crass insightfully explores ways of transforming divisions of race, class, and gender into catalysts for powerful vision, strategy, and movement building in the United States today.

Crass's collection begins with an overview of the anarchist tradition as it relates to contemporary activism and an in-depth look at Food Not Bombs, one of the leading anarchist groups in the revitalized radical Left in the 1990s. The second and third sections of the book combine stories and lessons from Crass's experiences of working as an anti-racist and feminist organizer, combining insights from the Civil Rights Movement, women of color feminism, and anarchism to address questions of leadership, organization building, and revolutionary strategy. In section four, Crass discusses how contemporary organizations have responded to the need for white activists to lead anti-racist efforts in white communities and how these efforts have contributed to multiracial alliances in building a broad-based movement for collective liberation. Offering rich case studies of successful organizing, and grounded, thoughtful key lessons for movement building, *Toward Collective Liberation* is a must-read for anyone working for a better world.

"In his writing and organizing, Chris Crass has been at the forefront of building the grassroots, multi-racial, feminist movements for justice we need. Towards Collective Liberation *takes on questions of leadership, building democratic organizations, and movement strategy, on a very personal level that invites us all to experiment and practice the way we live our values while struggling for systemic change."*
—Elizabeth 'Betita' Martinez, founder of the Institute for Multiracial Justice and author of *De Colores Means All of Us: Latina Views for a Multi-Colored Century*

Al-Mutanabbi Street Starts Here: Poets and Writers Respond to the March 5th, 2007, Bombing of Baghdad's "Street of the Booksellers"

Edited by Beau Beausoleil and Deema Shehabi

ISBN: 978-1-60486-590-5
$20.00   320 pages

On March 5th, 2007, a car bomb was exploded on al-Mutanabbi Street in Baghdad. More than thirty people were killed and more than one hundred were wounded. This locale is the historic center of Baghdad bookselling, a winding street filled with bookstores and outdoor book stalls. Named after the famed 10th century classical Arab poet al-Mutanabbi, it has been the heart and soul of the Baghdad literary and intellectual community. This anthology begins with a historical introduction to al-Mutanabbi Street and includes the writing of Iraqis as well as a wide swath of international poets and writers who were outraged by this attack.

This book seeks to show where al-Mutanabbi Street starts in all of us: personally, in our communities, and in our nations. It seeks to show the commonality between this small street in Baghdad and our own cultural centers, and why this attack was an attack on us all. This anthology sees al-Mutanabbi Street as a place for the free exchange of ideas; a place that has long offered its sanctuary to the complete spectrum of Iraqi voices. This is where the roots of democracy (in the best sense of that word) took hold many hundreds of years ago. This anthology looks toward al-Mutanabbi Street as an affirmation of all that we hope for in a more just society.

"This anthology celebrates the exquisite relationship between the book and the reader, humanity and culture, writing and life and love. It is a tribute to a street that grows into a large and archetypal symbol and spatial metaphor for books."
—Muhsin al-Musawi, professor of Arabic and Comparative Studies at Columbia University and editor of the *Journal of Arabic Literature*

"The collection of materials in this anthology is astounding and harrowing. Beausoleil and Shehabi have put together a book that will be adored by lovers of poetry, essays, journalism, and testimony. It will also be required reading for anyone interested in social justice."
—Steven Salaita, associate professor of English, Virginia Tech University

Until the Rulers Obey: Voices from Latin American Social Movements

Edited by Clifton Ross and Marcy Rein
with a Foreword by Raúl Zibechi

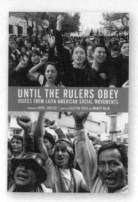

ISBN: 978-1-60486-794-7
$29.95   528 pages

Until the Rulers Obey brings together voices from the
movements behind the wave of change that swept
Latin America at the turn of the twenty-first century. These movements have
galvanized long-silent—or silenced—sectors of society: indigenous people,
campesinos, students, the LGBT community, the unemployed, and all those left
out of the promised utopia of a globalized economy. They have deployed a wide
range of strategies and actions, sometimes building schools or clinics, sometimes
occupying factories or fields, sometimes building and occupying political parties to
take the reins of the state, and sometimes resisting government policies in order to
protect their newfound power in community. This unique collection of interviews
features five dozen leaders and grassroots activists from fifteen countries
presenting their work and debating pressing questions of power, organizational
forms, and relations with the state. They have mobilized on a wide range of issues:
fighting against mines and agribusiness and for living space, rural and urban; for
social space won through recognition of language, culture, and equal participation;
for community and environmental survival. The book is organized in chapters by
country with each chapter introduced by a solidarity activist, writer, or academic
with deep knowledge of the place. This indispensable compilation of primary
source material gives participants, students, and observers of social movements a
chance to learn from their experience.

Contributors include ACOGUATE, Luis Ballesteros, Marc Becker, Margi Clarke,
Benjamin Dangl, Mar Daza, Mickey Ellinger, Michael Fox, J. Heyward, Raphael
Hoetmer, Hilary Klein, Diego Benegas Loyo, Courtney Martinez, Chuck Morse,
Mario A. Murillo, Phil Neff, Fabíola Ortiz dos Santos, Hernán Ouviña, Margot
Pepper, Adrienne Pine, Marcy Rein, Christy Rodgers, Clifton Ross, Susan Spronk,
Marie Trigona, Jeffery R. Webber, and Raúl Zibechi.

"This is the book we've been waiting for. Anyone interested in the explosion of social
movements in Latin America—and the complex interplay between those forces and
the 'Pink Tide' governments—should inhale this book immediately. Until the Rulers
Obey gives us country-specific context from a superb team of 'introducers,' who then
step aside so we can hear a chorus of voices from some of the most inspiring grassroots
organizations on the continent. This is a people's history in real time, bubbling up from
below."
—Avram David "Avi" Lewis, documentary filmmaker and former host of Al Jazeera
English show *Fault Lines* and Naomi Klein, author of *No Logo* and *Shock Doctrine: The
Rise of Disaster Capitalism*